Praise for *Grimoire of Aleister Crowley*

"There are presently very few individuals living today who are qualified by education and experience to write this, and even fewer with the writing talent and communication skills to bring it all to life on the printed page. Brother Orpheus is the incarnation of both these aspects of genius. Whether he is expanding upon classic Crowley rituals or creating and developing his own Thelemic ceremonies, the magician reader can be confident he or she is in good hands."

> —**Lon Milo DuQuette**, author of *The Magick of Aleister Crowley* and *Understanding Aleister Crowley's Thoth Tarot*

"Rodney Orpheus, the modern Minstrel of Thelema, is back with another vibrant, creative, and irreverent effort that is sure to please and enlighten as it broadcasts the good news that the Lord of the Aeon is alive and well. This is a practical, lively, and meticulously documented manual designed for group magical workings. It admirably fulfils its task—bringing new insight to both published and unpublished rituals with diagrams and detailed instructions for movement, apparel, and Temple setup. It includes rituals from Crowley and others, and its important appendices round out an excellent work."

> —**James Wasserman**, author of *To Perfect this Feast: A Performance Commentary on the Gnostic Mass*

"In addition to gifting us with a long-needed anthology of Aleister Crowley's group rituals, Rodney Orpheus's *Grimoire,* with its inclusion of rituals inspired by Crowley, is also a course on how to take older texts and adapt them to one's needs. The cookbook-style "list of ingredients and preparation time" that precedes each ceremony handily gives aspiring ritualists a heads up on how many Fratres or Sorores are needed, how much memorization is required, and how complex the ritual equipment and staging is. Eminently readable and (more importantly) usable, *Grimoire of Aleister Crowley* will keep many a magical group busy for years to come."

—**Richard Kaczynski,** author of *Perdurabo*

"Rodney Orpheus has produced the most significant Thelemic book written this century. *Grimoire of Aleister Crowley* adds a key missing fragment to the corpus of Crowley's Thelemic rituals—a coherent set of group rituals which enhance personal practices and expand effective magical interaction between practitioners. Drawing on unpublished Crowley material, the author has vitalized the rituals with the spirit of Thelemic practice, rather than slavishly following standard formulae. This book is going to end up being standard reading for numerous groups, and is sure to cause a stir, and may even start a revolution."

—**David Rankine**, author of *The Goetia of Dr. Rudd*
and *The Grimoire of Arthur Gauntlet*

"This book is all purple and pleasure, a revelation of fragments of rituals by Aleister Crowley which were half-concealed, expounding the mantras and the spells and propagating the essence of Thelema. Rodney Orpheus has provided an original and enchanting work for the twenty-first century which opens the gates to the palace and offers a pathway to the mysteries hidden therein. *Grimoire of Aleister Crowley* is sure to become a modern classic."

—**Sorita d'Este,** author of *Practical Qabalah Magick*
and *Hekate Liminal Rites*

GRIMOIRE *of* ALEISTER CROWLEY

Group Magick Rituals

RODNEY ORPHEUS
ALEISTER CROWLEY AND JOHN DEE, ET AL.

Foreword by Lon Milo DuQuette

WEISER BOOKS

This edition first published in 2019 by Weiser Books, an imprint of
Red Wheel/Weiser, LLC
With offices at:
65 Parker Street, Suite 7
Newburyport, MA 01950
www.redwheelweiser.com

Ordo Templi Orientis
International Headquarters
JAF PO Box 7666
New York, NY 10116-7666
USA

ISBN: 978-1-57863-675-4
Library of Congress Cataloging-in-Publication Data available upon request.

Cover design by Kathryn Sky-Peck

Printed in the United States of America
TS

10 9 8 7 6 5 4 3 2 1

CONTENTS

ILLUSTRATIONS

Foreword
by Lon Milo DuQuette

Do what thou wilt shall be the whole of the Law.

Magick is a lonely art. It must ever be so, because ultimately we are each a universe unto our self. The *'whatever-it-is-we-are'* was alone when it incarnated into this corporeal dimension; and it will be alone at the timeless instant we shuffle off this mortal coil. But as we labor through the measured ticks of space-time on this side of the pylons of birth and death our *'whatever-it-is-we-are'* is surrounded and assailed by a vast assortment of other *'whatever-it-is-we-ares'* – other monads of consciousness who are also universes unto themselves – and some of these other universes are fellow magicians.

Magick is also (first and foremost) a self-transformational art. It may be the magician's intent to effect changes in his or her outer life circumstances, *i.e.,* 'I want the girl next door to fall in love with me…' but the success of any magical operation designed to bring about that romantic outcome will most assuredly be in large part the consequences of the *magician becoming transformed* into the type of person the girl next door falls in love with.

I'm sure there are knowledgeable and skilled magicians who will disagree with my sweeping assertion that *the only thing I can change with Magick is myself.* It is of course a statement that is impossible for me to prove or disprove, and frankly I'm not inclined or motivated to try. I'm not trying to establish or defend magical doctrine. I simply know that for me – at this season of my life – at this moment in my magical career – the thing that needs to change the most in my world is *me.*

I have to confess, the prospect of magick being a form of consciously directed self-evolution was not what initially attracted to me to the art so many years ago. Naturally, I told myself that I was doing all this to gain 'enlightenment' – to achieve 'spiritual liberation,' but in truth it was the allure of wearing a black-hooded robe and strutting around in darkened temples brandishing my wand and sword against terrible demons cowering in terrified obedience before my radiant adeptship.

Man! Would I look *cool* doing that!

No matter how noble and altruistic my conscious pretenses were, Lon Milo DuQuette (the post-adolescent magician) inwardly desired power – power to master the cruel and chaotic circumstances of my life – power to right the wrongs I was witnessing in the world around me – power to set things straight and in harmony with my own (obviously *already enlightened*) vision of personal, moral, social, political, and spiritual absolutes.

As comically deluded as I might have been, there is of course nothing fundamentally wrong with such youthful and militant idealism – nothing wrong with wanting to change the world for the better and setting to work to do just that. I guess the biggest flaw in my aspirational game-plan was that I was overlooking the fact that in order for me to use magick to begin making these changes I would first have to consciously evolve into a real magician. As luck would have it, I would early in my career come under the influence and tutelage of magicians who would each in their unique way (either by positive example, negative example, or admonition) make sure I never forgot this fundamental fact of life.

Foremost among my senior mentors were Phyllis Secker (Soror Meral), Grady L. McMurtry (Hymenaeus Alpha, 777), Helen Parsons-Smith (Soror Grimaud), and Francis (Israel) Regardie. All of these dear people are now deceased.

McMurtry and Regardie trained directly under Aleister Crowley, and Seckler had been the student of Jane Wolfe, a student of Crowley's and a one-time resident of Crowley's famous *Abbey of Thelema* in Sicily. Parsons-Smith was the double widow of Jack Parsons (the famed magician and rocket scientist) and Wilfred T. Smith – both were, at different times, Masters of Agape Lodge, O.T.O. in Southern California.

These colorful people kept me from being entirely alone in the early years of my quest. Because of their efforts (and more often despite their efforts) I was in the mid 1970s baptized in the magick fire of Thelema. With their encouragement, cynicism, and guidance, I formally took up the disciplines of Crowley's magical orders, the A∴A∴ and Ordo Templi Orients.

My A∴A∴ work began under the guidance of Seckler and was (or should have been) an entirely private affair. My O.T.O. experience, on the other hand, required me to work in a more public manner and with other magicians all over the world – sometimes many other magicians. In fact, an important aspect of the O.T.O.'s magical curriculum is the development of the individual magician's ability to work in concert (and survive) within the complexities of a uniquely organized society populated by cast of militantly independent magicians (some of whom are as intractable, imperfect and flawed as myself!). It's a very important part of the magical training of an O.T.O. initiate.

As you might expect, Crowley didn't make the O.T.O. ordeal an easy one. In fact, I've known more promising magicians to wreck on the shoals of the Order's societal challenges than for any other reason. More often than not, however, I usually come to see the wisdom and genius of Crowley's magical vetting process.

Whether or not they have established a formal A.A. relationship, a great many O.T.O. initiates and others who consider themselves Thelemic magicians embark on the study and practice of the various rituals Crowley developed for the edification of A.A. magicians. The systematic practice of these rituals *vis a vis* the magician's personal initiatory climb up the *Tree of Life* of consciousness is generally viewed in Thelemic circles as "doing the work."

The work is certainly there to do. The rituals and a few commentaries are published in a plethora of sources. One of the finest collections is found in the magnificently ponderous Liber ABA, Book IV 1, but for many years most of us relied almost exclusively on those ritual 'Libers' that appeared in the Appendices of *Magick in Theory and Practice*.

Armed with little more than these Libers and the roadmap of the *Tree of Life*, four generations of magicians have set out alone on the Thelemic path of return; dissecting, cross-referencing, and trying to make sense of the bewildering subtleties of Crowley's evolving thought, and then attempting to transfer that understanding to the temple environment in coherent ceremonies that can be performed by (and for the benefit of) one person. To say it is a challenge to the lone magician would be a 'beastly' understatement.

Yes. Magick is a lonely art. But does it always need to be that lonely? I don't believe so – and neither does my Brother Rodney Orpheus. People – even magicians – sometimes need other people. There are moments in my life when I don't know *what* I am, *where* I am, or *who* I am unless I can see myself momentarily reflected in the souls of others around me.

The term *"Thelemic group ritual"* may sound like an oxymoron, but it needn't be one. As Brother Orpheus reveals, many of Crowley's most significant rituals started out as group operations. For me, it is profoundly helpful (at times even necessary) to see the complex dynamics of my own inner magical mechanisms portrayed as different 'officers' in a ritual. I can, and of course must eventually integrate all these officers into myself, but first I have to know who they are, what they do, and what they mean to me. That is most easily and elegantly done by seeing them operate in a group drama.

I took one look at Rodney's group treatments of the *Ritual of the Mark of the Beast* and the *Invocation of Horus* and was thrown back in my chair in stunned admiration, *"My gods! Why hasn't someone done this before?"* This might sound like a rhetorical question, but in fact it does indeed have an answer. The reason someone hasn't done this before is because there are presently very few individuals living today who are qualified by education and experience to do so, and even fewer with the writing talent and communication skills to bring it all to life on the printed page. Brother Orpheus is the incarnation of both these aspects of genius. Whether he is expanding upon classic Crowley rituals or creating and developing his own Thelemic ceremonies, the magician reader can be confident he or she is in good hands.

Magick may be a lonely art, but that doesn't mean we must always be alone on our journey – and it doesn't mean we won't always need friends.

Love is the law, love under will.

Preface

No man is an island. However looking at the plethora of self-help books littering the New Age Spirituality section of the average bookstore you'd be forgiven for thinking we were all islands awash in a sea of our own obsessive behavior. While it is true that our approach to the gods must be an intensely personal journey, and that each individual must find their own path, it is also clearly true that mankind is a social animal, with a hard-wired need to share experience and work together towards a common goal.

Generally speaking there have been two major evolutionary factors in humanity's rise to dominance of the Earth:

1. our ability to manipulate our environment so that it can fit us better, using tools and constructing clothing and shelter
2. our ability to work together in communities, sharing work out to those best fitted to do it, and communicating our individual thoughts to each other to educate and instruct

In my own previous work *Abrahadabra* I concentrated very much on the first of these two things - giving people tools to use for their own individual development. However I have noticed since then that alongside spiritual development comes a desire to share those experiences, and deepen them in the sharing. From this desire springs the phenomenon of cults, magical orders, and organised religions. Even the most introspective and individual of religious systems inevitably gives rise to the collective experience.

Both my first book and this one are based on the principles of Thelema. Thelema is a spiritual system designed by Aleister Crowley about a hundred years ago, which has become increasingly popular in recent years. It is ideally suited to spiritual practices in the post-Einstein modern world since it asserts that there is no absolute moral dogma, no big god in the sky that we have to bow down to, and no evil demon who will make us burn in hell for our sins. As Crowley so aptly summed it up:

> *"There is no grace: there is no guilt:*
> *This is the Law: DO WHAT THOU WILT!"*

xii GRIMOIRE OF ALEISTER CROWLEY

Ironically of course, this means that you don't actually have to call yourself a Thelemite to work with the Thelemic system. Thelema allows you to be what you want, and believe what you want, while still being able to focus on the practical application of your spiritual belief. This practical application is what Crowley refers to as *Magick* - the Science and Art of causing Change to occur in conformity with Will. So even if you don't identify yourself with being a Thelemite as such, you can still easily and happily work with the rituals given in this book. Whether you call yourself a Gnostic, a Wiccan, a Buddhist, or even a Christian, you will absolutely be able to work with the the material given here and achieve great results.

To many beginners, Thelema seems to be one of the most individually-oriented spiritual systems, since it is fundamentally based on the primacy of the Will of each individual person. Yet the very first principle of Thelema - Do what thou wilt shall be the whole of the Law - emphasises not the self, but the other. When I say this phrase I am not talking about my Will, I'm talking about yours. I am affirming that you have the right to do your Will. It is a statement that above all is about my relationship with other people, not about myself alone.

No matter how individual we are, we're still human beings, we still need to share our experiences and deepen it in interaction with others. Many people will see this as a contradiction in terms, because they think that there must always be a big difference between the desire of an individual and the dynamic of a group. However many Thelemites would refute this thesis, and state that the only worthwhile group is one made up of people working together voluntarily towards a common goal. However it's certainly not easy, which is why Thelemic magical orders like O.T.O. exist - to provide a solid framework for Thelemites to work within.

Aleister Crowley, in a letter to his successor Karl Germer in 1942, shows that he too had an awareness of this issue. He says:

> "*The broad base of public association is the Gnostic Mass... The other rituals will have to tail along as best they can... Of course, the minor secrets in them have their special magical value, so that they will always maintain a certain use to certain types of mind. Also, the actual magical effect on the candidate may be of the greatest value to him, and the training and discipline are always useful.*"

He was specifically referring to the O.T.O. initiation rituals here, but the general point stands. There is no doubt that the Gnostic Mass is the pinnacle of Crowley's achievement when it comes to group ritual working, and he would no doubt feel extremely gratified and proud that it is now celebrated on a weekly basis by O.T.O. bodies across the globe. However Crowley also wrote a considerable number of other group rites that have been largely overlooked and also "may be of the greatest value" to us.

When I first got involved in Thelema in the 1970s, the number of Thelemites in the world was probably in the low hundreds, scattered all over the globe. Very few of them ever met, and if they did it was infrequent at best. So there was really no need for a book on Thelemic group ritual, and the books that were published on Thelema reflected that, being largely aimed at the solo magician. Since then, only thirty years later, that situation has changed dramatically, and continues to change.

Globally there are now tens of thousands of Thelemites, with O.T.O. alone currently having around 4000 members, and growing year on year. Almost every major world city has at least one Thelemic group. In the past years since publishing my first book I've visited many O.T.O. bodies around the world, of all sizes and levels of experience. All of them have been formed of people coming together to try to create a true Thelemic community and to explore the mysteries of the human experience together. O.T.O., in common with most magical orders, is based on a series of initiation rites, which gradually reveal the mysteries of the cycle of existence to the initiate. However, since initiation rites tend to occur fairly infrequently (usually about once a year at most for each member of the group) practically speaking in most cases they cannot provide the kind of regular group magical experience that a spiritual community needs, especially in a smaller local group. So the most frequent question I'm asked by new (and not so new) magical groups when I visit is "Well, we have a group of people here, so what do we do now?" Hence this book.

Rituals only manifest magical power when they are performed. Without that experiential component they are, quite literally, meaningless. Reading a ritual and thinking you know what it means is like reading a love poem and thinking you know what love is. Anyone who has read the text of the Gnostic Mass, and then attended a performance of it, will know what I mean. Reading alone cannot bring over even a fraction of the beauty, power, and intensity of great ritual performance.

So in collating and editing the rituals presented here, performance has been my number one priority. Many of the rites have either never been published properly before, or when they have been, evidence suggests that they were rarely, if ever, performed beforehand. Many were clearly left unfinished or contained significant internal errors. Accordingly in many cases they've had to be greatly amended to make them performable. Crowley scholars looking for an exact reproduction of his unpublished notes are therefore likely to be disappointed. In making edits I have however tried to stick as closely as possible to the original texts, and where I've had to add dialogue I've borrowed from Crowley's own writings rather than add my own. I've tried to ensure that the end result remains faithful to the authors' original intent, while also making them practical and workable.

Another important thing to remember about the performance of ritual: you don't have to be some sort of expert to start doing magick! Even if you are a complete beginner to this stuff, don't let that stop you. Many of the rituals here were originally written to be performed by people with little or no magical background or deep knowledge. That's actually kind of the point: you learn about ritual by actually doing it. Doing one good ritual will teach you more than reading one hundred bad books. So don't assume you have to have a library of occult tomes, or need to be trained for years by some ancient magical Order before starting this stuff. Just get together with this book and a couple of friends and get going. Your performance might not win any Oscars, but it will get results, and you'll learn a lot in the process.

Although this is a specifically Thelemic compendium, and based largely on the works of Aleister Crowley, it should be borne in mind that no man is an island in time either. While researching these rites it has become ever more apparent to me that our work today is a continuation of a current that rolls throughout the centuries, from Ancient Egypt, through the Greek Mysteries, Roman Mithraism, Gnosticism, the Knights Templar, medieval demonology, the Rosicrucians, and many more. I think it's important that we honour these our ancestors, and respect the sacrifices they made to communicate this Hidden Tradition to us, often against great odds. Accordingly in this book you'll also find rituals originating several centuries ago, but which have a strong historical connection to modern Thelema, and updated for performance in the world today.

In some cases, especially in the sections of the book dealing with Goetia and Gnosticism, I've rewritten some historical rituals to conform with Thelemic ideas. Whereas I'd like to think that this is an innovation on my part, there is already quite a precedent for it, not least by Gerald B. Gardner. Gardner was a VII° member of O.T.O. and combined parts of the Book of the Law and the Gnostic Mass with older ritual texts to create his revived witch cult rites, with Crowley's encouragement; and it was these synthetic rites that led to the development of modern-day Wicca.

However this isn't just a book listing the texts of a bunch of rituals. There's a lot more to working in a group than simply getting together to recite a few mystical sentences once a week. A group's power lies in more than being a collection of individuals, it is also in the relationships that exist between individuals. So throughout the book I've tried to point out how important it is to foster healthy group dynamics. In this occult world of ours it's very easy for emotions to run high, which can lead to disastrous consequences if relationships are not carefully nurtured. On the other hand, it can also lead to some of the deepest and most fulfilling relationships you'll ever have with another group of people, and for that reason if no other has much to recommend it.

I am indebted to Hymenaeus Beta, Frater Superior O.T.O. for first bringing Crowley's unpublished ritual notes to my attention and thus providing the original inspiration for this book, and for his research assistance during the writing of it; Brother Lon Milo DuQuette for his unflagging support; Bishops Tau Apiryon and Helena for bringing together so much wisdom; David Rankine for sharing his profound knowledge of Goetia; Brother Richard Kaczinski for nitpicking in all the best ways; Brother Adrian Dobbie and Ulysses Black for design and layout, not an easy job in a book like this; the members of Quetzalcoatl Lodge (Brazil), Southern Cross Oasis (Australia), Tamesa Oasis, Tamion Camp, and Ameth Lodge (UK) for beta testing; all of the people around the world who wrote to tell me how much my first book meant to them; and last but most certainly not least, my Sister Cathryn Orchard for research, illustrations, feedback, and love. It would take a whole other book to describe fully how much I owe you.

I am also indebted to Richard M. Stallman, Tim Berners-Lee, Mark Shuttleworth and the Ubuntu team, the LibreOffice team, the Internet Sacred Text Archive, and to the Free Open Source Software community at large, for not only providing me with the tools to create this book, but also creating a truly Thelemic commonwealth of mutual respect, information sharing, and aid that is a model for modern society.

This book is not a comprehensive list of all Thelemic group rituals that exist, nor should it be. Thelema is a young religion, only a century old, and we are still creating it every day. By all means work with the rituals here, but I encourage you to examine them closely and learn how to extend and (hopefully) improve them. We're all learning (even me) and it would give me no greater pleasure than to see people using this work as a springboard to even greater efforts in the future.

Rodney Orpheus
Manchester, Europe, 2010

A Note on Safety

Magical rituals frequently make use of items that can be dangerous if misused: candles and other naked flames; daggers, swords, and other slashing and piercing weapons; water; and of course, those heavy, ungainly things we call our bodies. All of these things have killed and seriously injured people in the past, and it's up to you to make sure that you don't join their number in the future. Each time you add another person to your magical group you exponentially increase the likelihood of an accident happening. Don't just think that an accident might happen: the law of averages says that sooner or later it will happen! I'm a very careful person, yet I myself have had to be rushed to hospital in an ambulance when I was (accidentally) stabbed during a group ritual. I really don't want that to happen again - to me or anyone else.

To that end here are some important safety notes. And I do mean important - these are rules, not suggestions. Following these rules is not optional in a group setting! So when you start to work with any magical group, discuss these rules first, make sure everyone is aware of them, and that everyone agrees with them. If someone doesn't agree, then don't argue about it, just make it clear that they need to leave the temple. That's all there is to it.

1. Always have a fire extinguisher in the temple, and make sure that everyone knows where it is, and how to operate it. Only use it if the fire is very small or someone is actually alight. In general it's better to concentrate on getting everyone out of the building safely than try to fight a fire. Possessions are replaceable, you are not.

2. Make sure there is a clear exit route in case of emergency, and that everyone knows where it is.

3. Don't wear robes with big floppy sleeves and then reach over naked flames. Don't wear hairspray either. I've seen more than one person set themselves on fire during a ritual for just those reasons.

4. If you're working in some else's temple, or outdoors in a forest, make sure that you have permission to use naked flames. If you don't, lose the candles and charcoal and use battery torches instead.

5. Make sure that all burning items are in secure fireproof holders. Do not use small tea lights unless you have special candle holders to put them in - the metal surround that they come with is not a candle holder and can achieve ridiculous temperatures if left unattended. Don't leave smouldering charcoal laying around either, it can flare up and do some serious high temperature damage if you're not careful, especially outdoors. A forest fire is a very bad thing indeed, you really don't want to be stuck in the middle of one.

6. No sharp blades! Daggers and swords are called weapons for a reason: they are designed to kill people. All blades in temple must be blunted. I don't care how proud you may be of your original 18th century samurai sword, if it can cut me and hurt me, it doesn't belong in the same room as me. So either blunt it or dump it. There can be no exceptions to this rule.

7. Whereas flagellation has a long and noble history both as a spiritual and a sexual technique, if a ritual calls for whipping to be used, please go easy. There's no need to hurt someone, and in many countries beating someone until you cause a mark or draw blood is illegal and can have you thrown in prison *even if they fully consent*. If in doubt, keep it symbolic.

8. Don't draw blood in a public setting. There are some Thelemic rituals that call for blood-letting (most notably the Mass of the Phoenix) but this should be kept private, partly for the legal reasons stated above, but more importantly for reasons of hygiene. There are many pathogens borne by blood, don't pass them around. You don't want to catch some nasty disease, or cause someone else to catch it.

9. Don't flail your arms around, or spin round without looking. You'd be amazed at how many times I've seen someone get smacked in the face accidentally during a ritual. Remember that you will frequently be working in a confined space with several other people moving around, so move slowly and watch what you're doing.

10. Don't mix electricity and water. The result isn't nice.

11. When in doubt, safety first. If you think something might be unsafe, then assume that it is and don't do it.

12. Remember it's not just your safety you are dealing with during any group ritual, it's other people's safety as well. You might be prepared to take a risk with your own body, but you have no right to put someone else at risk too.

Chapter One
The Ritual of the Mark of the Beast

Aleister Crowley wrote a great number of magical rituals during his long and prolific career, but arguably his finest ritual is Liber V vel Reguli, which was originally published in Crowley's masterpiece *Magick in Theory and Practice* in 1929. This rite, also known as the Mark of the Beast ritual, is a version of one of the most fundamental rituals in the Hermetic magical tradition, the Pentagram Ritual.

Pentagram rituals belong to a class of ritual generally known as "Banishing" rituals, although that's rather a misleading term, since they don't really just "banish" things. They are designed to set up a neutral ritual space that a magician can work in, and to invoke energy into the magician in order to power the Will. A pentagram ritual is an entirely self-contained magical operation, and the regular practice of doing one of these pentagram rituals is highly recommended to beginning magicians.

Pentagram rituals were first popularised in the late 19th century by the Golden Dawn magical order, where Aleister Crowley received much of his early training. The Golden Dawn and its followers make much of the theory that all magical work should be opened and closed by a pentagram ritual being performed. This is far from being the universal law that some people might claim, and although it can certainly be beneficial in some cases, is rarely necessary. It also tends to reduce the pentagram ritual from the position of being a perfectly fine invocation in itself to being something that's little more than a prelude to other magical work, which is a terrible shame.

Aleister Crowley was a huge fan of the pentagram ritual, and taught the Golden Dawn version of it to all of his early students. However as time went on Crowley rightly saw that the G.D.'s pentagram ritual, despite its popularity, had some serious technical faults, and for many years attempted to amend and improve it. His first attempt was a ritual called the Star Ruby, published in the *Book of Lies* around 1912, and later even more amended.

Even that didn't seem to be enough for Crowley though, and in the 1920's he began work on the Mark of the Beast ritual, an even more radical revision of the Pentagram ritual. The O.T.O. Archives contain an early typescript of the ritual made by Crowley in about 1926, complete with several notes by him and one of his young students at the time, Gerald Yorke. The version presented in the typescript is obviously a work in progress, and contains sections later excised or radically changed in the final published version. In particular, in contrast to the final solo version of *Liber Reguli*, this early draft was intended to be a ritual for group working.

We know that Crowley had been using some kind of Pentagram ritual as part of O.T.O. group workings in 1921, when he wrote to the head of the American O.T.O., Charles Stansfeld Jones:

> *"We are having great success every night with rituals, the order being Pentagram, Creed, Collects, then anything special as occasion dictates, Benediction and O.T.O. applause. The effect has been magnificent."*
>
> Crowley to Jones, January 25, 1921

The Creed, Collects, and Benediction were taken from the text of *Liber XV*, The Gnostic Mass, which was designed from the outset as a group rite, however Pentagram rituals up until this point were primarily designed for solo practitioners. I think it quite likely then that the Mark of the Beast ritual may have been designed by Crowley around this period as an attempt to remedy this and create a more group-oriented Pentagram ritual.

The group sections in Crowley's early recension of the Mark of the Beast ritual are fairly minimal, being confined to a chorus adding Thelemic affirmations to the beginning/ending section of the rite (the "Qabalistic Cross" sections). The bulk of the rite is basically a fairly standard pentagram ritual performed by one person. As such it's not really an ideal group working, which is probably why Crowley dropped the group parts when he published it in 1929. However I do think that with the group sections added back in, it could be very useful as a ritual to open or close a general Lodge meeting, and a good way to get people involved in the performance of this excellent rite.

If your group is holding regular meetings or classes that don't have a major ritual component, one good exercise might be to have one member of the group (called the Magician in the ritual) perform this at the start or end of the evening, rotating this principal role at every meeting so that each member of the group gets to do the "starring role" at least once. Be careful not to fall into the trap of having the same person or couple of people do the principal role each time. If someone says "You know it better than me, so you should do it every time" then that's a message that they need to be taught how to do it better! The last thing any group needs is a couple of experienced people doing everything and not leaving room for new members to learn and flourish. So do please resist that temptation at all costs. Remember that one of the foundation stones of Thelema is that "every man and every woman is a star", so make sure everyone has a chance to shine.

The original typescript of the Mark of the Beast ritual has several points with question marks after them, and in a couple of places has several variations of the symbols marked out; clearly showing that Crowley didn't consider it complete, and was still trying to work out how it should all fit together. I spent some considerable time trying to reconstruct a working version of the rite from the original Crowley typescript notes, but eventually realised that if Crowley couldn't do it then I probably couldn't either.

In the end I decided to just use the published version from *Magick in Theory and Practice*, since clearly that was what Crowley considered the final revision; but with the addition of the original group parts from the early version. As soon as I added those back in and made a couple of minor tweaks, suddenly the ritual began to make sense as a viable group rite.

This synthetic version also has the advantage that if you already know the standard solo version of the Mark of the Beast ritual, it's quite easy to perform the role of the Magician in a group setting without having to shift gears radically; and conversely, being part of a group performance of it helps you learn it as a ritual for your own solo workings.

Note that in this ritual the pentagrams are drawn "averse", or upside-down to what is general usage in most Pentagram rituals. Contrary to popular belief, this does not imply that they are "evil" or "negative" in any way - really there's no such thing as the "correct" way to draw a pentagram, it's purely a convention. The pentagram is a star, and stars in the sky have no up or down, right way or averse way, they just are. I suspect that Crowley drew them this way because conventionally the single point upright pentagram symbolically refers to the divine spirit conquering matter, whereas the two points upward version refers to the divine descending into matter. Since the Mark of the Beast ritual is essentially about bringing divine energy down to the earth (as is invocation generally), then using the pentagrams in this form makes logical sense.

An interesting feature of this ritual is that it uses the so-called Invoking Pentagrams, rather than the Banishing Pentagrams used in most other Pentagram rituals. Frankly I don't consider it particularly important either way since all Pentagram rituals are essentially invocations of divine energy regardless of which pentagram you use or what way up you draw it. For more information on the pentagrams used in the Golden Dawn tradition see Appendix I of this book.

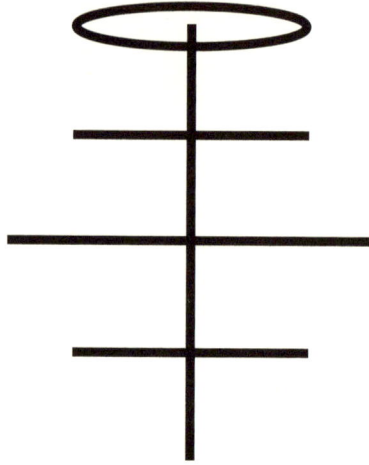

The Oath of the Enchantment

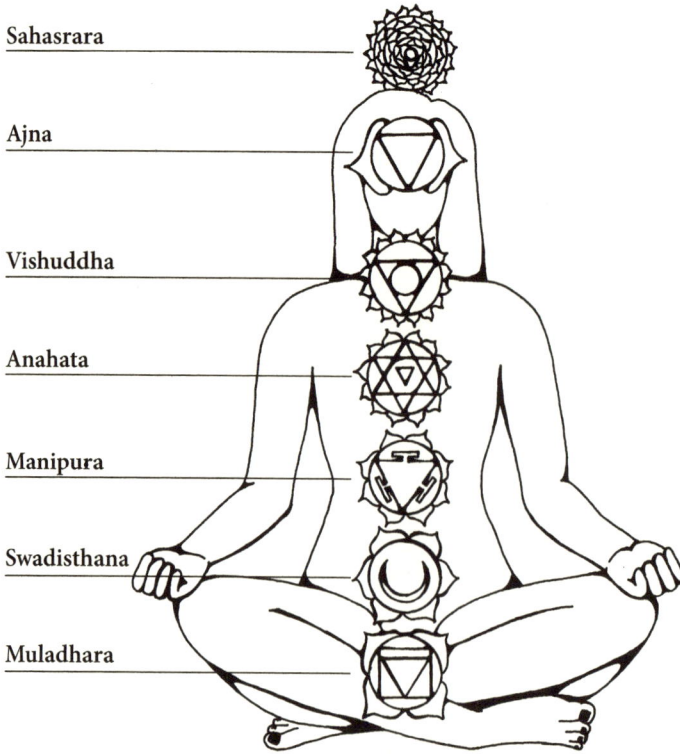

Sahasrara

Ajna

Vishuddha

Anahata

Manipura

Swadisthana

Muladhara

The Chakras

The Ritual of the Mark of the Beast: Group Version

Participants: Minimum 2. The rite works well with a small group.
Time required: 15 minutes.
Setup: Minimal.
Words: Relatively simple.
Equipment: • Wand
  • Robe

The FIRST GESTURE

The Oath of the Enchantment, which is called The Elevenfold Seal.

The Animadversion towards the Aeon.

1. Let the Magician, robed and armed as he may deem to be fit, turn his face towards Boleskine, that is the House of The Beast 666.
    {Note 1: Boleskine House is on Loch Ness, 17 miles from Inverness, Latitude 57.14 N. Longitude 4.28 W.}

    [The people should normally stand outside the circle, facing the Magician, unless you have a really big temple or are working outdoors, in which case you may have room for the people to stand inside the circle. In practice the Magician needs plenty of room to move around freely during the rite, so having the people within the circle rarely works well.

    Thelemic rituals are normally oriented towards Boleskine, the house where Aleister Crowley lived when he received the Book of the Law; *in a similar way to how Moslem rituals are oriented towards Mecca - it provides a common point of focus for everyone.]*

2. Let all strike the battery 1-3-3-3-1.

    [The best way to do this in a group setting is to have the Magician and all members of the group clap together, in a battery of one clap, three claps, three claps, three claps, one clap. Crowley's original notes have just the Magician doing the battery, but in practice I've found that having everyone do it together is greatly preferable.]

3. Let the Magician put the Thumb of his right hand between its index and medius, and make the gestures hereafter following.

Air

Fire

Earth

Water

The Averse Invoking Pentagrams

The Unicursal Hexagram

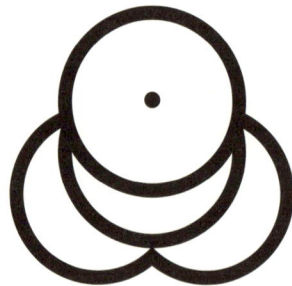

The Mark of the Beast

The Vertical Component of the Enchantment.

1. Let him describe a circle about his head, crying **NUIT!**

    [Note that generally when Crowley writes a word or phrase in all capital letters he means it to be intoned in a sonorous manner, rather than just spoken normally.]

2. Let him draw the Thumb vertically downward and touch the Muladhara Cakkra, crying, **HADIT!**

3. Let him, retracing the line, touch the centre of his breast and cry **RA-HOOR-KHUIT!**

All: Do what thou wilt shall be the whole of the Law.

The Horizontal Components of the Enchantment.

1. Let him touch the Centre of his Forehead, his mouth, and his larynx, crying **AIWAZ!**
2. Let him draw his thumb from right to left across his face at the level of the nostrils.
3. Let him touch the centre of his breast, and his solar plexus, crying, **THERION!**
4. Let him draw his thumb from left to right across his breast, at the level of the sternum.
5. Let him touch the Svadistthana, and the Muladhara Cakkra, crying, **BABALON!**
6. Let him draw his thumb from right to left across his abdomen, at the level of the hips.

All: **Love is the law, love under will.**

[A holograph note by Crowley states:
·   Nuit and Hadit are Brain and Seed (Brahmarandra and Muladhara)
·   Aiwaz is Silence and Speech (Ajna and Visuddhi)
·   Ra Hoor Khuit is Force and Fire (Anahata)
·   Therion is Manipura - or also Anahata?
·   Babalon is Svadistthana, the Womb

Here Crowley relates the primary Thelemic gods to the chakras, or energy centres in the body, according to the Indian yogic system. In Liber ABA, Book 4 Part 2, Crowley describes them as being lotuses:

Puella

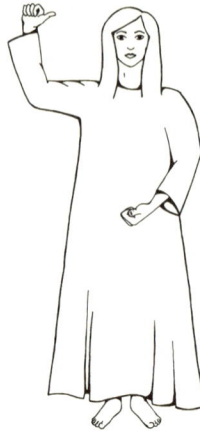

Puer

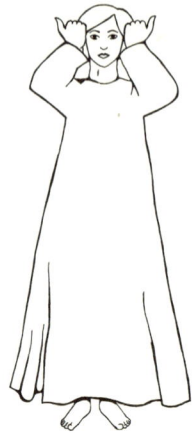

Vir

Mulier

Mater Triumphans

The NOX Signs

There is the lotus of three petals in the Sacrum, in which the Kundalini lies asleep. This lotus is the receptacle of reproductive force. There is also the six-petalled lotus opposite the navel—which receives the forces which nourish the body. There is also a lotus in the Solar plexus which receives the nervous forces. The six-petalled lotus in the heart corresponds to Tiphereth, and receives those vital forces which are connected with the blood. The sixteen-petalled lotus opposite the larynx receives the nourishment needed by the breath. The two-petalled lotus of the pineal gland receives the nourishment needed by thought, while above the junction of the cranial sutures is that sublime lotus, of a thousand and one petals, which receives the influence from on high; and in which, in the Adept, the awakened Kundalini takes her pleasure with the Lord of All.

These chakras also relate to the fundamental Man of Earth Degrees in Ordo Templi Orientis.

Crowley's notes to Liber Reguli go on to say:

...The Cross should include Hod and Netzach, Chokmah, and Binah

The "Qabalistic Cross" must be that of the Grand Hierophant, but crowned by Nuit.

Here Crowley references how this also relates to the Hebrew Qabalah. We can clearly see his lifelong obsession with the creation of what might be called a "Grand Unified System" of magick, containing a synthesis of all the best bits from many different traditions. If you are a complete beginner and these references to Egyptology, Yoga, and Qabalah are over your head, you might wish to consult my previous book Abrahadabra, which provides a comprehensive introduction to these concepts.]

The Asseveration of the Spells.

[Asseveration is the act of asserting something firmly and positively.]

1. Let the Magician clasp his hands upon his Wand, his fingers and thumbs interlaced, crying **LAShTAL! THELEMA! FIAOF! AGAPE! AUMGN!** (Thus shall be declared the Words of Power whereby the Energies of the Aeon of Horus work his will in the World.)

[These words are pronounced: Lash-tal, Thel-e-ma, Ee-A-O, Ag-a-pay, A-oom. Note that the Fs in FIAOF and the GN in AUMGN are silent.]

All: **The Word of the Law is Thelema!**

The Proclamation of the Accomplishment.

1.   Let all strike the Battery: 3-5-3, crying **ABRAHADABRA**.

[Have all members of the group clap together here, in a battery of three claps, five claps, three claps, then cry ABRAHADABRA together.]

The SECOND GESTURE

The Enchantment.

1.   Let the Magician, still facing Boleskine, advance to the circumference of his circle.

2.   Let him turn himself towards the left, and pace with the stealth and swiftness of a tiger the precincts of his circle, until he complete one revolution thereof.

3.   Let him give the Sign of Horus (or The Enterer) as he passeth, so to project the force that radiateth from Boleskine before him.

[This sign is made by leaning forward, advancing the left foot and throwing the arms out horizontally before you, as if to fire energy out of them.]

4.   Let him pace his path until he comes to the North; there let him halt, and turn his face to the North.

[That is you go round one and a quarter times]

5.   Let him trace with his wand the Averse Pentagram proper to invoke Air (Aquarius).

[An averse pentagram is one with the single point down, two points up. The Averse Air pentagram is drawn by starting at the lower left point and going horizontally across to the right, then up left, down middle, up right, down left. i.e. go widdershins (anti-clockwise).]

6.   Let him bring the wand to the centre of the Pentagram and call upon **NUIT!**

[All of the people should assist the Magician by visualising the particular God or Goddess called in each quarter. If in doubt use the imagery shown in the Trump

cards of a Crowley Tarot pack. For Nuit, see Atu XVII, The Star; Atu XX, The Aeon; or Atu XXI, The Universe.]

7.   Let all make the sign called Puella, standing with the feet together, head bowed, the left hand shielding the Muladhara Cakkra, and the right hand shielding the breast (attitude of the Venus de Medici).

[Puella, Puer, Mulier, Vir, Mater Triumphans are Latin for Girl, Boy, Woman, Man, Triumphant Mother. These signs are attributed to the five elements, and to the various stages that their energy manifests through.]

8.   Let the Magician turn again to the left, and pursue his Path as before, projecting the force from Boleskine as he passeth; let him halt when he next cometh to the South and face outward.

[i.e. go round one and a half circles. See Crowley manuscript note below which explains why.]

9.   Let him trace the Averse Pentagram that invoketh Fire (Leo).

[Start bottom middle and go deosil (clockwise) i.e. go up left and then round until you've completed the entire pentagram.]

10.   Let him point his wand to the centre of the Pentagram, and cry, **HADIT!**

[See Atu XX, The Aeon - Hadit is the winged disk.]

11.   Let all give the sign Puer, standing with feet together, and head erect. Let the right hand (the thumb extended at right angles to the fingers) be raised, the forearm vertical at a right angle with the upper arm, which is horizontally extended in the line joining the shoulders. Let the left hand, the thumb extended forwards and the fingers clenched, rest at the junction of the thighs (Attitude of the gods Mentu, Khem, etc.).

12.   Let the Magician proceed as before; then in the East, let him make the Averse Pentagram that invoketh Earth (Taurus).

[Another one and a quarter circles. The pentagram is drawn from bottom middle widdershins towards the upper right point and so on.]

13.   Let him point his wand to the centre of the pentagram, and cry, **THERION!**

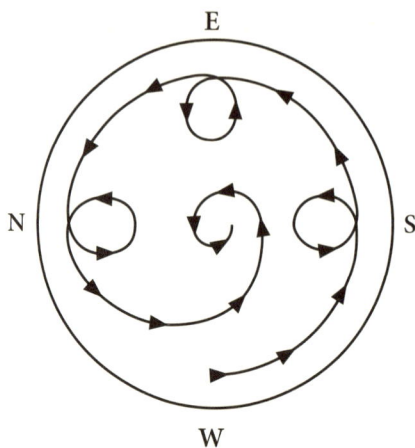

Spiral Dance 1

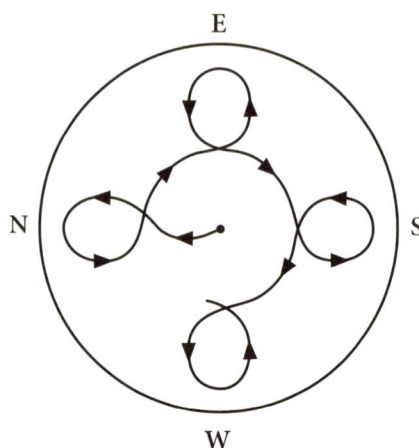

Spiral Dance 2

Sign of the Enterer

Sign of Silence

[See Atu XI, Lust - Therion is the Beast pictured.]

14.   Let all give the sign called Vir, the feet being together. The hands, with clenched finger and thumbs thrust out forwards, are held to the temples; the head is then bowed and pushed out, as if to symbolize the butting of an horned beast (attitude of Pan, Bacchus, etc.).

15.   Proceeding as before, let the Magician make in the West the Averse Pentagram whereby Water is invoked.

[Another one and a half circles. A Crowley manuscript note says: "11 half-circles, or 5 1/2 circles to unite 5 & 6. Puer makes him Vir; Vir makes Puella - Mulier."
The Averse pentagram of Water: start at the lower right and go horizontally across to the lower left and thus round deosil. Note that the pentagrams change direction each time - first widdershins, then deosil, then widdershins again, then deosil.]

16.   Pointing the wand to the centre of the Pentagram, let him call upon **BABALON!**

[See Atu XI again - Babalon is the Goddess riding on the Beast.]

17.   Let all give the sign Mulier. The feet are widely separated, and the arms raised so as to suggest a crescent. The head is thrown back (attitude of Baphomet, Isis in Welcome, the Microcosm of Vitruvius). (See *Book 4*, Part II).

18.   Let the Magician break into the dance, tracing a centripetal spiral widdershins, enriched by revolutions upon his axis as he passeth each quarter, until he come to the centre of the circle. There let him halt, facing Boleskine.

[You go round the circle one complete revolution here.]

19.   Let him raise the wand, trace the Mark of the Beast, and cry **AIWAZ!**

[Crowley's notes say: Trace the mark where Sol is Hadit, Luna Nuit, and the Testes 666 and 156. The Mark of the Beast is composed of three sections: the top circle with point in the middle represents the sun, Sol, and is assigned to the Thelemic god Hadit; the crescent just below is the moon, Luna, and assigned to the goddess Nuit; and the two semi-circles at the bottom (Testes) are assigned to 666 (To Mega Therion) and 156 (Babalon).
Aiwaz should be visualised as "a tall dark man in his thirties, well-knit, active and strong, with the face of a savage king, and eyes veiled lest their gaze destroy what

they saw." A Crowley typescript note refers to the wand here as a "Prometheus-tube", the inference being that the Magician is drawing down divine energy to the Earth in this section.]

20.   Let him trace the invoking Hexagram of The Beast.

[This is the Unicursal Hexagram, drawn from the top middle point deosil towards the bottom right, top left, bottom middle, top right, bottom left, top middle.]

21.   Let him lower the wand, striking the Earth therewith.

22.   Let all give the sign of Mater Triumphans (The feet are together; the left arm is curved as if it supported a child; the thumb and index finger of the right hand pinch the nipple of the left breast, as if offering it to that child). Let all utter the word **THELEMA!**

23.   Let the Magician perform the spiral dance, moving deosil and whirling widdershins. Each time on passing the West he should extend the wand to the Quarter in question, and bow:

[Note that he extends the wand to the quarter, not bows to the quarter. Each time he bows to the West.]

   a. **"Before me the powers of LA!"** (to West.)
   b. **"Behind me the powers of AL!"** (to East.)
   c. **"On my right hand the powers of LA!"** (to North.)
   d. **"On my left hand the powers of AL!"** (to South.)
   e. **"Above me the powers of ShT!"** (leaping in the air.)
   f. **"Beneath me the powers of ShT!"** (striking the ground.)
   g. **"Within me the Powers!"** (in the attitude of Phthah erect, the feet together, the hands clasped upon the vertical wand.)
   h. **"About me flames my Father's face, the Star of Force and Fire."**
   i. **"And in the Column stands His six-rayed Splendour!"**
      (This dance may be omitted, and the whole utterance chanted in the attitude of Phthah.)

[The attitude of Phthah is standing upright, the feet together, with the wand clenched with both hands upright against the chest]

The FINAL GESTURE

This is identical with the First Gesture.

Chapter Two
The Invocation of Horus
According to the Divine Vision of W., the Seer

The Invocation of Horus was first performed by Aleister Crowley in March 1904 in Cairo, at the instigation of his recently married bride Rose, called W, or Ouarda (Arabic for Rose) in the text. Over a period of a few days Aleister had been performing rituals to introduce his new bride to magick, a subject about which she knew nothing. Much to his surprise, each time he did so Rose would fall into a trance and receive instructions that they should invoke the Egyptian god Horus. She gave detailed instructions as to the setting of the ritual, which was quite different to what Aleister had been used to from his training in the Golden Dawn; but he reluctantly went ahead with it at noon on March 19th as he had been instructed. He was not impressed with the results, but Rose told him he should perform it again at midnight as well. This time, the rite was a huge success, and Aleister was informed (presumably again via the mediumship of Rose) that "The Equinox of the Gods had come", and that he was to prepare a link "between the solar-spiritual force and mankind".

It was this ritual that led to the writing of *The Book of the Law* in the same room a few days later on April 8-10, and the inauguration of what would become the Thelemic system of magick. So if your and your companions are planning to start performing rituals together, or to establish yourselves as a group, this is a fitting ritual to start work with; it's relatively simple to perform and very powerful.

It may not be obvious at first glance that this is a group ritual, and indeed since then it has frequently been performed as a solo rite; but it should be remembered that the setup instructions do specify "white robes" plural, and that there were two people involved in the original performance, both Aleister and Rose Crowley. We can assume that Aleister was the one saying all the words, while Rose acted as the Seer, or focus for the divine energy, and spoke with the voice of the God. Although she may not have had any experience with magick before she was clearly fully able to play a vital role in the performance of this ritual. There's an important lesson there: that even if you are completely inexperienced you may be perfectly capable of performing powerful and important magick; so never let lack of experience stop you from doing what you need to do.

Something else that may not be obvious is that this was written as a divinatory rite - the idea was to invoke Horus so that he could transmit a message that was waiting for Aleister. In practice this rite can still be used for divinatory purposes by us today, but I think it needs to be borne in mind that we aren't the Crowleys, nor is this still the dawn of the New Aeon of Thelema - the New Aeon that this ritual initially heralded is here now and we are in the midst of it. We are already living through the results of the original performance of this ritual and the message transmitted by it. As such, I think it's more fitting for us to use it as a commemorative or celebratory ritual.

Whereas the rite was presumably originally written for recitation by one person only, it lends itself easily to adaptation for a larger group, and the version I give here is built around the classic call and response format. Call and response is a great way to run any group ritual, especially in a group where some are less experienced than others - one person can lead the invocation with everyone else joining in the response. This format is a very common ritual technique across many different cultures and religions around the world, from African shamanism to High Christian Masses. However you shouldn't assume that because one person leads and the others follow that this means that only one person is "active" in the rite - everyone is an active participant and adds power to the invocation.

The ritual contains rich visual imagery, much of it derived from the classical Egyptian myths about Horus. Each participant should try to visualise what is being described during the rite, in order to formulate the god's presence more strongly. Studying a book on Egyptian myths beforehand might be very useful. E. A. Wallis Budge's *Gods of the Egyptians* came out in the same year as this ritual was originally written, and although it's not considered to be the most scholarly work these days, it is a good snapshot of the prevailing wisdom at the time, and is easily available.

If one person is going to perform most of the Horus invocation, it may be an idea for them to be robed as described in the later section of the text i.e. a white robe edged in gold with a red descending triangle affixed to the chest; a head wrapping in white and gold; a sword; and a wand of some sort.

The original text simply ends with the line "The Adoration - Impromptu"; presumably the idea was that by this stage the Seer would be sufficiently overcome that Horus would take over and direct the ritual himself from there. In *Magick*, Chapter 19, On Dramatic Rituals, Crowley writes:

"Following the climax there should always be an unrehearsed ceremony, an impromptu. The most satisfactory form of this is the dance. In such ceremonies appropriate libations may be freely used."

I'm far from convinced that this is a good universal rule. In my experience, "impromptu" can be a rather dangerous word in a group ritual situation. Impromptu sections can sometimes degenerate into egoistic posturing or grandstanding by one or more members of the group; or equally bad, into a bunch of people looking at each other sheepishly wondering what to do next that won't be totally embarrassing for each of them. For these reasons I usually try not to leave any loose ends like this in a group setting. I'd suggest that rather than leaving the Adoration to be completely impromptu, that the group decide beforehand roughly what format the Adoration should take, and stick to it. Possibilities for the Adoration could include:

1. Have a statue of Horus in the temple, or an altar dedicated to him. Then at the end of the ritual, have each person come before it and place an offering there - this could be a garland of flowers, an offering of food or drink, or perhaps to anoint the statue with a small amount of holy oil.

2. Simply have each person stand, sit, or kneel in silent meditation, either with their eyes closed or perhaps focused on an image of the god, or on a copy of the Stele of Revealing.

The Adoration period doesn't have to be too long, but I would recommend that it be at least a few minutes. A good ten minutes or more would be ideal - after the preceding invocations you'll probably need that amount of time just to deal with the energy coursing through your system.

During this period of adoration, each person should attempt to communicate with Horus, build up an image of him in their mind, feel his energy coursing through their body, etc. If there's something that they particularly desire the god's help with, now would be a good time to focus on that magical intention too. Remember that in this rite, the participants are invoking Horus into themselves (see the last paragraph of the invocation, where it says "Come thou forth and dwell in me"). So you are adoring the god incarnating inside yourself, and through that adoration attaining direct communication with his essence.

The Invocation of Horus

Participants:	Two or more. The rite works well with a large group.
Time required:	About an hour
Setup:	Not too complex, but does require preparation of a rosary beforehand.
Words:	Medium
Equipment:	• Sword
	• Rosary of 44 beads (preferably pearl)
	• White robes (optionally edged in gold with red triangle affixed to breast)
	• Head wrap in white & gold (optional)
	• Wand (optional)

(To be performed before a window open to the E. or N. without incense. The room to be filled with jewels, but only diamonds to be worn. A sword, unconsecrated, 44 pearl beads to be told. Stand. Bright daylight at 12:30 noon. Lock doors. White robes. Bare feet. Be very loud. Saturday. Use the sign of Apophis and Typhon.)

[These are the setting instructions originally received by Rose Crowley. The ritual was originally to be performed in Cairo at the Spring Equinox, so standing by an open window would have been quite pleasant. It may not be so pleasant in March in Sweden or Wisconsin. So use common sense here. If for practical reasons you can't get things to work precisely to these specifications, I think that the important thing is that a sunny room with lots of natural light is to be preferred.

The time is specified as 12.30 noon, but when it was first performed at this time the results seemed poor, and it was the second performance at midnight when spectacular results were achieved. That leaves us with a dilemma in trying to reproduce it: do we aim for 12.30 in the afternoon or after midnight? I can only suggest that you try whichever seems to suit your situation best and see what happens.

The "Be very loud" instruction may be dispensed with if you're doing this rite in a large apartment block with thin walls on a Saturday afternoon - or even worse after midnight! And of course if you're going to be doing this with a group of people it will tend to get loud naturally, so watch out for that, especially if you have open windows. You really don't want people in the street to be calling the police to investigate their evil black magician neighbours next door!

The "44 pearl beads to be told" means a beaded necklace to be used as a rosary - in other words hold the necklace in your hand, moving one bead through your fingers with every line of invocation. Since the rite contains four sections, each with eleven lines of invocation, I think it's a safe bet to assume that one bead of the rosary is to be told for each line of each section. Making one of the beads slighter larger or different than the others helps you to know where to start and stop. For this particular rite, perhaps the best bet would be to have four groups of eleven beads, each group having ten normal beads plus one large bead. Although the ritual specifies pearl, I see no harm is using glass or stone beads as a substitute if that's all that you have handy.

The sign of Apophis and Typhon consists of holding your arms upwards in a V shape, roughly about 90 degrees apart (i.e. 45 degrees each side of your head). If you're going to be flinging your arms in the air while holding a beaded necklace in one hand, be careful you don't smack the person beside you in the face with a swinging necklace. It can be quite painful, and certainly disruptive to the ritual at the very least. It also helps if you know your lines so you don't have to fling around a script as well as a rosary.

In the following sections text in normal type should be performed by the main Magician, and text in bold should be performed by all of the participants in the rite as a response.]

Confession

Most Holy and Divine Lord of the Aeon, Ra-Hoor-Khuit, Crowned and Conquering Child:
Hear Thou this humble but bold invocation of Thy Presence:
O, Lord of the Sun, O God of War and Vengeance, I, [your magical name], ask to enter Thy Presence and ask that Thou willst aid and guard me in this work of Thine Art.

[Your magical name can be your motto as a magician, or if you don't have one, your full civil name. If the ritual is being performed by a group the text could be altered from "I" and "me" to "we" and "us", perhaps with the name of the magical group performing the rite]

I.

Strike, strike the master chord!
Draw, draw the Flaming Sword!
Crowned Child and Conquering Lord,
Horus, Avenger!

(At every "Thee I invoke," throughout the whole of the ritual, give the sign of Apophis.)

[If performing as a group ritual, one person may be chosen to recite the main part of the invocation with all the other members of the group doing the signs and the "Thee I invoke!" part. Alternately you could split it up and have one person leading

Osiris Slain

Isis Mourning

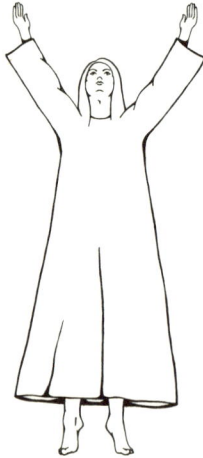

Apophis and Typhon

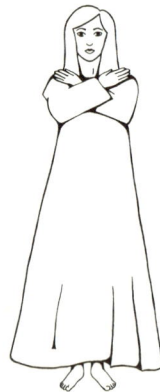

Osiris Risen

The LVX Signs

Rosary

Part I, another leading Part II, and so on through the four sections.
Note that in all four sections the "Invoke" response words are slightly different each time, but the sign of Apophis should be made with every response regardless of the exact wording.
This first section consists of calls to Horus in the third person, describing his attributes.]

O Thou of the Head of the Hawk!
Thee, Thee, I invoke!

Thou only-begotten-child of Osiris Thy Father, and Isis Thy Mother.
He that was slain;
She that bore Thee in Her womb flying from the Terror of the Water.
Thee, Thee I invoke!

O Thou whose Apron is of flashing white, whiter than the Forehead
of the Morning!
Thee, Thee I invoke!

O Thou who hast formulated Thy Father and made fertile Thy Mother!
Thee, Thee I invoke!

O Thou whose garment is of the golden glory with the azure bars of sky!
Thee, Thee I invoke!

Thou, who didst avenge the Horror of Death; Thou the slayer of Typhon!
Thou who didst lift Thine arms, and the Dragons of Death were as dust;
Thou who didst raise Thine Head and the Crocodile of Nile was abased
before Thee!
Thee, Thee I invoke!

O Thou whose Nemyss hideth the Universe with night, the impermeable
Blue!
Thee, Thee I invoke!

Thou who travellest in the Boat of Ra, abiding at the Helm of the Aftet
boat and of the Sektet boat!
Thee, Thee I invoke!

Thou who bearest the Wand of Double Power!
Thee, Thee I invoke!

Thou about whose presence is shed the darkness of Blue Light,
the unfathomable glory of the outmost Ether, the untravelled,
the unthinkable immensity of Space.
Thou who concentrest all the Thirty Ethers in one darkling sphere
of Fire!
Thee, Thee I invoke!

O Thou who bearest the Rose and Cross of Life and Light!
Thee, Thee I invoke!

> The Voice of the Five.
> The Voice of the Six.
> Eleven are the Voices.
> Abrahadabra!

II.

> Strike, strike the master chord!
> Draw, draw the Flaming Sword!
> Crowned Child and Conquering Lord,
> Horus, Avenger!

[In a group setting the following section could be performed, with each member taking a line in turn. Alternately one person could be chosen to do all the lines. This second section consists of calling Horus by all his various names.]

By Thy name of Ra, I invoke Thee, Hawk of the Sun, the glorious one!
I invoke Thee!

By Thy name Harmachis, youth of the Brilliant Morning, I invoke Thee!
I invoke Thee!

By Thy name Mau, I invoke Thee, Lion of the Midday Sun!
I invoke Thee!

By Thy name Tum, Hawk of the Even, crimson splendour of the sunset,
I invoke Thee!
I invoke Thee!

By Thy name of Khep-Ra I invoke Thee, O Beetle of the hidden Mastery of Midnight!
I invoke Thee!

By Thy name Heru-pa-Kraat, Lord of Silence, Beautiful Child that standest on the Dragons of the Deep, I invoke Thee!
I invoke Thee!

By Thy name Apollo, I invoke Thee, O man of Strength and Splendour, O Poet, O Father!
I invoke Thee!

By Thy name of Phoebus, that drivest Thy Chariot through the Heavens of Zeus, I invoke Thee.
I invoke Thee!

By Thy name of Odin, I invoke Thee, O warrior of the North, O Renown of the Sagas.
I invoke Thee!

By Thy name Jeheshua, O Child of the Flaming Star, I invoke Thee!
I invoke Thee!

By Thine own, thy secret name Hoori, Thee I invoke!
I invoke Thee!

The Names are Five.
The Names are Six.
Eleven are the Names!
Abrahadabra!

Behold! I stand in the Midst. Mine is the symbol of Osiris; to Thee are mine eyes ever turned.
Unto the splendour of Geburah, the magnificence of Chesed, the mystery of Daath, thither I lift up mine eyes.
This have I sought, and I have sought the Unity: hear Thou me!

III.

[In the third section we call Horus within us - he is no longer an external entity. If one person is taking on the part of Horus it might be a good idea to robe them in the items described below.]

Mine is the Head of the Man, and my insight is keen as the Hawk's.
By my head I invoke Thee!

I am the only-begotten child of my Father and mother.
By my body I invoke Thee!

About me shine the Diamonds of Radiance white and pure.
By their brightness I invoke Thee!

Mine is the Red Triangle Reversed, the sign given of none, save it be of Thee, O Lord!
By the Lamen I invoke Thee!

Mine is the garment of white sewn with gold, the flashing abbai that I wear.
By my robe I invoke Thee!

Mine is the sign of Apophis and Typhon!
By the sign I invoke Thee!

Mine is the turban of white and gold, and mine the blue vigour of the intimate air!
By my crown I invoke Thee!

My fingers travel on the Beads of Pearl; so run I after Thee in thy car of glory.
By my fingers I invoke Thee!

I bear the Wand of Double Power in the Voice of the Master - Abrahadabra!
By the word I invoke Thee!

Mine are the dark-blue waves of music in the song that I made of old to invoke Thee-

Strike, strike the master chord!
Draw, draw the Flaming Sword!
Crowned Child and Conquering Lord,
Horus, Avenger!

By the song I invoke Thee!
In my hand is thy Sword of Revenge; let it strike at Thy bidding!
By the Sword I invoke Thee!

The Voice of the Five.
The Voice of the Six.
Eleven are the Voices.
Abrahadabra!

IV.

[The fourth section continues with Horus now manifested within the participants.]

(At every "Abrahadabra" throughout this section, give the sign of Apophis)

Mine is the Head of the Hawk!
Abrahadabra!

I am the only-begotten-child of Osiris My Father, and Isis My Mother.
He that was slain;
She that bore Me in Her womb flying from the Terror of the Water.
Abrahadabra!

My Apron is of flashing white, whiter than the Forehead of the Morning!
Abrahadabra!

I have formulated My Father and made fertile My Mother!
Abrahadabra!

Mine is the garment of the golden glory with the azure bars of sky!
Abrahadabra!

I did avenge the Horror of death, I am the slayer of Typhon! I did lift
Mine arms, and the Dragons of Death were as dust;

I did raise Mine Head, and the Crocodile of Nile was abased before Me!
Abrahadabra!

My Nemyss hides the Universe with night, the impermeable Blue!
Abrahadabra!

I travel in the Boat of Ra, abiding at the Helm of the Aftet boat and of the
Sektet boat!
Abrahadabra!

I who bearest the Wand of Double Power!
Abrahadabra!

About my presence is shed the darkness Blue Light, the unfathomable
glory of the outmost Ether, the untravelled, the unthinkable immensity
of Space.
I concenter all the Thirty Ethers in one darkling sphere of Fire!
Abrahadabra!

(Remaining in the Sign, the invocation concludes:)

Therefore I say unto thee: Come Thou forth and dwell in me; so that
every spirit, whether of the Firmament, or of the Ether, or of the
Earth or under the Earth; on dry land or in the Water, of Whirling air
or of Rushing Fire; and every spell and scourge of God the Vast One
may be THOU!

Abrahadabra!

The Adoration.

Chapter Three
Invocation of the Holy Spirit (Isis)

The Invocation of the Holy Spirit was a litany apparently used by the residents of the Thelemic Abbey of Cefalu in Sicily during the early 1920s, and preserved amongst the papers of the one of the Abbey's residents, the Australian Frank Bennett, otherwise known as Frater Progradior. Crowley never published it, and thus the version that has come down to us isn't quite as polished as something like the Mark of the Beast. However it's still fairly complete and very workable.

A litany is another form of "call and response" ritual, where the officers recite various invocatory statements and the other participants respond with a repeated phrase or phrases, as we saw in the Invocation of Horus earlier.

This ritual requires a main opening officer, noted in the text as M.A., a Congregation (to perform the responses), and preferably several other officers who take on the various Egyptian god forms. This ideally would require one female to play the role of Nepthys and three males to play Harpocrates, Horus and Osiris respectively. Optionally one female can be chosen to play Isis, although she doesn't actually have any speech in the rite. However it might be useful to have someone attired as this goddess to act as a focus (see note on this below). If your group is small the M.A. could perform all the calls, with the other members present performing the appropriate responses.

It's not stated anywhere in the ritual notes we have what M.A. stands for - it probably means Major Adept. It's not really vital for us to know, since the title used isn't significant within the context of this ritual. In practice it just means "the person running the ritual". This might be the leader of your group, but it doesn't have to be.

It's important to bear in mind that the leader of a magical group might be the overall administrator and decision maker for the group's progress, but the leadership of specific magical workings can and should be passed around the membership of the group. And during the time of the ritual performance itself, whoever is in the lead role is the leader until the ritual is over. It doesn't matter if it's the most timid and least experienced member of the group, if they are performing the role of M.A. (or any other lead role in a ritual) they are in charge until the end of the working, and should be respected as such; as long as they stay within the rules of the constitution of the group, and within the limits of the safety instructions. So don't go second-guessing the ritual leader in the middle of a working, it's not usually very helpful.

However there's another side of that you should remember: no-one in a group should ever have absolute power. The group should have a set of clear rules and guidelines for how people are expected to comport themselves, and where authority begins and ends. If a group you join don't have their basic constitution written down and available to all the members, then suggest that they should. Rules like these don't have to be particularly complex, they can be just a couple of simple sentences spelling out the basic attitude that the group expects of everyone. And I do mean everyone, there should never be one rule for the members and a different rule for the leaders.

The group must also have a clearly understood set of safety procedures, and stick to them. If anyone ever tries to force you to ignore the safety procedures I've given at the beginning of the book, do feel confident to simply stand up and refuse. No-one has the right to put you in danger, no matter what spurious magical reasons they might come up with. And under no account ever join any group where the leader is expected to hold absolute power over the other members. I don't care how exalted and wise he or she is, or whether they really are the Son of God - we're all the Children of the Gods, so this isn't much of a big deal when you get down to it. Your life is every bit as important as theirs. It's not the job of a magical group leader to dictate your morality or your sexuality, or what you say and do in your daily life. It's their job to run a magical group, and that's all. A good rule of thumb is that if the members of a group - and that means all the members, including the leaders - don't treat each other with mutual respect, it's not a group you should be in.

But back to the ritual...

As regards attire and general setup, nothing is specified in the surviving typescript. So really it can be as simple or complex as desired. Normal magical robes could be worn, but better still the officers could be dressed in costumes traditionally associated with ancient Egypt or with the gods they are playing. Setting up statues of the gods invoked, or Egyptian hangings and pictures helps to set the mood; and having some incense burning is a good thing in almost any ritual. Feel free to use your imagination with this one, and build a good, but fitting, setting for the performance - your efforts will be well rewarded.

The ritual itself is basically in two parts: an introductory dialogue and the litanies proper. In the introduction, the M.A. asks certain questions which are replied to by the Brothers present or by the Sisters present. This dialogue between them sets up the focus of the rite and prepares the participants for the invocation that follows.

In the original text the speech given here for Osiris was not associated with any god. However the text itself in that section clearly identifies the speaker as Osiris, so I've taken the liberty of adding him in formally.

Unfortunately, although the ritual is quite beautiful, it doesn't really end; it just stops, with no resolution or climactic point - a common problem with many of Crowley's group rituals. During testing, participants often reported that when they reached the last litany they felt "all dressed up with nowhere to go". I suspect that the typescript we have here may actually be missing another page with more text for the rite, or some explanation of it.

Since the intent of the operation is clearly to invoke the goddess Isis, and invocation means to call spirit into something material, I think it pertinent to ask into what exactly is Isis to be invoked? We need some sort of material basis to contain the Holy Spirit, yet the ritual as it comes down to us makes no mention of such a thing. We have several options:

1. Invoke the goddess into a fixed inanimate object, such as a statue, which can then be used an a visible object of worship or meditation in the future

2. Invoke the goddess into an appropriate necklace, ring, or other piece of jewellery which can be worn as a talisman, and thus keep the influence of the goddess near at all times

3. If there are enough participants, nominate one to play the role of Isis, and have the Holy Spirit invoked into them. That person can then use the power of the Goddess to bless the participants in turn; or perhaps to act as an oracle, by drawing Tarot cards, casting a Yi King hexagram, or other appropriate divinatory mechanism.

So before setting up the ritual decide which of these options is going to fit best with your group and prepare accordingly. If you are going to elect one person to play the role of Isis, a nice addition might to have that person recite one of Crowley's better poetic works, *Isis am I*, at the climax of the ritual; either before or after generating the oracle or blessing the people. If the person playing Isis can learn the poem by heart, it might make sense to have them recite it immediately after the last litany, at the moment of supreme possession; otherwise it might be better to have them read it a little while later, after the work of the goddess is done.

Invocation Of The Holy Spirit (Isis)

Participants:	Minimum two, though four would be better. The rite works well with a large group.
Time required:	30+ minutes
Setup:	Relatively simple, but can be made more complex if desired.
Words:	Medium
Equipment:	• Egyptian costumes (optional)

  - Nepthys
  - Harpocrates
  - Horus
  - Osiris
  - Isis

[Note that in the following dialogue M.A. addresses both Brothers and Sisters directly as Brethren, showing that in a ritual context "Brethren" is not a gender specific term, but applies equally to women and men.]

Dialogue

M.A.:	Fratres et Sorores, assist me in making clear the one Mystic Ceremony. Brethren - what is the Hour?
Brothers.:	It is the Hour when Luna is simulating the MidHeaven.
M.A.:	Brethren - what is the place?
Sisters.:	It is the summit of the Sacred Mount whereon is the Assembly of the Gods.
M.A.:	Brethren - for what purpose are we gathered together?
Brothers.:	For the purpose of invoking our Lady Isis, the Holy Spirit, that being purified in heart and of right aspiration, we may be initiated into the Sublime Mysteries of Her nature.
M.A.:	Brethren - how do we hope to attain an end so sublime and exalted?
Sisters.:	By the aid of the Most High, the Lord of the Universe; by

the Love and Devotion which we bear to our Lady Isis; by the Unity of our purpose, the Unity of our aim, the strength of our unconquered Will, and by our knowledge of the names whereby the Holy Goddess may be most readily invoked.

M.A.: Brethren - it is sufficient: Let us now, being of one heart, one mind, and of one accord, exalt ourselves with fervour, that in very truth, our Goddess, the Holy Spirit, may descend upon us from Her Throne on High; and may we, being uplifted in ecstasy, comprehend the Love, Beauty and Truth that is in Her, who is indeed the very Spouse of God.

All: So mote it be.

[Litany]

[The Litany proper is divided into four sections, each being a call and responses of a specific god: Nepthys, Harpocrates, Horus, and Osiris. Each section contains a set of call lines, and each call line is followed directly by a response. In each case the officer playing the god should perform the main call lines in their particular section with all the other members of the group performing the responses. If there are no other officers all the calls may be done by the M.A.]

Nepthys

All: Hail unto Thee Holy Spirit!

Nepthys: Thy Sister Nepthys invokes Thee.

All: O Isis, Hear us!
Hail unto Thee Holy Spirit!

Nepthys: Nepthys, who dost aid Thee in gathering together the Scattered Members.

All: O Isis, Hear us!
Hail unto Thee Holy Spirit!

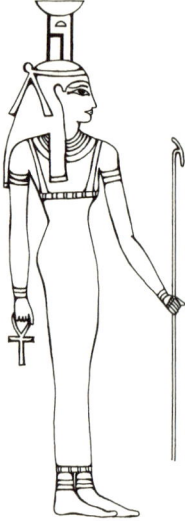

Nepthys   Isis   Harpocrates

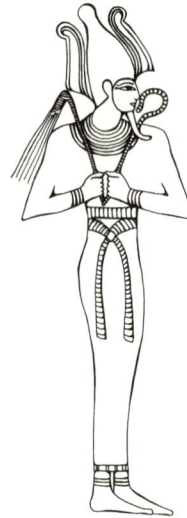

Horus   Osiris

Nepthys:	Nepthys, who supportest with Thee our Lord Osiris, invokes Thee
All:	O Isis, Hear us! Hail unto Thee Holy Spirit!
Nepthys:	Nepthys, who weepest with Thee at the resurrection of Osiris, invokes thee.
All:	O Isis, Hear us! Hail unto Thee Holy Spirit!
Nepthys:	Nepthys, who cometh rejoicing with the sound of the drum and the Sistrum, invokes thee.
All:	O Isis, Hear us! Hail unto Thee Holy Spirit!
Nepthys:	I, Nepthys, bid Thee come to thy Temple.
All:	O Isis, Hear us! Hail unto Thee Holy Spirit!
Nepthys:	Thou Lady beloved of us all.
All:	O Isis, Hear us! Hail unto Thee Holy Spirit!
Nepthys:	Come without fear; behold thy enemies are scattered.
All:	O Isis, Hear us! Hail unto Thee Holy Spirit!
Nepthys:	I, Nepthys, Thy Sister, love Thee.
All:	O Isis! Hear us! Hail unto Thee Holy Spirit!
Nepthys:	Bring thy gladness into the heart of thy sister,
All:	O Isis, Hear us! Hail unto Thee Holy Spirit!

Nepthys:	O Isis! Hasten unto us! delay not! for our hearts are open to receive Thee.

All:	O Isis, Hear us! Hail unto Thee Holy Spirit!

Nepthys:	Nepthys, the initiator into the Mysteries, awaits thy coming.

All:	O Isis, Hear us!

Harpocrates

(Standing in the Sign of Silence)

[Stand upright, thumb or first finger on lips]

All:	Hail, O Hail, Holy Spirit!

Harpocrates:	Hoor-pa-kraat, invokes Thee.

All:	O Isis! Hear us! Hail, O Hail, Holy Spirit!

Harpocrates:	Thy son, born maimed from the womb, invokes Thee.

All:	O Isis, Hear us! Hail, O Hail, Holy Spirit!

Harpocrates:	Thy son, exalted in glory, invokes Thee, O Isis!

All:	O Isis, Hear us! Hail, O Hail, Holy Spirit!

Harpocrates:	Hoor-pa-kraat, Enthroned upon the Lotus, invokes Thee.

All:	O Isis, Hear us! Hail, O Hail, Holy Spirit!

Harpocrates: O Isis! the Lord in the Silence invokes Thee.

All: O Isis, Hear us!

Horus

(Standing in the Sign of the Enterer)

All: **Hail Holy Spirit**

Horus: **Horus thy Son invokes Thee.**

All: **O Isis! We invoke Thee.**
                 Hail Holy Spirit

Horus: **The Avenger of the Death of Osiris invokes Thee.**

All: **O Isis! We invoke Thee.**
                 Hail Holy Spirit

Horus: **O Isis! The Slayer of Thy Enemies invokes Thee.**

All: **O Isis! We invoke Thee.**
                 Hail Holy Spirit

Horus: **O Isis! The Hawk-Headed One invokes Thee.**

All: **O Isis! We invoke Thee.**
                 Hail Holy Spirit

Horus: **O Isis! The Slayer of Set invokes Thee.**

All: **O Isis! We invoke Thee.**
                 Hail Holy Spirit

Horus: **O Isis! Horus, Lord of the Two Worlds, invokes Thee.**

All: **O Isis! We invoke Thee.**

Osiris

All:	Hail Holy Spirit Hail!
Osiris:	Thou Spouse of God!
All:	Hear us! Hail Holy Spirit Hail!
Osiris:	Thou Queen of Heaven!
All:	Hear us! Hail Holy Spirit Hail!
Osiris:	Thou Mother of Nature!
All:	Hear us! Hail Holy Spirit Hail!
Osiris:	Thou Bride, Mother and Daughter of the Crucified!
All:	Hear us! Hail Holy Spirit Hail!
Osiris:	Thou Immaculate Virgin of Eternity!
All:	Hear us! Hail Holy Spirit Hail!
Osiris:	Thou Scarlet Woman who ridest on the Beast!
All:	Hear us! Hail Holy Spirit Hail!
Osiris:	Thou Radiant Queen of Beauty!
All:	Hear us! Hail Holy Spirit Hail!
Osiris:	Thou, our Lady of Sorrow!

All: Hear us!
            Hail Holy Spirit Hail!

Osiris: Thou, clothed with the Sun!

All: Hear us!
            Hail Holy Spirit Hail!

Osiris: Thou, who standest on the Moon!

All: Hear us!
            Hail Holy Spirit Hail!

Osiris: Thou, whose head is the Diadem of the Twelve Stars

All: Hear us!
            Hail Holy Spirit Hail!

Osiris: Thou, who art Crowned with the Throne

All: Hear us!
            Hail Holy Spirit Hail!

Osiris: Thou, who art horned as the Moon!

All: Hear us!
            Hail Holy Spirit Hail!

Osiris: Thou, our Lady of the Earth!

All: Hear us!
            Hail Holy Spirit Hail!

Osiris: Thou, our Lady of the Amber Skin!

All: Hear us!
            Hail Holy Spirit Hail!

Osiris: Thou, whose Countenance is as grass refreshed by rain

All: Hear us.
            Hail Holy Spirit Hail!

Osiris:	Thou, Lady of Love and Victory!
All:	Hear us! Hail Holy Spirit Hail!
Osiris:	Thou, Crowned with Light, Life & Love
All:	Hear us!

(Extended arms)

[The Sign of Osiris Slain.]

Hail Holy Spirit Hail!

Osiris:	Osiris, thy Lord, awaits Thee
All:	Hear us! Hail Holy Spirit Hail!
Osiris:	Osiris, Slain and Crucified, awaits thee
All:	Hear us!

(Cross arms)

[The sign of Osiris Risen.]

Hail Holy Spirit Hail!

Osiris:	Osiris, Risen and Justified, awaits thee
All:	Hear us! Hail Holy Spirit Hail!
Osiris:	Osiris, the Great Bull of Ameritus awaits thee
All:	Hear us! Hail Holy Spirit Hail!
Osiris:	Osiris, bearing the Royal Uraeus upon his forehead awaits thee

All: Hear us!
                  Hail Holy Spirit Hail!

Osiris: Lo!~ The Opener-of-ways, bids thee come

All: Hear us!

"Isis am I" from Tannhauser

Isis am I, and from my life are fed
All showers and suns, all moons that wax and wane,
All stars and streams, the living and the dead,
The mystery of pleasure and of pain
I am the mother! I the speaking sea!
I am the earth and its fertility!
Life, death, love, hatred, light, darkness, return to me –
To me!

Hathoör am I, and to my beauty drawn
All glories of the Universe bow down
The blossom and the mountain and the dawn,
Fruit's blush, and woman, our creation's crown.
I am the priest, the sacrifice, the shrine,
I am the love and life of the divine!
Life, death, love, hatred, light, darkness, are surely mine –
Are mine!

Venus am I, the love and light of earth,
The wealth of kisses, the delight of tears.
The barren pleasure never comes to birth,
The endless, infinite desire of years.
I am the shrine at which thy long desire
Devoured thee with intolerable fire
I was song, music, passion, death, upon thy lyre –
Thy lyre!

I am the Grail and I the Glory now:
I am the flame and fuel of thy breast;
I am the star of God upon thy brow;

I am thy queen, enraptured and possessed.
Hide thee, sweet river; welcome to the sea,
Ocean of love that shall encompass thee!
Life, death, love, hatred, life, darkness, return to me –
To me!

Reprise
Isis am I, and from my life are fed
All stars and suns, all moons that wax and wane,
Create and uncreate, living and the dead,
The Mystery of Pain.
I am the Mother, I the silent sea,
The Earth, its travail, its fertility.
Life, death, love, hatred, light, darkness, return to me –
To me!

Chapter Four
A Ritual to Invoke HICE

*The Wheel turns to those effectual methods of invocation employed in
the ancient Mysteries and by certain secret bodies of initiates to-day.
The object of them is almost invariably the invocation of a God, that
God conceived in a more or less material and personal fashion. These
Rituals are therefore well suited for such persons as are capable of
understanding the spirit of Magick as opposed to the letter.*

- Aleister Crowley, *Magick*

This rite first appeared in *The Equinox* Vol I, Number 10 in 1913 as
one of two pieces under the heading of *Two Fragments of Ritual.* An
introductory note gives it as being a translation of an ancient German
manuscript found amongst the papers of Adam Weishaupt, founder of the
Illuminati. This is a typical Aleister Crowley joke - it's fairly obvious that
both rituals were actually written by Crowley himself.

This particular ritual is supposedly to invoke HICE, which is the Coptic
form of the Egyptian goddess Isis. As you can see from the previous chapters
Crowley clearly enjoyed invoking this particular deity. However in this
case the ritual is presented in the form of a dramatic presentation for three
performers who between them play several Egyptian gods, and enact a
variation of an Egyptian myth cycle in which Typhon and Apophis conspire
to kill Osiris, who the goddess Isis then brings back to life in the person of
their child Horus, who in turn seeks to avenge his father's death. As such, I
think the title of the ritual is extremely misleading - it's not just Isis or HICE
that is being invoked here, but an entire pantheon of Egyptian deities.

Apophis, or Apep, is the Egyptian serpent demon of destruction, who
lived in the Underworld and attacked and swallowed the sun every night,
using his hypnotic gaze to paralyse his victims. Typhon was a similar Greek
demon, a destructive monster with a hundred serpent heads, whose eyes
dripped venom, and mouths breathed red-hot lava. Isis was the mother
goddess, whose name means literally "She of the Throne"; she is a goddess of
nature, caring, and wisdom. Isis was married to her brother Osiris, Lord of
the Dead (sister/brother relationships are common in divine pantheons all
over the world). Osiris was also the god of the grain, which is planted in the

dark ground in winter and springs up alive again later. Horus was the hawk-headed child of Isis and Osiris, a strong warlike deity who was brought up to avenge the death of his father.

This whole ritual is of the nature of a "passion play" - the symbolic re-enactment of a primal myth of the gods. As such, it hearkens back to an earlier tradition in ancient Egypt, where the temples of Osiris would perform a similar re-enactment of this story starting around November 13th, the day that grain was planted. This tradition later inspired the Christian Passion Play, which is a dramatic re-enactment of the death and rebirth of Jesus, put on by early Christians as a way of bringing the story of Christ to the common people. So in this ritual we have the foundation for a Thelemic Passion Play which could be performed as a public celebratory rite, perhaps as an Equinox or Solstice celebration. If your group has the opportunity to put on a Thelemic working for the public (perhaps at a pagan meeting, alternative religious convention, or something similar), this ritual is well worth considering.

The original title of the ritual says that it can be used to invoke "any other divine one". I suppose in the sense that the rite refers to the solar death and rebirth myth it is a common background story, but calling it a rite to invoke *any* divine one is pushing it a bit. Crowley was very much influenced by pioneering anthropologist J.G. Frazer's massive twelve volume study of comparative religion *The Golden Bough* (even going so far as to write a collection of short stories based on it called *Golden Twigs*). It contained Frazer's theory that the myth of the dying and resurrected solar god was a universal one shared across many cultures in slightly varying forms. Although there is some surface veracity in it, most modern scholars agree that Frazer's theory isn't really that universal outside of a relatively small cultural region, and that even then he may have interpreted things in a rather loose manner to fit his theory (a problem that Crowley himself sometimes suffered from - as do we all). So rather than this being a universal ritual as such, I see it as being very specifically based on the Isis/Osiris/Horus story. That the myth that lies behind it is one that resonates strongly with many people is a bonus point.

The ritual is a lot simpler to learn and stage than some of Crowley's other mystic dramas such as *The Rites of Eleusis* or *The Ship*. In comparison to those it's a fairly short ritual with relatively few lines and a small cast - which is quite remarkable considering the excessive wordiness of some of Crowley's earlier attempts at portraying the solar death and rebirth myth. The story told is quite easy to follow even for someone with no prior knowledge of Thelema or magick. In this we may see an evolution of Crowley's thought away from the complex, dense poetry of his youth to a more mature and simplified form. In *Magick*, published sixteen years later, he would write:

...the story of the God should be dramatised by a well-skilled poet accustomed to this form of composition. Lengthy speeches and invocations should be avoided, but action should be very full.

In the original rite printed in *The Equinox* the three principal players were referred to by different titles than I have used here. The original titles were far too confusing and played no real purpose in the ritual at all. Instead I have used the titles of First Adept, Second Adept, and Third Adept, and added in brackets which god they are playing at each point in the ritual, which makes the rite much easier to understand and perform. Also for the sake of clarity I have reformatted the opening sequence, which made no logical sense in the original version.

First Adept plays the roles of Apophis and Isis, and is thus ideally taken by a woman. Second Adept plays Typhon and is probably best done by a man. Third Adept plays Osiris and Horus and thus is also best played by a male.

The ritual specifies lots of striking of the Third Adept with a rod and a scourge (i.e. a wooden cane and a whip) - please take care to not actually *hurt* anyone. In particular, please bear in mind that in some countries it is illegal to beat or whip someone in any way that leaves a mark or breaks the skin *even if the other person fully consents to the beating.* Remember that you are acting out the role of gods, you're not actually literally supposed to be doing the things mentioned in the text. As always, *safety first!*

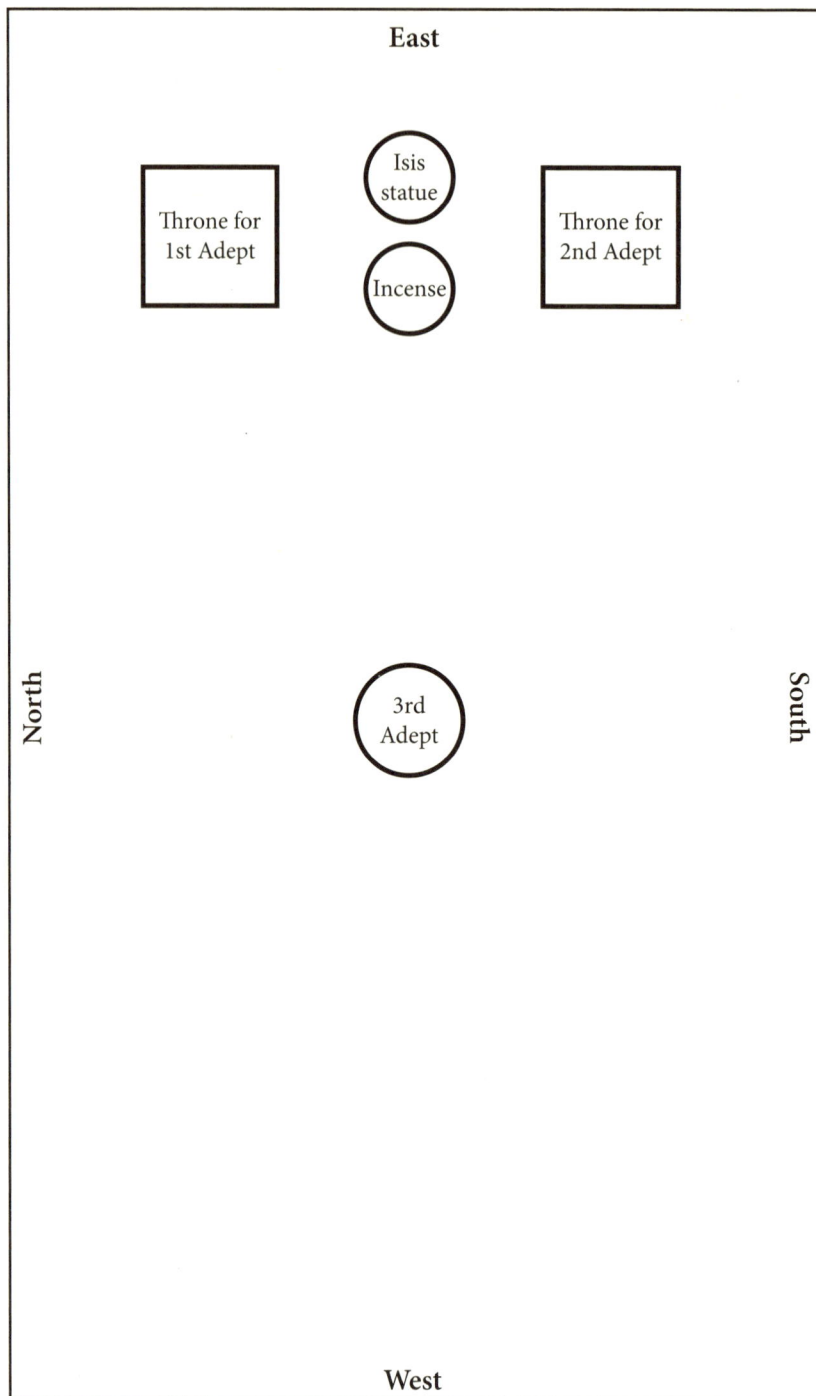

East

Isis
statue

Throne for
1st Adept

Throne for
2nd Adept

Incense

North

South

3rd
Adept

West

A Ritual To Invoke HICE

Participants:	Minimum three. The rite can be performed before a large size group.
Time required:	About half an hour
Setup:	Medium
Words:	Medium
Equipment:	• Statue of Isis
	• Incense & burner
	• Lamp
	• Two thrones
	• First Adept:
	• Red robe with blue over-robe
	• Rod and dagger
	• Second Adept:
	• Green robe with red over-robe
	• Scourge and sword
	• Third Adept:
	• White robe

The Opening

(The assistants being all without, First Adept and Second Adept perform the ritual appropriate:

> *[If the ritual is being performed as a dramatic presentation for the public, I assume they fall under the heading of "assistants" and thus should also be outside the room during this opening section. The ritual appropriate is the following sequence of Knocks, Hymn, Pentagram]*

Second Adept knocks as appropriate to god invoked.)

> *[I assume that by "appropriate" Crowley means that the number of knocks given is in some way indicative of the deity. However another interpretation might be that the nature of the knocks should have a symbolic connection with the god; for example in dealing with Isis shaking a sistrum might be the most appropriate solution.]*

(First Adept performs the Hymn appropriate to banishing.)

> *[I'm unsure what the "Hymn appropriate to banishing" might be in this context.]*

(Second Adept performs the Banishing Ritual of the Pentagram, as revised.)

[When Crowley talks of the "revised" version of the Pentagram ritual here, he was presumably referring to The Star Ruby ritual, which he had written a couple of years before this ritual and published in the Book of Lies. However any good later revision of the Pentagram ritual would also be appropriate. The group version of the Mark of the Beast ritual might work well here, or given the Egyptian nature of this ritual, The Rite of the Infinite Stars might be a good choice (published in the appendix to my previous book Abrahadabra).]

First Adept: **Bahlasti!**

Second Adept: **Ompehda!**

[These banishing words are from The Book of the Law, Chapter III, verse 54. Crowley says in his Commentaries: "By sound Bahlasti suggests 'hurling' or 'blasting;' Ompehda is not too phantastically onomatopoeitic for 'an explosion.'" After these words are spoken would be an appropriate time for the Third Adept to enter and take his place in the temple.]

(Let the symbol or image of HICE be in the East of the Temple.)

[This statue of Isis is facing towards the West of the temple. A statue of Horus or Osiris might also be employed - they both also play a large part in the ritual.]

(Let incense burn before her. Let there be two other thrones: on her right that of First Adept, on her left that of Second Adept; the child is Third Adept.)

[That is, the throne of the First Adept is in the North-East of the temple, and that of the Second Adept in the South-East, with the statue of Isis in between them.]

(First Adept is dressed in blue, Second Adept in red; the child [Third Adept] is naked at first.)

[In practice this works best if First Adept begins wearing a red robe with blue over-robe and Second Adept begins wearing a green robe with red over-robe. Compare with the colours worn by the Priestess and Priest in the Gnostic Mass. While clothed with these blue and red over-robes the First and Second Adepts are performing a similar role as manifestors of the female and male magical energies]

(The lamp shall be burning above Third Adept, who crouches in the centre, in the prescribed posture.)

[This posture is not described anywhere that I can find, but it would make sense for it to be a foetal position, like a babe in the womb.]

(If there be assistants, they shall all wear the robes of their grade; they shall be seated in balanced disposition about the temple; and they shall enter only after the opening.)

The Death Of Osiris

(Second Adept and First Adept divest themselves of their blue and red robes, appearing merely in their magick robes of red and green as the temporal and spiritual powers, Typhon and Apophis.)

Second Adept (Typhon): **Sister, I burn upon the throne.**

First Adept (Apophis): **I am in agony, Typhon!**

Second Adept (Typhon): **Who hath disturbed our ageless peace?**

First Adept (Apophis): **Threatened our mystery?**

Second Adept (Typhon): **Isis**
Hath borne a child.

First Adept (Apophis): **We are twins.**

Second Adept (Typhon): **What word**
Insults us?

Third Adept (Osiris): (Springs up.)
Lo! I am, the third.

Second Adept (Typhon):

(Comes forward with the scourge, and forces Third Adept to kneel.)

Then bow thee to the two above!
(Strikes him twice.)

First Adept (Apophis):

(Comes forward with the rod.)

We need no witnesses of our love.
(Strikes him twice.)

Second Adept (Typhon): **Who art thou?**

First Adept (Apophis): **Whence art thou?**

Third Adept (Osiris): **My name**
Is surely I am that I am.

Second Adept (Typhon): **Blaspheme not!**
(Strikes him twice.)

First Adept (Apophis): **Lie not!**
(Strikes him twice.)

Third Adept (Osiris): **I am come**
From Isis, from the Virgin Womb.

Second Adept (Typhon): **Blaspheme not!**
(Strikes him twice.)

First Adept (Apophis): **Lie not!**
(Strikes him twice.)

Third Adept (Osiris): **I am he**
Appointed from eternity
To rule upon the folk of Khem.

Second Adept (Typhon): **We are the gods and kings of them.**

First Adept (Apophis): **Upstart!**
(Strikes him twice.)

Second Adept (Typhon): **Usurper!**
(Strikes him twice.)

First Adept (Apophis): **We defy thee.**

Second Adept (Typhon): **We have the power to crucify thee.**

(First Adept forces Third Adept back, and they stretch out his arms.)

[That is, back on to the floor, where Third Adept lays with his arms outstretched in the crucifixion position. He stays laying in this position until The Arising of Horus part of the rite later.]

Third Adept (Osiris):   **Amen! I am willing to be slain.
                          Verily I shall rise again!**

First Adept (Apophis):   **With four wounds thus I nail thee.**

(Wounds brow, hands, and feet with the dagger.)

[Do not actually cut Third Adept! As always, the dagger used should not have a sharp edge or point! Simply touch the dagger gently to the given areas. Be especially careful on the brow, you don't want the point of the dagger anywhere near his eyes!]

Second Adept (Typhon):   **With one wound I impale thee.**

(Wounds breast with sword.)

[See note above.]

Second Adept (Typhon):   **Hail, sister! We have slain the god.**

First Adept (Apophis):   **Ours is the termless period.**

Second Adept (Typhon):   **Bending across the bloodless face
                           Let us embrace!**

First Adept (Apophis):   **Let us embrace!**

(They embrace, leaning across the corpse. First Adept returns to her throne, and dons the blue robe, thus assuming the power of Isis. Second Adept remains, his sword upon the heart of Third Adept.

The Arising Of Horus

First Adept (Isis):   **Lo! I lament. Fallen is the sixfold Star:
                        Slain is Asar.
                        O twinned with me in the womb of Night!
                        O son of my bowels to the Lord of Light!**

O man of mine that hath covered me
From the shame of my virginity!
Where art thou? Is it not Apep thy brother,
The snake in my womb that am thy mother,
That hath slain thee by violence girt with guile,
And scattered thy limbs on the Nile?

Lo! I lament. I have forged a whirling Star:
I seek Asar.
O Nepti, sister! Arise in the dusk
From thy chamber of mystery and musk!
Come with me, though weary the way,
To bring back his life to the rended clay!
See! are not these the hands that wove
Delight, and these the arms that strove
With me? And these the feet, the thighs
That were lovely in mine eyes?
Lo! I lament. I gather in my car
Thine head, Asar.
And this—is this not the trunk he rended?
But—oh! oh! oh!—the task transcended,
Where is the holy idol that stood
For the god of thy queen's beatitude?
Here is the tent—but where is the pole?
Here is the body—but where is the soul?
Nepti, sister, the work is undone
For lack of the needed One!

Lo! I lament. There is no god so far
As mine Asar!
There is no hope, none, in the corpse, in the tomb.
(She rises and Second Adept falls back to his knees)
But these—what are these that war in my womb?
There is vengeance and triumph at last of Maat
In Ra-Hoor-Khut and in Hoor-pa-Kraat!
Twins they shall rise; being twins they are one,
The Lord of the Sword and the Son of the Sun!
Silence, coeval colleage of Voice,
The plumes of Amoun—rejoice!

(Comes down to the corpse, and raises it with kisses upon the stigmata, wrapping it then in her blue robe. She then clothes it in the white robe.)

[I think the inference here is that First Adept should wrap her arms around the Third Adept, enveloping him in her robe while she is still wearing it, as a mother cradling a child. After that she then dresses the Third Adept in the white robe to complete his transformation from Osiris to Horus.]

> Lo! I rejoice. I heal the sanguine scar
> Of slain Asar.
> I was the Past, Nature the Mother.
> He was the Present, Man my brother.
> Look to the Future, the Child—oh pæan
> The Child that is crowned in the Lion-Æon!
> The sea-dawns surge and billow and break
> Beneath the scourge of the Star and the Snake.
> To my lord I have borne in my womb deep-vaulted
> This babe for ever exalted!

(Third Adept takes the sword of Second Adept and pins his throat therewith. First Adept returns to her throne.)

[Third Adept picks up the red robe and tosses it over the dead body of Second Adept, then Third Adept sits the throne in the Southeast; so you have Isis and Horus sitting on the two thrones. Second Adept then rises and puts on his red robe to symbolise that he is now returning to his priestly function.]

The Awakening Of The Divine Force

(The remaining sheets of MSS. are missing or indecipherable.)

[This was Crowley's original end note from The Equinox. *It could mean that he lost the rest of the original manuscript that he had written (this happened to him on more than one other occasion), or possibly that he wrote this much and then couldn't figure out what should happen next. Since it does say that this part should be "The Awakening of the Divine Force" I have therefore added a short section from the Invocation of Horus that fits well. If the rite is being put on as a public or semi-public passion play one option would be to hand everyone a small piece of paper as they enter the temple with this verse printed on it and have Second Adept indicate at this point of the ritual that everyone should join in. It works very well in practice to finish off the rite on a triumphal note.]*

Second Adept
(and all the people):   **Strike, strike the master chord!**
Draw, draw the Flaming Sword!
Crowned Child and Conquering Lord,
Horus, Avenger!

(All give the sign of Apophis.)

[A good ending is to have this be the signal for general feasting and celebration of the resurrection of the sun i.e. break out the wine and good food, blessed by Isis Triumphant and Horus on their thrones, and handed out by Second Adept.]

Chapter Five
A Rite of Isis

This ritual is one of the first non-Crowleyan Thelemic rites. It was originally written by one of the early Thelemites, Howard E. White (Frater Ad Alta), under the direction of Charles Stansfield Jones (Frater Achad), and had its premiere public performance at the Vancouver Labour Temple, November 27th, 1914, with Jones as Magus and White as Assistant Magus. The performance was an attempt to increase interest in British Columbia Lodge No. 1, the first O.T.O. body to be established in North America. Apparently it was successful, for they put on a second performance in June of the next year, selling fifty-five tickets.

I say the ritual is non-Crowleyan, but perhaps that's pushing it a bit, since much of it was clearly inspired by and derived from Crowley's own work - so not surprisingly when they sent it to Crowley for his opinion he was apparently much impressed, replying to Jones:

> I am more than pleased at your letter just received with ritual enclosed. It is very fine. Mr. White is to be congratulated heartily; no criticism seems necessary. I hope you will arrange to repeat this all the time, say every new moon or every full moon, so as to build up a regular force. You should also have a solar ritual to balance it, to be done at each time the Sun enters a new sign, with special festivity at the Equinoxes and solstices.

> In this way you can establish a regular cult; and if you do them in a truly magical manner, you create a vortex of force which will suck in all the people you want. The time is just ripe for a natural religion. People like rites and ceremonies, and they are tired of hypothetical gods. Insist on the real benefits of the Sun, the Mother-force, the Father-force, and so on, and show that by celebrating these benefits worthily the worshippers unite themselves more fully with the current of life. Let the religion be Joy, but with a worthy and dignified sorrow in death itself, and treat death as an ordeal, an initiation... In short, be the founder of a new and greater Pagan cult.

We can see from this that Crowley envisioned O.T.O. bodies to be performing at least two major rituals a month: one lunar and one solar. From my own experience in running magical groups I think this is a pretty good target to aim at. Having a fairly sizable ritual every fortnight or so means you don't have too much time pressure on a small group, yet means that you also don't have too long a period with people sitting around with nothing to do. If you want to follow this schedule you could use one or more of the Isis rituals given in the last few chapters for your lunar rites, and have the Invocation of Horus, The Bacchanal (see Chapter 7), or perhaps the Gnostic Mass as your solar rites.

A large chunk of the middle section of this ritual is derived from the "Cancer" section of *Liber 963: The Treasure House of Images* by J.F.C Fuller from *The Equinox Vol 1, 3*, split up for three part working. Fuller was a British Army officer and one of the very first Thelemites, later to achieve fame as an expert on mechanised warfare, and supposedly inventor of the Blitzkrieg system used to notable effect by the German military in the 1930s. Much to Crowley's chagrin we can assume, since Crowley detested the Nazis with a passion.

Another part that is certainly not by Aleister Crowley is the use of *Ave Maria* near the climax of the ritual. Some people, especially those from a Roman Catholic background, might find this odd in a Rite of Isis; but it isn't really, since so much of Marian iconography is directly taken from Isis worship. Historian Will Durant wrote in his monumental *The Story of Civilization*:

> *Early Christians sometimes worshiped before the statues of Isis suckling the infant Horus, seeing in them another form of the ancient and noble myth by which woman (i.e., the female principle), creating all things, becomes at last the Mother of God.*

Since the Christians stole the Mother Goddess in the first place in order to create the myth of Mary, Queen of Heaven, I think it only fitting that we borrow her back now and again. Quite apart from that, there are several lovely musical settings of this prayer that can be used to add atmosphere to the ritual, perhaps the most famous of which is that by Charles Gounod, who set the prayer to music from Bach's *Well Tempered Clavier*.

The original opening of this ritual is very much based on the Golden Dawn style of working, as transmitted by Crowley through the pages of the early numbers of *The Equinox*, the magical journal he had been publishing for several years. However by 1914 Crowley himself was already beginning to move away from this style of ritual towards a less wordy, more ecstatic approach based on poetry and music, and the main body of the ritual is more closely modelled on that style, featuring excerpts from several different poems by Crowley.

Evidence suggests that Jones and White were never really happy with the original opening, as it was rewritten three times. The one reproduced here is based on the second version, which according to Crowley archivist Gerald Yorke was written by Crowley as a replacement for the first opening that White had written. I think this unlikely, it just doesn't sound like the kind of thing Crowley would have written at this period of his life, when he had pretty much abandoned the Golden Dawn style of ritual working that this opening is based on. Also since he had written to Jones that "no criticism seems necessary" it would seem pretty illogical to then go on to rewrite the entire opening! I think it much more likely that this second opening was written by Jones (possibly in conjunction with White) since the original typescript has Jones' handwritten notes all over it, and it reads more like it was written by someone who had been following Crowley's writing in *The Equinox* slavishly.

Regardless of who actually wrote it, and how much editing was done on it, somewhere in the whole process confusion crept in, because the temple directions as given in the opening became completely reversed compared to the setup in the main body of the ritual, leading to a fairly unworkable mess if you try to do the rite as written. Consequently I've had to edit it again to sort out the directions, so the "original" opening as given here is actually slightly different to the version in the typescript.

This opening is quite complex and features not only both the entire Lesser Pentagram and Hexagram rituals, but also some extra Fire and Spirit pentagrams thrown in for good measure. The Golden Dawn made much of these different types of pentagrams and hexagrams for different purposes, but to be honest I find them completely extraneous and rather contrived. However if you wish to use these rituals and symbols as written, be my guest - the full original Lesser rituals of the Pentagram and Hexagram are reproduced in the Appendix to this book. Personally I haven't used any of this Golden Dawn derived stuff in decades, and I've never missed it.

Another problem with the original opening is that it is stylistically very different than the main body of the rite. The opening is based on Biblical divine and angelic names, and sonorous King James Version speeches, whereas the main section is very pagan and poetic. Consequently I've written a Revised Opening (yes, a fourth version!) that I hope is a little more focused and harmonises better with the main ritual text – and more closely follows Crowley's injunction to concentrate on the pagan aspects. It also has the additional benefit of being much shorter and simpler - the main ritual already has plenty of text and action, so I think the whole operation benefits from having a simplified opening, especially for public performance.

Whether or not the ritual is really suitable for public performance is debatable I think. It certainly has a lot going on within it, but may be a little long-winded to really keep people's attention focused, especially if the opening is performed as written - Pentagram rituals don't tend to work very well in a public setting. I would definitely recommend that you use the Revised Opening in public, and omit the optional Pentagram part.

However despite originally being a bit overburdened with formalities the ritual is quite beautiful, and certainly recommended if your group wants to get their teeth into a bigger, more complex working.

Note that the original piece was written for three specific male Officers of B.C. Lodge No. 1 playing the Magi. In the interest of preserving historical accuracy I have left the text with male pronouns in place, but of course in future performances any or all of the Officers may be played by women; in which case simply change the pronouns to suit.

The ritual specifies that the officers should each wear a Nemmes. This is the classic Egyptian headdress so beloved of the Golden Dawn rites. If you're not sure how to make one, have a look round the Internet for instructions, or simply do without, it's not essential.

A Rite of Isis

Participants:	Minimum four.
Time required:	About an hour
Setup:	Relatively complex
Words:	A lot
Equipment:	

- Magus
  - White and gold robe
  - Nemmes (optional)
  - Bowl of consecrated water

- Assistant Magus
  - White robe
  - Nemmes (optional)

- Magus of Fire:
  - Black robe, with red triangle upon the breast (or just plain black)
  - Lighted candle

- Soror Luna
  - White robe or Egyptian dress

- Altar with
  - Statue of Isis
  - Four candles, unlit at start
  - Blue lamp
  - Bell

- North and South small altars each having a candle

- Altar of Incense with
  - Three candles, unlit at start
  - Censer, charcoal & incense

- Musician or music playback system
- Veil in the Eastern part of the temple (optional)

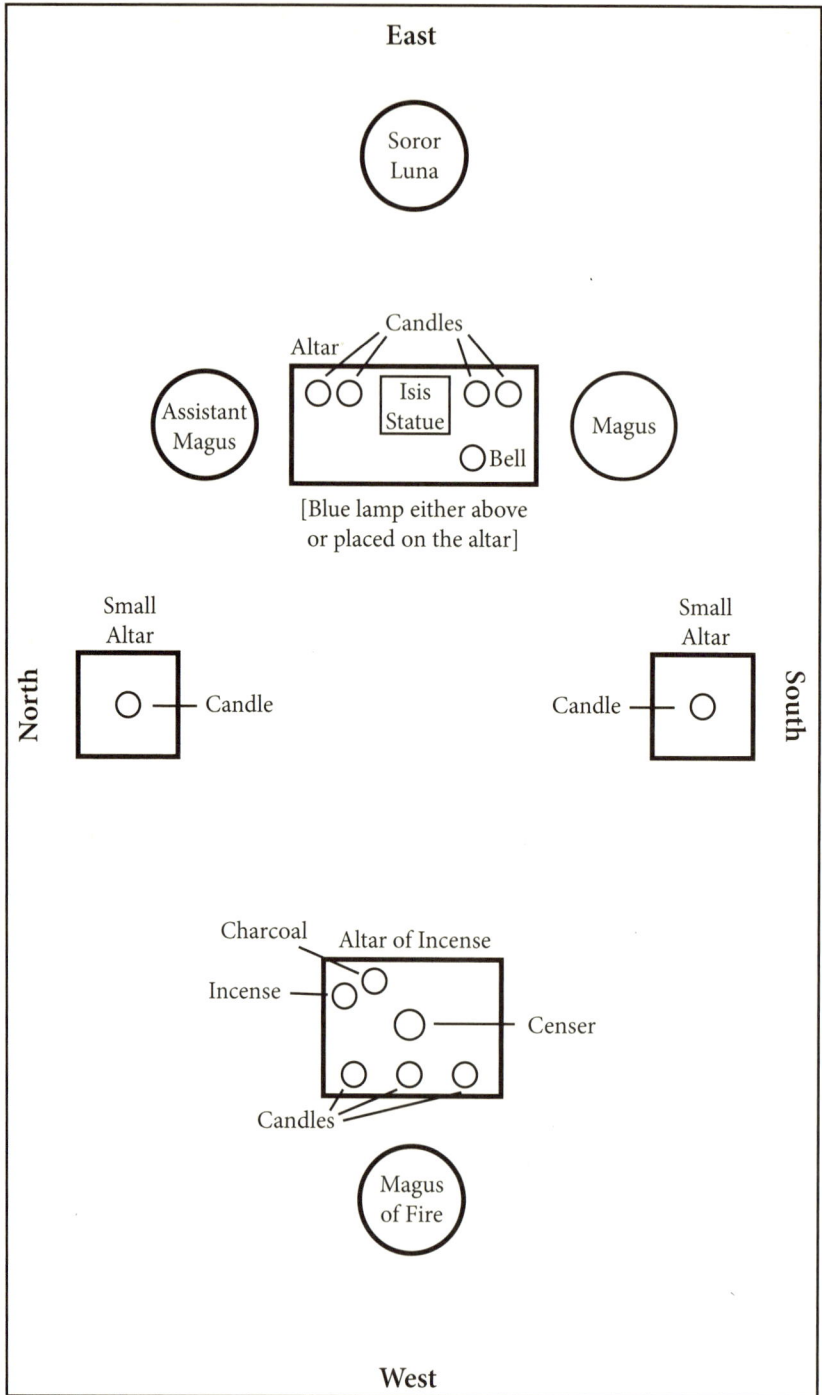

East

Soror
Luna

Candles

Altar

Isis
Statue

Bell

Magus

Assistant
Magus

[Blue lamp either above
or placed on the altar]

North

Small
Altar

Candle

Small
Altar

Candle

South

Charcoal   Altar of Incense

Incense

Censer

Candles

Magus
of Fire

West

Original Opening

In the East is the Altar having upon it a statue of Isis and four candles, and above it a blue lamp burning. In the North and South are two small altars each having upon them a candle. On the Altar of Incense are three candles.

> [There is also a bell upon the Altar in the East. The blue lamp can be a electric light with a blue lampshade. Although not stated in the original text, presumably the Altar of Incense is in the West, since the other three directions are already taken. The censer, charcoal, and incense should also be on this Altar of Incense (obviously).]

The station of the Magus is South of the Altar, that of the Assistant Magus is North of the Altar, and that of the Magus of Fire is West of the Altar of Incense.

> ["The Altar" referred to is the the High Altar in the East. The text does not specify a station for Soror Luna, but I suggest in the far East of the Temple, beyond the High Altar. In one performance I have seen of this rite Soror Luna was seated in the East within a bower of roses, which was extremely effective dramatically. Another good option is to have Soror Luna seated behind a veil in the East, similar to the Gnostic Mass. Any other participants or audience should be spread around the North and South edges of the temple space at the beginning of the rite, with the three Magi outside the room.]

All lights are burning.

> [This appears to refer to ambient lighting around the temple - which would be the case if the ritual is being put on in a large space with an audience.]

(When all are assembled a simple melody is played. After a pause the Magus, Assistant Magus, and Magus of Fire enter, the Magus of Fire going first bearing a lighted candle. The Magus carries a bowl of consecrated water which he sprinkles round the Temple. They pass from the East once round the Temple.

> [The direction they move is not specified - I would assume deosil (clockwise). The water is supposed to be consecrated before the ritual begins - this could be done as part of a previous ritual, for example by using water taken from the font after a Gnostic Mass. Alternately the Magus could just bless the water before entering the temple. The order of officers in this part is to have Magus of Fire lead, followed by Magus, then Assistant Magus. The Magus of Fire should go round one full circle with the other officers and then continue on round a further half circle to his station.]

The Magus of Fire takes his station and the Magus and Assistant Magus pass to the high altar.

[The original typescript had the Magus of Fire carrying the censer into the Temple, which appears to have been an error.]

Magus:　　　GLORIA DEO ALTISSIMO RA-HOOR-KHUIT.

[Glory to the Most High God Ra-Hoor-Khuit.]

(He faces West.)

Magus:　　　Fratres: Let us consecrate the Fire and purify the Temple, in order that the Divine Light alone may be manifest, and all the powers of darkness be scattered. In and through the holy Seven-fold word ARARITA.

[Frates is Latin for Brothers. If there is only one male officer this should be Frater; with one female officer you might add "et Soror" (and Sister); with more than one female officer add "et Sorores" (and Sisters).]

(The Magus of Fire passes to the East, bearing the lighted candle which he hands to the Assistant Magus. The Magus performs the banishing Pentagram of Fire over the candle and says:)

Magus:　　　I exorcise ye, o ye spirits of evil and powers of darkness, in and through the Name of the Most High God, Elohim, and in the name of the great Archangel of Fire, Michael, that ye abide not in this creature of Fire, but depart hence and seek not to enter again into this Temple of the Magick of Light.

[The Magus of Fire should wait by the High Altar during this section.]

(He makes the invoking pentagram of spirit active and says:)

EHIEH. BITOM

(He makes the invoking Pentagram of Fire.)

Magus:　　　I consecrate thee, creature of fire in and through the name of IHVH and in the name TzBAVTh and by the might of the Spirit of the Primal Fire, that, through the power of the great Archangel Michael who standeth at the Right Hand of the Altar of Incense, thou mayest become of service in the Temple of Light, a defense against the assaults of the evil ones, and a source of strength in the Holy Mysteries.

[IHVH is usually pronounced Jehovah, and TzBaVTh is pronounced Tzabaoth. The words are Hebrew and are references to the god and angelic hosts of the Bible]

(The Magus of Fire takes the consecrated candle, bears it to the Altar of Incense, and from it lights all the candles in the Temple and the charcoal. He returns to his station.)

Magus: **Frater (motto of Magus of Fire), purify the Temple by fire.**

(The Magus of Fire casts incense thrice upon the charcoal and passes round the Temple, bearing the censer, and saying:)

Magus of Fire: **Incensum istud a te benedictum, ascendat ad te Domine, descendat super nos misericordia tua.**

[This phrase is from the Roman Catholic Latin Mass and means "May this incense, which Thou hast blessed, ascend to Thee O Lord, and may Thy mercy descend upon us".]

(He passes to the centre of the Temple and censes the four quarters, saying, while censing to the East:)

Magus of Fire: **In the Name of Raphael.**

(To the South)
In the Name of Michael.

(To the West)
In the Name of Gabriel.

(To the North)
In the Name of Auriel.

(He returns to his station.)

Magus: **Fratres: Let us further purify the Temple. Frater (motto of Assistant Magus), perform the Banishing Ritual of the Pentagram.**

(This is done.)

Magus: **Let the purification be completed by the Banishing Ritual
                of the Hexagram.**

(The Magus performs this Ritual.)

(All stand at their stations.)

Magus: **KHABS AM PEKHT.**

Assistant Magus: **KONX OM PAX.**

Magus of Fire: **LIGHT IN EXTENSION.**

> *[Khabs Am Pehkht and Konx Om Pax are versions of the term Light In Extension,
> used in various Golden Dawn rituals, and supposedly derived from the ancient
> Greek Rites of Eleusis.]*

(Facing East. All kneel and repeat in a low tone.)

All: **HOLY ART THOU, LORD OF THE UNIVERSE.
                HOLY ART THOU, WHOM NATURE HATH NOT FORMED.
                HOLY ART THOU, THE VAST AND THE MIGHTY ONE.
                HOLY ART THOU, HADIT, THOU SECRET FLAME.
                HOLY ART THOU, NUIT, THOU STARRY ONE.
                HOLY ART THOU, LORD OF THE AEON.
                HOLY ART THOU RA-HOOR-KHUIT.
                HOLY, ALL HOLY**

> *[Presumably "All" does not include Soror Luna here, but does include all other
> participants.]*

(They rise. The Assistant Magus strikes upon the bell 3-3-3, and the Magus
goes West of the Altar, facing East, and says:)

Magus: **Unity uttermost showed,
                I adore the might of thy breath
                Supreme and terrible God
                Who makest the Gods and death
                To tremble before thee:
                I, I adore thee!**

(The Magus returns to his station.)

Assistant Magus: **Let us meditate upon the Supreme Unity: as it is written below the statue of Our Lady Isis:**
"I am all that was, and that is, and that shall be; and no mortal hath lifted my veil."

(Here follows a few minutes silent meditation.)

[All sit during this meditation.]

Revised Opening

In the East is the Altar having upon it a statue of Isis, a bell, and four candles, and above it a blue lamp burning. On the North and South are two small altars each having upon them a candle. On the Altar of Incense in the West are three candles and the censer, charcoal, and incense.

The station of the Magus is South of the Altar, that of the Assistant Magus is North of the Altar, and that of the Magus of Fire is West of the Altar of Incense. Soror Luna is in the far East of the Temple beyond the High Altar.

All ambient lights around the Temple are burning, the candles on the altars are unlit.

(When all are assembled a simple melody is played. After a pause the Magus, Assistant Magus, and Magus of Fire enter, the Magus of Fire going first bearing a lighted candle. The Magus carries a bowl of consecrated water which he sprinkles round the Temple. They pass from the East deosil once round the Temple. The Magus of Fire takes his station and the Magus and Assistant Magus pass to the High Altar.)

Magus: **GLORIA DEO ALTISSIMO RA-HOOR-KHUIT.**

[Glory to the Most High God Ra-Hoor-Khuit.]

(He faces West.)

Magus: **Fratres: Let us consecrate and purify the Temple, in order that the Divine Light alone may be manifest, and all the** powers of darkness be scattered. In and through the holy Seven-fold word ARARITA.

Frater (motto of Magus of Fire), purify the Temple by fire.

(The Magus of Fire takes the lighted candle, and from it lights all the candles in the Temple and the charcoal.

The Magus of Fire casts incense thrice upon the charcoal and passes round the Temple, bearing the censer, and saying:)

Magus of Fire: **Incensum istud a te benedictum, ascendat ad te Domine, descendat super nos misericordia tua.**

> *[This phrase is from the Roman Catholic Latin Mass and means "May this incense, which Thou hast blessed, ascend to Thee O Lord, and may Thy mercy descend upon us".]*

(He passes to the centre of the Temple and censes the four quarters, saying, while censing:)

Magus of Fire:

(To the East)

In the Name of Therion.

(To the South)

In the Name of Hadit.

(To the West)

In the Name of Babalon.

(To the North)

In the Name of Nuit.

(He returns to his station.)

Magus: **Fratres: Let us further purify the Temple. Frater (motto of Assistant Magus), perform the Banishing Ritual of the Pentagram.**

> *[Optional.]*

(This is done.)

(All stand at their stations.)

Magus: **KHABS AM PEKHT.**

Assistant Magus: **KONX OM PAX.**

Magus of Fire: **LIGHT IN EXTENSION.**

(Facing East. All kneel and repeat in a low tone.)

All: **HOLY ART THOU, LORD OF THE UNIVERSE.**
                   HOLY ART THOU, WHOM NATURE HATH NOT FORMED.
                   HOLY ART THOU, THE VAST AND THE MIGHTY ONE.
                   HOLY ART THOU, HADIT, THOU SECRET FLAME.
                   HOLY ART THOU, NUIT, THOU STARRY ONE.
                   HOLY ART THOU, LORD OF THE AEON.
                   HOLY ART THOU RA-HOOR-KHUIT.
                   HOLY, ALL HOLY

(They rise. The Assistant Magus strikes upon the bell 3-3-3.)

   [i.e. three times three strikes on the bell.]

(The Magus goes West of the Altar, facing East, and says:)

Magus: **Unity uttermost showed,**
                   I adore the might of thy breath
                   Supreme and terrible God
                   Who makest the Gods and death
                   To tremble before thee:
                   I, I adore thee!

(The Magus returns to his station.)

Assistant Magus: **Let us meditate upon the Supreme Unity: as it is written**
                   below the statue of Our Lady Isis:

                   "I am all that was, and that is, and that shall be; and no
                   mortal hath lifted my veil."

(Here follows a few minutes silent meditation.)

[All sit during this meditation.]

Ritual

(When this is done, the Magus of Fire passes to the East of the Temple and addresses those assembled.)

[The original text had a long reading from Aleister Crowley on the nature of Ecstasy at this point, recited as a kind of "sermon" to the people. If you wish to include a sermon here, you may also do so, but frankly I think it can happily be dispensed with, and you could move directly to the next section, the adorations from Liber 963, which is a great deal more interesting.]

(He returns to his station, and there casts incense upon the censer. He remains standing West of the Altar of Incense. The Magus and Assistant Magus rise and stand facing the Altar.)

Magus: **O Thou Sovran Warrior of steel-girt valour, whose scimitar is a flame between day and night, whose helm is crested with the wings of the Abyss. I know Thee!**

Assistant Magus: **O Thou four-eyed guardian of heaven, who kindleth to a flame the hearts of the downcast, and girdeth about with fire the loins of the unarmed.**

(All present repeat together:)

[What we mean by "All" during the main body of the ritual depends on how many people are in attendance. Generally the officers and Soror Luna should not recite the parts for All, but if there are not many other people attending the performance they may wish to fill in.]

All: **O Glory be unto Thee through all Time and though all space: Glory and Glory upon Glory, Everlastingly. Amen, and Amen, and Amen.**

Magus: **O Thou Sovran Light and fire of loveliness, whose flaming locks stream downwards through the aethyr as knots of lightning deep-rooted in the Abyss. I know Thee!**

Assistant Magus: O Thou winnowing flail of brightness, the passionate lash of whose encircling hand scatters mankind before Thy fury as the wind-scud from the stormy breast of Ocean.

All: O Glory be unto Thee through all Time and though all space: Glory and Glory upon Glory, Everlastingly. Amen, and Amen, and Amen.

Magus: O Thou Sovran Singer of the revelling winds, whose voice is as a vestal troop of Bacchanals awakened by the piping of a Pan-pipe. I know Thee!

Assistant Magus: O Thou dancing flame of frenzied song, whose shouts, like unto golden swords of leaping fire, urge us onward to the wild slaughter of the Worlds.

All: O Glory be unto Thee through all Time and though all space: Glory and Glory upon Glory, Everlastingly. Amen, and Amen, and Amen.

Magus: O Thou Sovran Might of the most ancient forests, whose voice is as the murmur of unappeasable winds caught up in the arms of the swaying branches. I know Thee!

Assistant Magus: O Thou rumble of conquering drums, who lulleth to a rapture of deep sleep those lovers who burn into each other, flame to fine flame.

All: O Glory be unto Thee through all Time and though all space: Glory and Glory upon Glory, Everlastingly. Amen, and Amen, and Amen.

Magus: O Thou Sovran Guide of the star-wheeling circles, the soles of whose feet smite plumes of golden fire from the outermost annihilation of the Abyss. I know Thee!

Assistant Magus: O Thou crimson sword of destruction, who chasest the comets from the dark bed of night, till they speed before Thee as serpent tongues of flame.

All: O Glory be unto Thee through all Time and though all space: Glory and Glory upon Glory, Everlastingly. Amen, and Amen, and Amen.

Magus:	O Thou Sovran Archer of the darksome regions, who shooteth forth from Thy transcendental crossbow the many-rayed suns into the fields of heaven. I know Thee!
Assistant Magus:	O Thou eight-pointed arrow of light, who smiteth the regions of the seven rivers until they laugh like Maenads with snaky thyrsus.
All:	O Glory be unto Thee through all Time and though all space: Glory and Glory upon Glory, Everlastingly. Amen, and Amen, and Amen.
Magus:	O Thou Sovran Paladin of self-vanquished knights, whose path lieth through the trackless forests of time, winding through the Byss of unbegotten space. I know Thee!
Assistant Magus:	O Thou despiser of the mountains, Thou whose course is as that of a lightening-hoofed steed leaping along the green bank of a fair river.
All:	O Glory be unto Thee through all Time and though all space: Glory and Glory upon Glory, Everlastingly. Amen, and Amen, and Amen.
Magus:	O Thou Sovran Surging of wild felicity, whose love is as the overflowing of the seas, and who makest our bodies to laugh with beauty. I know Thee!
Assistant Magus:	O Thou outstrider of the sunset, who deckest the snow-capped mountains with red roses, and strewest white violets on the curling waves.
All:	O Glory be unto Thee through all Time and though all space: Glory and Glory upon Glory, Everlastingly. Amen, and Amen, and Amen.
Magus:	O Thou Sovran Diadem of crowned Wisdom, whose work knoweth the path of the sylphs of the air, and the black burrowings of the gnomes of the earth. I know Thee!

Assistant Magus: O Thou Master of the ways of life, in the palm of whose hand all the arts lie bounden as a smoke-cloud betwixt the lips of the mountain.

All: O Glory be unto Thee through all Time and though all space: Glory and Glory upon Glory, Everlastingly. Amen, and Amen, and Amen.

Magus: O Thou Sovran Lord of primaeval Baresarkers, who huntest with dawn the dappled deer of twilight, and whose engines of war are blood-crested comets. I know Thee!

Assistant Magus: O Thou flame-crowned Self-luminous One, the lash of whose whip gathered the ancient worlds, and looseth the blood from the virgin clouds of heaven.

All: O Glory be unto Thee through all Time and though all space: Glory and Glory upon Glory, Everlastingly. Amen, and Amen, and Amen.

Magus: O Thou Sovran Moonstone of pearly loveliness, from out whose many eyes flash the fire-clouds of life, and whose breath enkindleth the Byss and the Abyss. I know Thee!

Assistant Magus: O Thou fountain-head of fierce aethyr, in the pupil of whose brightness all things lie crouched and wrapped like a babe in the womb of its mother.

All: O Glory be unto Thee through all Time and though all space: Glory and Glory upon Glory, Everlastingly. Amen, and Amen, and Amen.

Magus: O Thou Sovran Mother of the breath of being, the milk of whose breasts is as the fountain of love, twin-jets of fire upon the blue bosom of night. I know Thee!

Assistant Magus: O Thou Virgin of the moonlit glades, who fondleth us as a drop of dew in Thy lap, ever watchful over the cradle of our fate.

All: O Glory be unto Thee through all Time and though all space: Glory and Glory upon Glory, Everlastingly. Amen, and Amen, and Amen.

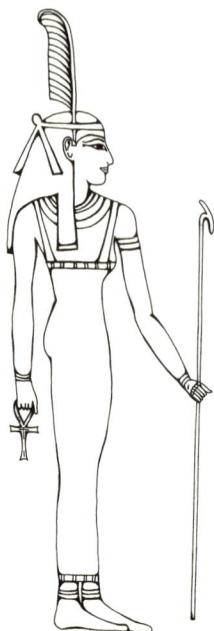

Maat

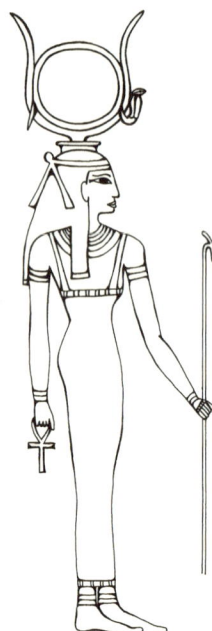

Hathor

Magus:	O Thou Sovran All-Beholding eternal Sun, who lappest up the constellations of heaven, as a thirsty thief a jar of ancient wine. I know Thee!
Assistant Magus:	O Thou dawn-wing'd courtesan of light, who makest me to reel with one kiss of Thy mouth, as a leaf cast into the flames of a furnace.
All:	O Glory be unto Thee through all Time and though all space: Glory and Glory upon Glory, Everlastingly. Amen, and Amen, and Amen.

(They kneel. Slight pause. The Assistant Magus strikes upon the bell.)

Magus: Deep, deep thy sombre Sea,
Spouse of eternity!
Mother, we cry to Thee:
Hear us, Maut, Mother!

[Maut or Maat is the Egyptian goddess of the Natural-Order, usually translated as Truth and Justice.]

Magus of Fire: Beauty and life and love!
                  Let fly thy darling dove!
                  Bend to us from above
                  Lady Ahathor!

[Ahathor or Hathor is the Egyptian goddess of the Milky Way, usually portrayed as a woman with the horns of a cow.]

Assistant Magus: Virginal Queen of Earth,
                  Late, love, and last of birth,
                  Loose, loose the golden girth,
                  Nephthys, the crowned one!

All: Sound, sistron, sound afar!
                  Shine, shine, O dawning Star!
                  Flame, flame, O Meteor Car!
                  Isis, Our Lady!

[From Crowley's poem "A Litany".]

(They stand.)

Assistant Magus: (3-3-3)

[Knocks three times three.]

Magus: **Hail unto Isis! Hail!**

Soror Luna: (As a recitative:)

[Recitative is halfway between talking and singing, as is used for dialogue in opera for example.]

            I AM ALL THAT WAS AND THAT IS AND THAT SHALL BE AND NO MORTAL HATH LIFTED MY VEIL.

All: **Hail unto Isis Our Lady of Life! Hail! All Hail!**

(The Magus of Fire passes to the East bearing the censer, and kneels before the Altar. The Magus and Assistant Magus approach, the latter bearing the incense. The Magus throws the incense upon the censer, and he and the Assistant Magus return to their stations.

The Magus of Fire elevates the censer.)

Assistant Magus: **Crown Her, O crown Her with stars as with flowers for a virginal gaud!**

Magus: **Crown Her, O crown Her with Light and the flame of a down-rushing Sword!**

Assistant Magus: **Crown Her, O crown Her with Love for maiden and mother and wife!**

Magus: **Hail unto Isis! For She is the Lady of Life!**

[From Cowley's "Rite of Luna", part of his modern Rites of Eleusis.]

(The Magus of Fire rises and carries the censer to the Altar of Incense. All seat themselves in Asana.)

[A lot of nonsense is written about asana. Patanjali says it is any posture which is "steady and easy", which is a fairly broad definition. It can be as simple as sitting upright in a chair, or as complex as the classic Yoga Lotus position. The important thing is that it should be a posture that will keep your body steady, and be easy for you to perform.]

Magus: **A KA DUA**
   TUF UR BIU
   BI A'A CHEFU
   DUDU NER AF AN NUTERU

(This mantra is chanted by the Magus and is then taken up by the Assistant Magus and all present, and is repeated continuously with ever increasing speed and loudness, until the Magus is satisfied that all are united in the Divine Harmony.

During the repetition the lights are lowered until there remains only the blue lamp above the Altar and the candles burning.

At the conclusion the Assistant Magus strikes once loudly upon the bell. The Magus of Fire takes up the censer and passing to the East places it upon the Altar. He then goes to the North taking the place of the Assistant Magus who advances to the West of the Altar, facing East. The Magus and Magus of Fire seat themselves in Asana. The Assistant Magus kneels, rises, places incense upon the censer, and recites:)

Assistant Magus: **Mother of Light, and the Gods! Mother of Music, awake!**
Silence and Speech are at odds: Heaven and Hell are at stake.
By the Rose and the Cross I conjure;
I constrain by the Snake and the Sword;
I am he that is sworn to endure -
Bring us the word of the Lord!
By the brood of the Bysses of Brightning,
whose God was my sire;
By the Lord of the Flame and the Lightning,
the King of the Spirits of Fire;
By the Lord of the Waves and the Waters,
the King of the Hosts of the Sea,
The fairest of all whose daughters was mother to me;

By the Lord of the Winds and the Breezes,
the King of the Spirits of Air,
In whose bosom the infinite ease is that cradled me there;
By the Lord of the Fields and the Mountains,
the King of the Spirits of Earth
That nurtured my life at his fountains
from the hour of my birth;
By the Wand and the Cup I conjure,
by the Dagger and Disk I constrain;
I am he that is sworn to endure; make thy music again!
I am the Lord of the Star and the Seal;
I am the Lord of the Snake and the Sword;
Reveal us the riddle, reveal! Bring us the word of the Lord;
As the flame of the sun, as the roar of the sea,
as the storm of the air,
As the quake of the earth - let it soar for a boon,
for a bane, for a snare,
For a lure, for a light, for a kiss, for a rod,
for a scourge, for a sword -
Bring us thy burden of bliss - Bring us the word of the Lord!

[From Crowley's poem "The Interpreter".]

(He kneels. Ave Maria is then sung, softly, by Soror Luna accompanied by a muted violin. Silence.)

[There are various musical settings of Ave Maria (or as it is known in English, "Hail Mary"). The text dates from the 15th century, and was originally derived from the

combination of the Biblical words of the Archangel Gabriel at the Annunciation (Luke 1:28) with Elizabeth's greeting to Mary at the Visitation (Luke 1:42), complete with later additions. Owing to its popularity as a Roman Catholic prayer it has been put into music by composers such as Mozart, Elgar, and Dvorak, among a great many others. The original Latin text is:

> *Ave Maria, gratia plena, Dominus tecum.*
> *Benedicta tu in mulieribus,*
> *et benedictus fructus ventris tui, Iesus.*
> *Sancta Maria, Mater Dei,*
> *ora pro nobis peccatoribus, nunc,*
> *et in hora mortis nostrae.*
> *Amen.*

which means:

> *Hail Mary, full of grace, the Lord is with thee;*
> *blessed art thou amongst women,*
> *and blessed is the fruit of thy womb, Jesus.*
> *Holy Mary, Mother of God,*
> *pray for us sinners now*
> *and at the hour of our death.*
> *Amen.]*

(The Assistant Magus rises, place incense upon the censer and goes to the South of the Altar to the station of the Magus and takes up his Asana. The Magus goes to the East of the Altar, and faces West.)

Magus: **Roll through the caverns of matter, the world's irremovable bounds!**
Roll, ye wild billows of ether!
The Sistron is shaken and sounds!
Wild and sonorous the clamour,
vast in the region of death.
Live with the fire of the Spirit,
the essence and flame of the breath!
Sound, O sound!
Gleam in the world of the dark,
where the chained ones shall tremble and flee!
Gleam in the skies of the dusk,
for the Light of the Dawn is in me!

Light on the forehead and life in the nostrils,
and love in the breast,
Shine, O Thou Star of the Dawning,
thou Sun of the Radiant Crest!
Shine, O shine!
Flame through the sky in the strength
of the chariot-wheels of the Sun!
Flame, ye young fingers of light,
on the west of the morning that run!
Flame, O thou Meteor Car, for my fire is exalted in thee!
Lighten the darkness and herald the daylight,
and waken the sea!
Flame, O flame!

[From Crowley's Rite of Luna, part of the Rites of Eleusis.]

(The Magus goes West of the Altar and places incense upon the censer.)

Magus: Crown Her, O crown Her with stars
               as with flowers for a virginal gaud!
               Crown Her, O crown Her with Light
               and the flame of a down-rushing Sword!
               Crown Her, O crown Her with Love
               for maiden and mother and wife!
               Hail unto Isis! For She is the Lady of Life!

(He kneels. Slight pause.)

Magus: **ISIS CROWNED!**

(All remain in perfect silence. After a pause the Assistant Magus strikes upon the bell softly three times, after another and longer pause he again strikes three times, and yet again after a still longer pause he again strikes three times. Then in another room is played a low simple melody, dying off very softly at the conclusion.

The Magus rises after a long pause. The Assistant Magus strikes upon the bell once loudly.)

Magus: **GLORIA PATRI ET MATRI ET FILIO ET FILIAE ET
               SPIRITUI SANCTI EXTERNO ET SPIRITUI SANCTI**

INTERNO UT ERAT EST ERIT IN SAECULA SAECULORUM: SEX IN UNO PER NOMEN SEPTEM IN UNO ARARITA

AMN

[Glory to the Father and to the Mother and to the Son and to the Daughter and to the Holy Spirit Without and to the Holy Spirit Within that was, and is, and is to come, forever and ever: six in one through the name of the seven in one ARARITA. Amen

ARARITA is an acronym of the Hebrew phrase "Achad Rosh; Acdotho Rosh Ichudo; Temurahzo Achad", meaning "One is his Beginning; One his Individuality; his Permutation One".]

(The Magus resumes his Asana. Silence for a few minutes. The Officers rise and pass out of the Temple. Then all depart in perfect silence, there being only sufficient light to permit of this.)

Chapter Six
Roots of Thelema I
- A Mithraic Liturgy

Mithras (or Meithras) was during the time of the Roman Empire the most widely worshipped god in the world. Since that time however his worship has been largely forgotten. However he is mentioned in a Thelemic context in several places in the works of Aleister Crowley, most notably in the Gnostic Mass, where the Priest invokes him in the words "Kurie Meithras" (Lord Mithras). In his *Confessions* Crowley describes a conversation with the discarnate wizard Amalantrah about the true derivation of Baphomet:

> *I had taken the name Baphomet as my motto in the O.T.O. For six years and more I had tried to discover the proper way to spell this name. I knew that it must have eight letters, and also that the numerical and literal correspondences must be such as to express the meaning of the name in such a ways as to confirm what scholarship had found out about it, and also to clear up those problems which archaeologists had so far failed to solve. Here, then, was an ideal test of the integrity and capacity of the Camel's Wizard. I flung the question in his face. "If you possess the superior knowledge which you claim, you can tell me how to spell Baphomet!" The Camel knew nothing of the Hebrew and little of the Greek. She had no idea that a conventional system existed by which one could check the accuracy of any given orthography. Her Wizard answered my question without hesitation. "Wrong," said I, "there must be eight letters." "True," he answered, "there is an R at the end." The answer struck me in the midriff. One theory of the name is that it represents the words Beta alpha phi eta mu eta tau epsilon omicron sigma, the baptism of wisdom; another, that it is a corruption of a title meaning "Father Mithras". Needless to say, the suffix R supported the latter theory. I added up the word as spelt by the Wizard. It totalled 729. This number had never appeared in my Cabbalistic working and therefore meant nothing to me. It however justified itself as being the cube of nine. The word chi eta phi alpha sigma, the mystic title given by Christ to Peter as the cornerstone of the Church, has this same value. So far, the Wizard had shown great qualities! He had cleared up the etymological problem and shown why the Templars should have given*

the name Baphomet to their so-called idol. Baphomet was Father Mithras, the cubical stone which was the corner of the Temple.

(The Camel mentioned in the text was Roddie Minor, a girlfriend of Crowley's who had contacted Amalantrah via mediumship in 1918.)

We can thus see that Mithras plays an important background role in the Thelemic canon, particularly in relationship to O.T.O. So although the following ritual was not written by Aleister Crowley (it pre-dates him by a couple of thousand years) I think that any Thelemic group performing it will find that it fits in extremely well with our magical current.

Although widespread across the Roman Empire, the worship of Mithras appears to have emerged in Persia sometime between 2000 BCE and 1 CE. We know that it survived there after the fall of the Roman Empire (Mithraic festivals were still being held in Iran up until the 20th century), so one plausible explanation for the connection of Mithras and Baphomet is that when the Templars based themselves in the Middle East during the Crusades they stumbled upon, and were influenced by, a surviving cult of Mithras. Mithraism was a religion that was traditionally practised by soldiers, since Mithras was a deity of victory and conquest whose initiates were male only, so it certainly would have been attractive to a group of warrior-monks far from home and sworn not to touch women.

Thanks to the success of the Roman Empire's military there are many well-preserved temples to Mithras still around today. Thus we have a fairly good idea of how original Mithraic temples were laid out. I think it very useful to try to recreate this temple layout wherever possible. The Mithras creation myth states that he was born inside a rock (which was actually the cosmos, as seen from outside), and Mithraic temples or Mithraeums (or Mithrea) were thus traditionally built inside caves or underground cellars, though a windowless room could also be used. Mithraeums weren't traditionally very large, usually only about 25 metres by 10 metres, and holding about 20-30 initiates at a time - so even a large modern living room could be turned into a reasonable facsimile of a Mithraeum.

The temple should be quite dark, perhaps with just a few candles or very low ambient lighting. The interior of the temple is a rectangular room with an altar set up at one end (the "East" of the temple), with benches running down each of the two long sides for the worshippers to sit or recline on. There should also be tables containing wheat, bread, beer, "bull's blood" wine, or other traditional foodstuffs sacred to Mithras. Also set up in the East should be an image of Mithras, known as the Tauroctony. There is a very formalised depiction of Mithras found in his temples all over the world, where the god is slaying a bull surrounded by various holy animals. See the illustration for

Tauroctony

details. Every Mithraic temple should feature a version of this image, either as a statue or as a two-dimensional reproduction.

The Tauroctony depicts the central mystery of Mithras. The god Ahura Mazda sent a raven to Mithras to order him to kill the sacred bull. Mithras was reluctant to do so, but knew he must comply, hence in this scene of slaying Mithras is always shown as having his head averted from the killing he is doing. Recent studies have shown that a desire to kill other men is quite rare in most humans, and in the past it was extremely difficult to get soldiers to kill people in conflict with this basic reluctance (that's why the military spends so much time and energy training soldiers to follow orders). So the portrayal of Mithras' reluctance to kill may have had a strong resonance with the soldiers who invoked him. From the sacrificed bull's body grew useful plants & herbs, from its blood came the vine, and from its semen came all useful animals - hence in many Tauroctonies the bull's wound has leaves or grain coming out of it.

To either side of Mithras there are two other humanoid figures - Cautes and Cautopates, who carry torches, one held aloft, the other pointing down, who represent the sunrise and the sunset. Although Mithras used to be generally thought of as a solar deity, he's not at all - he's a starry deity who manifests on Earth using the energy of our sun. You can see this by looking inside the cape of Mithras, which depicts the night sky, specifically the constellation of Perseus. It seems likely that one of the hidden teachings of the Mithraic cult was that Mithras was thought to inhabit this constellation, "the secret sun behind the sun".

The animals portrayed in the scene are representations of other star constellations. The bull itself is Taurus, who is being attacked by the Dog (Canis Minor), the Snake (Hydra), the Scorpion (Scorpio), and the Raven (Corvus). Also frequently shown are a lion and a cup, representing Leo and Aquarius, which were the signs at the solstices during the Age of Taurus. Few people realise that because of a "wobble" in the Earth's orbit, the positions of the stars in the sky change (over a very long period of time admittedly). This is known as the Precession of the Equinoxes, and astrologically is seen as heralding huge changes in society and the human race. The last few astrological periods like this were:

- Age of Cancer (ca. 8600 BCE - 6450 BCE): domestication
- Age of Gemini (ca. 6450 BCE - 4300 BCE): invention of writing, trade
- Age of Taurus (ca. 4300 BCE - 2150 BCE): Ancient Egypt and pyramids, bull worship
- Age of Aries (ca. 2150 BCE - 1 CE): Iron Age, solar cults
- Age of Pisces (ca. 1 CE - present day): Christianity, Islam

We know that Mithraism started sometime after 2000 CE, at the end of the Age of Taurus, the sign of the bull, so the Tauroctony, or slaying of the bull, may well have begun as a myth dealing with the change from the age of bull worship to the Age of Aries, with its emphasis on fire, iron, and the power of the virile sun (symbolised by the sword which Mithas carries to slay the bull). It's certainly fairly obvious that the astronomy (and astrology, which was the same thing back then) played a very large role in Mithraic belief.

Today we are once more in the midst of a great change in astrological Age, as we enter the Age of Aquarius, and overthrow the patriarchal monotheistic beliefs of the Piscean Age. Mithras is thus an excellent god for Thelemites to invoke, in his role as the destroyer of the outmoded ways of the past Age, and the bringer in of the New Age. Also Mithras is a god of the stars, and our religion is one where stars play a primary role. "Every man and every woman is a star" after all. Perhaps it's time for a new Aquarian Tauroctony, where Mithras slays not a bull, but a fish?

Mithraism was a mystery religion, in which the secrets were gradually given through a graded system of initiation (similar to the modern-day

O.T.O. for example). There were seven Degrees of initiation, the first four of which were open to everyone, the latter three by special invitation only. These Degrees were:

1. Corax (Raven - Mercury)
2. Nymphus (Bridegroom - Venus)
3. Miles (Soldier - Mars)
4. Leo (Lion - Jupiter)
5. Perseus (Persian - Moon)
6. Heliodromus (Sun-courier - Sun)
7. Pater (Father - Saturn)

Corax

Nymphus

Miles

Leo

Perseus

Heliodromus

Pater

The symbols of each Degree were often painted on the floor of the Mithraeum, in the form of a ladder that the initiates must "ascend". At each initiation the candidate would have to undergo ordeals, based on cold, heat, and fasting. Few details of these rites have come down to us, but we do know that at least one ritual (possibly that of Corax) included the Pater of the temple firing a bow at a rock, recreating the "water miracle" of Mithras when he made water flow from a rock in this manner. We can assume that during this rite the candidate was baptised with water, especially since every temple of Mithras had a well or sacred spring near the doorway at the West end.

Augustine, writing at the end of the fourth century, also mentions the use of water in Mithraic initiation:

> "But what kind of play is that which is played for them in the Cave with veiled eyes? For they have their eyes veiled... Some like birds flap their wings imitating the cry of ravens; others again roar like lions; while others with hands bound with the entrails of fowls are made to leap over trenches filled with water, and then some one comes and severs the bond, and calls himself their liberator."

The binding of the hands with bird entrails again might be a reference to the Corax rite of initiation, since in many initiatory systems the candidates' first entrance to the temple is with their hands bound.

Tertullian in his work On the Crown, written about 210 CE, talks about Soldiers of Mithras:

> "For when this Soldier is initiated in the Cave - in the Camp of Darkness as may well be said - and a crown is offered him at the sword's point - as though it were a mimicry of martyrdom - and then placed on his head, he is bidden to put up his hand and change it from his head to, it may be, his shoulder, declaring that Mithra is his Crown.
>
> And henceforth he never allows a crown or wreath to be put on him; and this he has as a mark whereby to prove himself, if on any occasion he should be tried concerning his mystery; immediately he is recognised as a Soldier of Mithra, if he cast down the crown, and declare that his Crown is his God."

I assume this to be a reference to the third degree of initiation, that of Miles, the Soldier.

We also know that in the initiation to the Degree of Leo the candidate was not baptised with water, but with honey (since water was not fitting in such a "fiery" Degree), and honey was placed in the initiate's mouth to symbolise pure and cleansing words.

The classical pagan philosopher Porphyry writes:

> *The theologers have used 'honey' in many different symbolic ways owing to its being a same deduced from many powers, and especially because it has both a purifying and preservative virtue; for by honey many things are preserved from decay, and with honey long open wounds are purified. Moreover it is sweet to taste, and collected from 'flowers' by 'bees' who happen to be 'ox-born.'*

> *When, therefore, they pour into the hands of those who are receiving the Leontic initiation, honey for washing instead of water, they bid them keep their hands pure from everything that causes pain or harm, or brings defilement; just as when the purifying medium is fire, they bring the candidate appropriate means of washing, declining water as inimical to fire.*

> *Moreover it is with honey too they purify their tongues from every sin.*

> *Further, when they bring honey to the Persian, as to the 'Keeper of the Fruits,' they symbolically signify the power of keeping or preserving.*

The "Persian" here being the Degree above that of the Leo - this last line may refer to part of the initiation of that Degree, or to a ritual act performed to that officer during other rites.

Porphyry goes on to quote Eubulus who states that the highest initiates in the Mithraic religion were apparently vegetarians, and that they believed in reincarnation of souls:

> *The first and most highly trained of them neither eat nor kill anything possessed of soul, but adhere to the ancient rule of abstinence from animals. The second use flesh, but do not slay tame creatures. While the third though they eat domesticated animals do not use all of them as do the rest of the people.*

> *For the chief doctrine of all of them is that of metempsychosis. And this they also seem to make clear in the Mysteries of Mithra; for they are accustomed to indicate us that is the grade or nature to which we belong by means of animal forms, thus mystically symbolizing the nature which we have in common with the animals.*

*Thus they call the initiates who take part in the actual rites Lions...,
and the subordinates Ravens. In the case of the Fathers moreover the
same symbolism is used, for they are called Eagles and Hawks.*

*These are the distinguishing marks of the three great grades; in addition,
he who receives the initiations in the Lion-grade is dressed in many
animal-forms.*

Note that the seven Degrees of Mithraism are here divided into "three
great grades". The first of these grades would appear to contain the I°-III°, the
second grade contain the next three Degrees, starting with the Leo Degree,
and the final grade be composed of the Fathers of the temples.

Apart from the above, we have little evidence of what actually occurred
in a Mithraeum. One notable exception is a work published in the late 19th
century by noted occultist, translator, and writer G.R.S. Mead under the title
A Mithraic Ritual. The work itself was discovered in the Paris Magic Papyrus
574 (Supplement grec de la Bibliotheque nationale), and is thought to date
from the 4th century, although it appears that it may have originated as early
as 100-150 CE. It is of Egyptian origin, most likely from a temple at Thebes.
As such it contains Egyptian magical themes as well as Mithraic ones, and
seems to be a combination of the two currents. How much of it is Mithaic
and how much Egyptian is still a matter of some academic dispute, but for
our purposes it works, and that's enough.

Mead's introduction to the ritual states:

*...the most likely supposition is that we have before us (when the latter
insertions are removed) a Ritual translated or paraphrased into Greek,
and adapted for use in Egypt, and that, too, for picked members of the
most esoteric circles. For our Ritual is not for the initiation of a neophyte
of the lower grades, but for a candidate who is to self-initiate himself in
the solitary mystery of apotheosis, whereby he became a true "Father"
of the inmost rites, one possessing face to face knowledge and gnosis.*

*...It is exceedingly probable, therefore, that we have in this Ritual of
initiation certain theurgic practices of Egyptian tradition combined
with the traditional Mithraic invocations done into Greek.*

Although G.R.S. Mead gives this as a solo self-initiation ritual I think this
is unlikely. The cult of Mithras was a mystery religion in which candidates
were led to initiation by those already of higher Degrees in the system. It's
very possible that this was a ritual of initiation to one of the higher Degrees

(perhaps Heliodromus or even Pater), or it may well have been some kind of meditative rite performed in the presence of the whole temple.

The ritual as written contains a great deal of instruction as to what should be visualised during its performance. There are many of these visualisations and it seems likely that the participant(s) may have been guided through them by the Father of the Temple or a ritual assistant. Accordingly I have adapted this work to serve as a group ritual, which is the way I think it may have been designed originally.

I have recreated it with three parts: Pater, Postulant, and People. The Pater is the Father of the Temple (this could be changed to Mater if the part is being performed by a woman), and serves to introduce the ritual working and guide the participants in visualisation; the Postulant does most of the direct invocation of Mithras; and the People back this up with sounds and chanting to energise the working. When there are only two people performing the rite the Postulant may also perform the parts given to the People. As a solo rite it could be performed without the Pater's speech at all, if the solo celebrant either reads or memorises the visualisations and performs them in the appropriate places. However I strongly recommend at least three people in this working, and it could be successfully used with a group as large as thirty.

Note that the personal pronouns used in the ritual are male, but don't have to be: Son may be changed to Daughter etc. where appropriate.

In several places in the ritual unarticulated sounds are made, which in the original Greek text are described as surigmoj and poppusmoj. The closest English translations are hissings and poppings. According to Mead:

The first denotes a shrill piping sound or hissing, the Latin stridor. It is used of such different sounds as the rattling of ropes, the trumpeting of elephants and a singing in the ears.

The second is used of a clicking or clucking with the lips and tongue, and of the whistling, cheeping, chirruping, warbling or trilling of birds. It is used of the smack of a loud kiss and also of the cry "hush." Both Aristophanes and Pliny tell us that it was used as a protection against, or rather a reverent greeting of, lightning; and the latter adds that this was a universal custom.

Basically it would appear that by surigmoj they were attempting to explain what we would now call white noise; and by poppusmoj some kind of clicking with the tongue or smacking of the lips as is used by certain African languages. Participants will have to work out for themselves how best to recreate these during the rite. In the text I have rendered the hissing with a triple S (as does Mead) and the popping as a triple P.

The text mentions amulets, which were very important in classical magick, and it is recommended that the participants either create or bring amulets to be used and thus consecrated during the rite. Also percussion, particularly of a metallic or booming nature might come in handy. Gongs, sistrums, or cowbells of gold, brass, iron, or steel would be perfect, as well as large drums preferably with animal skin heads (both to get that primeval atmosphere, and as "sacrifices" to Mithras).

A Mithraic Liturgy

Participants:	3-30
Time required:	An hour or so to perform.
Setup:	Fairly simple, though can be made more complex if desired - see notes on the traditional Mithraic temple design.
Words:	Quite a lot.
Equipment:	• Percussion instruments or other noise-making items
	• Food & drink
	• Amulet (preferably each person attending should bring one of these)
	• Tauroctony

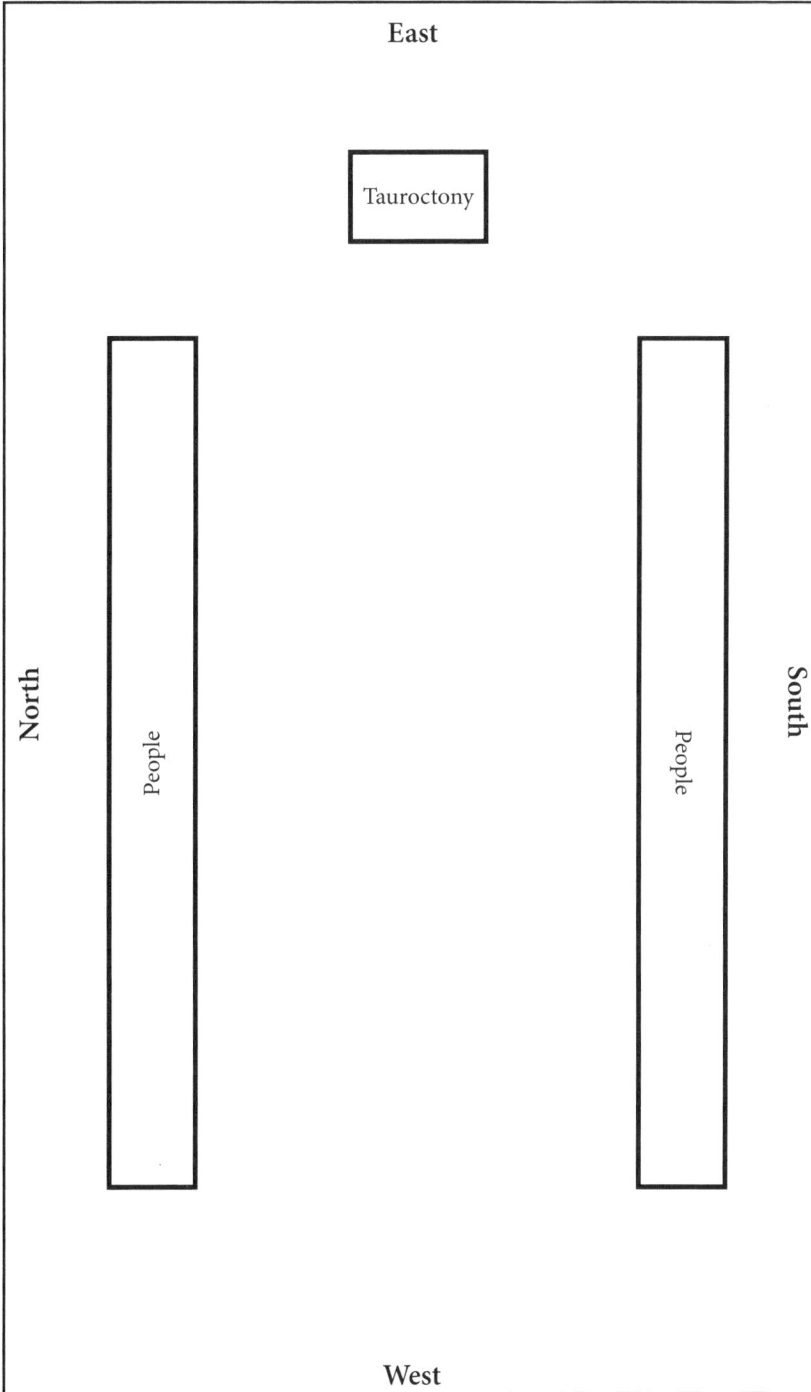

East

Tauroctony

North

People

People

South

West

The Father's Prayer

Pater:

O Providence, O Fortune, bestow on me Thy Grace - imparting these the Mysteries a Father only may hand on, and that, too, to a Son alone - his Immortality - a Son initiate, worthy of this our Craft, with which Sun Mithras, the Great God, commanded me to be endowed by His Archangel; so that I, Eagle as I am, by mine own self alone, may soar to Heaven, and contemplate all things.

The Invocatory Utterance (Logos)

Postulant:

O Primal Origin of my origination; Thou Primal Substance of my substance; First Breath of breath, the breath that is in me; First Fire, God-given for the Blending of the blendings in me, First Fire of fire in me; First Water of my water, the water in me; Primal Earth-essence of the earthy essence in me; Thou Perfect Body of me - N.N. son of N.N. [father], son of N.N. [grandmother] - fashioned by Honoured Arm and Incorruptible Right Hand, in World that's lightless, yet radiant with Light, in World that's soulless, yet filled full of Soul!

[When the letters N.N. are mentioned in the text this is classical shorthand for "Name of a particular person". The "Incorruptible Right Hand" is probably a reference to a previous introductory Mithraic initiation, in which the new candidate was welcomed by a handshake with the right hand; implying that this initiation ritual was designed to be performed by someone already initiated into at least the preliminary degrees of the system.]

If, verity, it may seem good to you, translate me, now held by my lower nature, unto the Generation that is free from Death; in order that, beyond the insistent Need that presses on me, I may have Vision of the Deathless Source, by virtue of the Deathless Spirit, by virtue of the Deathless Water, by virtue of the Deathless Solid, and by virtue of the Deathless Air; in order that I may become re-born in Mind; in order that I may become initiate, and that the Holy Breath may breathe in me; in order that I may admire the Holy Fire; that I may see the Deep of the New Dawn, the Water that doth cause the Soul to thrill; and that the Life-bestowing Æther which surrounds all things may give me Hearing.

For I am to behold today with Deathless Eyes - I, mortal, born of mortal womb, but now made better by the Might of Mighty Power, yea, by the Incorruptible Right Hand - I am to see today by virtue of the Deathless Spirit, the Deathless Æon, the master of the Diadeins of Fire - I with pure purities now Purified, the human soul-power of me subsisting for a little while in purity; which power I shall again receive transmitted unto me beyond the insistent Bitterness that presses on me, Necessity whose debts can never go unpaid - I, N.N., son of N.N. [mother] - according to the Ordinance of God that naught can ever change.

For that it is beyond my reach that, born beneath the sway of Death, I should unaided soar into the Height, together with the golden sparklings of the Brilliancy that knows no Death.

Stay still, O nature doomed to Perish, nature of men subject to Death! And straightway let me pass beyond the Need implacable that presses on me; for that I am His Son; I breathe; I am!

The First Instruction

Pater:

[During this section all should visualise the following: Breathe in the sun's rays three times. Fly upwards high into the air and gaze at the sun, and through it see into the realm of the Gods. Feel a turbulent wind coming from the East (front) of the temple, sweeping down and to the West (rear). Then the Gods will start to swoop down from their realm beyond the sun and towards the temple. At the end of the visualisation put your right index finger to your lips.]

Take from the Sun-rays breath, inhaling thrice as deeply as thou canst; and thou shalt see thyself being raised aloft, and soaring towards the Height, so that thou seem'st to be in midst of Air.

Thou shalt hear naught, nor man nor beast; nor shalt thou see aught of the sights upon the earth, in that same hour; but all things thou shalt see will be immortal.

For thou shalt see, in that same day and hour, the Disposition of the Gods, the Ruling Gods ascending heavenwards, the other ones descending. And through his Disk - the God's, my Father's - there shall be seen the Way-of-going of the Gods accessible to sight.

And in like fashion also shall be seen the Pipe, as it is called, whence comes the Wind in service for the day. For thou shalt see as though it were a Pipe depending from His Disk; and toward the regions Westward, as though it were an infinite East Wind. But if the other Wind, toward the regions of the East should be in service, in the like fashion shalt thou see, toward the regions of that side, the converse of the sight.

And thou shalt see the Gods gazing intently on thee and bearing down upon thee. Then straightway lay thy dexter finger on thy lips and say:

The First Utterance

Pater:	Silence! Silence! Silence!
People:	Silence! Silence! Silence!
Pater:	The Symbol of the Living God beyond Decay. Protect me, Silence! Ppp!
People:	Protect me, Silence! Ppp!
Pater:	Sss! Sss! Ppp!
People:	Sss! Sss! Ppp!
Pater:	And thereon shalt thou see the Gods gazing benignly on thee, and no longer bearing down upon thee, but proceeding on the proper order of their doings.

The Second Instruction

Pater:
When, then, thou see'st the Upper Cosmos clean and clear, with no one of the Gods (or Angels) bearing down on thee, expect to hear a mighty thunder-clap so as to startle thee.

[Pater should use a gong or other percussion instrument to make a loud noise here]

Then say again:

The Second Utterance (Logos)

Pater:
O Silence! Silence!
I am a Star, whose Course is as your Course, shining anew from out the depth

People:
O Silence! Silence!
I am a Star, whose Course is as your Course, shining anew from out the depth

Pater:
Upon thy saying this, straightway His disk will start expanding.
Sss! Sss!
Ppp! Ppp!

People:
Sss! Sss!
Ppp! Ppp!

Pater:
And after thou hast said this, straightway shalt thou see a mighty host of stars, five-pointed, emerging from His Disk, and filling all the Air.
Then say again:
O Silence! Silence!

People:
O Silence! Silence!

Pater:
And when His Disk is opened fully out, thou shalt behold an infinite Encircling and Doors of Fire fast closed.

Straightway set going then the utterance that follows, closing thy eyes:

The Third Utterance (Logos)

Postulant: Hear me, give ear to me - N.N., son of N.N. [mother] - O Lord, who with Thy Breath hast closed the Fiery Bars of Heaven; Twin-bodied; Ruler of the Fire; Creator of the Light; O Holder of the Keys; Inbreather of the Fire; Fire-hearted One, whose Breath gives Light; Thou who dost joy in Fire; Beauteous of Light; O Lord of Light, whose Body is of Fire; Light-giver and Fire-sower; Fire-loosener, whose Life is in the Light; Fire-whirler, who sett'st the Light in motion; Thou Thunder-rouser; O Thou Light-glory, Light-increaser; Controller of the Light Empyrean; O Thou Star-tamer!

Oh! Open unto me! For on account of this, the bitter and implacable Necessity that presses on me, I do invoke Thy Deathless Names, innate with Life, most worshipful, that have not yet descended unto mortal nature, nor have been made articulate by human tongue, or cry or tone of man:

Pater: Utter all these with Fire and Spirit once unto the end; and then begin again a second time, until thou hast completed all the Seven Immortal Gods of Cosmos. When thou hast uttered them, thunders and crashings shalt thou hear in the Surround, and feel thyself a-shake with every crash.

All: ëeö · oëeö · iöö · oë · ëeö · ëeö · oëeö · iöö · oëëe · öëe · öoë · ië · ëö · oö · oë · ieö · oë · öoë · ieöoë · ieeö · eë · iö · oë · ioë · öëö · eoë · oeö · öië · öiëeö · oi · iii · ëoë · öuë · ëö · oëe · eöëia · aëaeëa · ëeeë · eeë · eeë · ieö · ëeö · oëeeoë · ëeö · euö · oë · eiö · ëö · öë · öë · öë · ee · ooouiöë!

[This could be replaced with a simpler mantra, especially for a group who are less familiar with ritual working. The mantra IAO chanted a number of times would seem ideal for this purpose. Alternately a group could experiment with having each participant use a random selection of vowel sounds. The text gives 53 sets of vowels, which are then repeated seven times, making 371 in total. If desired the narrator could keep a count and stop the others at the correct places - or it could simply be left up to the feelings of all the participants to judge. The use of a rosary with 53 beads makes counting much easier.

It might be a useful practice here for members of the group to bang percussion such as gongs or sistrums, at the end of each cycle of vowels.]

Pater:	Silence! Silence! Silence!
People:	Silence! Silence! Silence!
Pater:	Protect me, Silence! Ppp!
People:	Protect me, Silence! Ppp!
Pater:	Sss! Sss! Ppp!
People:	Sss! Sss! Ppp!
Pater:	Thereon open thy eyes; and thou shalt see the Doors thrown open, and the Cosmos of the Gods that is within the Doors; so that for joy and rapture of the sight thy Spirit runs to meet it, and soars up. Therefore, hold thyself steady, and, gazing steadily into thyself, draw breath from the Divine. When, then, thy Soul shall be restored, say:

The Fourth Utterance

Pater:	Draw nigh, O Lord!
People:	Draw nigh, O Lord!
Pater:	Upon this utterance His Rays shall be turned on thee, and thou shalt be in midst of them.
	When, then, thou hast done this, thou shalt behold a God, in flower of age, of fairest beauty, and with Locks of Flame, in a white Tunic and a scarlet Mantle, wearing a Crown of Fire. Straightway salute Him with the Salutation of the Fire:

The Fifth Utterance

Postulant:	Hail Lord! O Thou of mighty Power; O King of mighty Sway; Greatest of Gods; O Sun; Thou Lord of Heaven

and Earth; O God of Gods! Strong is Thy Breath; strong is Thy Might!

O Lord, if it seem good to Thee, make Thou announcement of me unto God most high, who hath begotten and created Thee!

For that a man - N.N., son of N.N. [mother], born of the mortal womb of N.N. [grandmother], and of spermatic ichor, yea, of this ichor, which at Thy Hands today hath undergone the transmutation of rebirth -, one, from so many tens of thousands, transformed to immortality in this same hour, by God's good-pleasure, of God transcendent Good, a man, I say, presumes to worship Thee, and supplicates with whatsoever power a mortal hath.

Pater: Upon this utterance He shall come to the Pole, and thou shalt see Him moving round as on a path.

Then gaze intently, and send forth a prolonged "bellowing," like to a horn-note, expelling the whole breath, with pressure on the ribs,

[People should be instructed to join in with the bellowing.]

and kiss the amulets,

[Those of the People who have amulets should kiss them here too.]

and say first to that upon the right:

The Sixth Utterance

Pater: Protect me! Ppp!

People: Protect me! Ppp!

Pater: When thou hast uttered this. thou shalt behold the Doors thrown open, and, issuing from the Depth, Seven Virgins, in byssus-robes, with serpent-faces. and golden sceptres in their hands. These are they who are called Heaven's Fortunes.

When thou dost see these things, make salutation thus:

The Seventh Utterance

Postulant: Hail Heaven's Seven Fortunes, Virgins august and good, ye sacred ones who live and eat with Ppp!

Ye holiest Protectors of the Four Supports!

[The People may repeat each of these lines]

Hail thou, the First, Ppp!
Hail thou, the Second, Ppp!
Hail thou, the Third, Ppp!
Hail thou, the Fourth, Ppp!
Hail thou, the Fifth, Ppp!
Hail thou, the Sixth, Ppp!
Hail thou, the Seventh, Ppp!

Pater: There come forth others, too - Seven Gods, with faces of black bulls, in linen loincloths, with seven golden fillets on their heads. These are they called Heaven's Pole-lords.

And in like fashion unto each of them thou must make salutation with his special name.

The Eighth Utterance

Postulant: Hail Guardians of the Pivot, ye, sacred sturdy Youths, who all, at once, revolve the spinning Axis of Heaven's Circle, ye who let loose the thunder and the lightning, and earthquake-shocks and thunder-bolts upon the hosts of impious folk, but who bestow on me, who pious am and worshipper of God, good-health, and soundness of my frame in every Part, and Proper stretch of hearing and of sight, and calm, in the now Present good-hours of this day, O mighty Ruling Lords and Gods of me!

[The People may repeat each of these lines]

Hail thou, the First, Ppp!
Hail thou, the Second, Ppp!
Hail thou, the Third, Ppp!
Hail thou, the Fourth, Ppp!

Hail thou, the Fifth, Ppp!
Hail thou, the Sixth, Ppp!
Hail thou, the Seventh, Ppp!

Pater: Now when they all are present in their order, here and there, gaze in the Air intently, and thou shalt see lightnings down-flashing, and lights a-quiver, and the earth a-shake;

[You may want to use your percussion and noise-makers here once more, it works well.]

and then a God descending, a God transcending vast, of radiant Presence, with golden Locks, in flower of age, clad in a Robe of brightness, with Crown of gold upon His Head, and Garments on His Legs, holding in His Right Hand the golden Shoulder of the Calf.

This latter is the Bear that moves the Heaven-dome, and changes its direction, now up now down, according to the hour.

Then shalt thou see lightnings leap from His Eyes and from His Body stars.

Straightway send forth a "bellowing" prolonged, with belly-pressure, to start thy senses going all together-prolonged unto the very end,

[The People should also do this]

kissing again the amulets

[Again, those of the People with amulets should do this too.]

and saying:

The Ninth Utterance

Postulant: O Lord of me - N.N. - abide, with Me, within my Soul! Oh! leave me not! For N. bids thee remain.

Pater: And gaze intently on the God, with "bellowing" prolonged,

[All bellow here again]

and thus salute Him:

The Tenth Utterance

[This is the climax of the rite, and the Postulant should state the words with an emphasis on finality.]

Postulant:

Hail Lord, Thou Master of the Water! Hail, Founder of the Earth! Hail, Prince of Breath!

O Lord, being born again, I Pass away in being made Great, and, having been made Great, I die.

Being born from out the state of birth-and-death that giveth birth to mortal lives, I now, set free, pass to the state transcending birth, as Thou hast stablished it, according as Thou hast ordained and made, the Mystery.

[Ritual may now end with the Postulant dispensing food and drink from the altar to the other participants. All eat while basking in the radiance of the divine. Music may be played. When feasting is done, all leave the temple in joy and fulfillment.]

Chapter Seven
Roots of Thelema II
- The Bacchanal

The "Third Method" [of invoking any Deity] is the Dramatic, perhaps the most attractive of all; certainly it is so to the artist's temperament, for it appeals to his imagination through his aesthetic sense.

Its disadvantage lies principally in the difficulty of its performance by a single person. But it has the sanction of the highest antiquity, and is probably the most useful for the foundation of a religion. It is the method of Catholic Christianity, and consists in the dramatization of the legend of the God. The Bacchae of Euripides is a magnificent example of such a Ritual; so also, though in a less degree, is the Mass.

- Aleister Crowley, *Magick*

We have seen in the preceding chapter how the two thousand year old religion of Mithraism became one of the antecedents to the work we are doing today, but it's far from the only example. Although Thelema is one of the most modern religions around, its roots are from many cultures and mysteries. One of the beauties of our system is that we have this incredibly varied history that has been passed down to us, and that we can still connect to and draw from today. So here is another of our magical roots - the Bacchanal.

The Bacchanalia were originally annual festivals held to celebrate the Graeco-Roman god Bacchus, and (in contrast to the Mithraic religion) were originally a secret mystery cult almost entirely composed of women. Over time they became so popular that they were held several times a month, and men were eventually admitted also, though frequently only if they dressed as women. They were characterised by liberal consumption of wine, accompanied by dancing and chanting: wine, women, and song taken to its ultimate extreme. In many ways not unlike a modern day rave or rock festival - except these were a lot more extreme. People who think that the youth of today are much more wild and uninhibited than their forebears have a lot to learn about history.

Yet the Bacchanal was not just about getting drunk and having a good time - it was about loosing the artificial boundaries of everyday life and returning to a primal state where we can reconnect ourselves with the natural world around us. In that sense these were deeply spiritual practices, with a strong transformatory effect on those who participated. Also there were practical magical effects too, for as the playwright Euripides wrote:

> *This god too hath prophetic power, for there is no small prophecy inspired by Bacchic frenzy; for whenever the god in his full might enters the human frame, he makes his frantic votaries foretell the future. Likewise he hath some share in Ares' rights; for oft, or ever a weapon is touched, a panic seizes an army when it is marshalled in array; and this too is a frenzy sent by Dionysus.*

> *[The Bacchantes / Euripides; translated by Edward P. Coleridge, 1891.]*

So who was Bacchus (or Dionysus as he was often known), this god who could cause ordinary housewives to desert their families and revel in the woods by night? Mythologically he was the son of the God Zeus, though according to some accounts he had two mothers: the first being Persephone, Queen of the Underworld. After his birth to her he was torn apart by Titans, who left nothing but his heart; Zeus then blasted the Titans into ash, which he mixed with the flesh of Dionysus to create the human race. Humans thus partake of both natures, that of the divine Dionysus, and the material Titans.

Zeus then implanted the heart of Dionysus into the womb of the mortal woman Semele, who bore him, giving him his title of *Dithyrambos*, or twice-born. After that he was hidden in Zeus' thigh for a while to keep him safe, and then raised by woodland nymphs. (It should be noted that "thigh" was often used in earlier times as a euphemism for another prominent part of the male anatomy). Perhaps unsurprisingly, he was a disturbed child. He wandered the Mediterranean region for some time in madness, until he came to Phrygia (modern-day Turkey), where he was "cured" by his grandmother Cybele. After that he was just prone to androgyny, random acts of violence and slaying, continual drunkenness, and leading masses of people to desert their families to follow him into wanton revelling and the killing and dismembering of wild animals; so obviously the cure worked.

Bacchus had a great affinity with trees and fruit, and while on his travels discovered how to cultivate vines and create wine, and for this invention he was justly celebrated far and wide. Farmers would pray to him for a good harvest, and his earliest shrines seem to have been representations of his image carved into sacred trees. Also on his travels he met and married Ariadne, daughter of King Minos of Crete (whose famous thread had led Theseus through the Labyrinth). He topped this off by then descending to the Underworld and rescuing his mother, to give her a good retirement among the gods on Mount Olympus. And so the wild youth became the noble family man, as so many do.

We can see the classic death and rebirth theme in the life of Dionysus - not only is he killed and returned to life, but he later goes to the Underworld and brings his mother out of death. Although it might be tempting to see this as a solar myth, it may be more accurate to see it as the life-cycle of the crops, which die in Winter to fertilise the land and be renewed in Spring. In this sense there are parallels to the life of Osiris, also a god of vegetation who was dismembered and reborn. And of course, the later myth of Jesus of Nazareth, who was also supposedly killed, went to the Underworld, and was reborn. It seems likely that much of the myth of Jesus was actually derived from that of Bacchus. Aleister Crowley wrote in Chapter 7 of *The Book of Lies*:

> *The legend of 'Christ' is only a corruption and perversion of other legends. Especially of Dionysus: compare the account of Christ before Herod/Pilate in the Gospels, and of Dionysus before Pentheus in 'The Bacchae'.*

And in *Magick*, chapter 1:

> *...the identity of this legend with the course of Nature, its madness, its prodigality, its intoxication, its joy, and above all its sublime persistence through the cycles of Life and Death. The pagan reader must labour to understand this in Pater's "Greek Studies", and the Christian reader will recognise it, incident for incident, in the story of Christ. This legend is but the dramatization of Spring.*

> *The magician who wishes to invoke Bacchus by this method must therefore arrange a ceremony in which he takes the part of Bacchus, undergoes all His trials, and emerges triumphant from beyond death. He must, however, be warned against mistaking the symbolism. In this case, for example, the doctrine of individual immortality has been dragged in, to the destruction of truth. It is not that utterly worthless part of man, his individual consciousness as John Smith, which defies death - that consciousness which dies and is reborn in every thought. That which persists (if anything persist) is his real John Smithiness, a quality of which he was probably never conscious in his life.*

The myth of Dionysus was originally celebrated in two festivals, one rural and one urban. The rural festival was celebrated around the Winter Solstice, whereas the city celebrations where held around the Spring Equinox. The main public rite was the pompe, or procession, in which the worshippers carried carved images of the phallus, long loaves of bread, jars of water and jars of wine. Then would come dancing and singing, and choruses would perform 'Dithyrambs', hymns about the life of Dionysus sung by a chorus of up to fifty people dancing in circles. These often took a call and response style, with the chorus leader taking on the main role and the rest of the chorus following.

The Bacchantes loved music of all sorts, and used an incredible variety of instruments, especially drums, cymbals, and flutes. Basically if it could make a noise and you could dance to it, it was in. They also liked to clothe themselves in whatever they found in the woodlands. Deer skins, goat skins, and bull's hides were a favorite, and easily obtained, since the revellers also liked to tear any deer, goats and bulls they came across apart with their bare hands and eat the raw flesh as a way of getting closer to the spirit of Dionysus. They also wove crowns of ivy and bindweed for themselves, and each carried a stave topped with a pine-cone, called a Thyrsus.

The Thyrsus was traditionally made from the hollow stalk of the giant fennel plant, or *ferula*. The asafoetida variety of giant fennel grows up to 2 metres tall, which gives an idea of possible length of the Thyrsus, and 5-8 centimetres wide; since it was also hollow it would thus make a low resonant sound when banged on the floor. Asafoetida is closely related to the now extinct variety of giant fennel Silphium, an important medicinal plant in ancient times, and which may have been the one originally used in the Bacchanal.

A giant fennel stalk was also used by Prometheus to bring down fire from heaven to assist the evolution of mankind. This is referenced in the Gnostic Mass, in the Priest's Anthem:

> *Thou, the true fire within the reed*
> *Brooding and breeding, source and seed*
> *Of life, love, liberty, and light*

If you want to make your own Thyrsus and can't get hold of a giant fennel stalk, perhaps thick bamboo would be a good substitute.

Obviously there is a phallic reference in the Thyrsus, the hollow reed topped with the pine cone representing male fertility. Also pine cones with seeds still in will rattle like a shaker (similar to poles with bottle tops nailed to them that modern-day Morris Dancers use). Sometimes the pine cones at the top were also filled with honey, which would run down the shaft during the rites (perhaps not a good idea if you're doing this indoors...).

Crowley depicted Dionysus on the card of the The Fool in his Tarot pack, and wrote in *The Book of Thoth*:

> *The legend of Bacchus is, first of all, that he was Diphues, double-natured, and this appears to mean more bisexual than hermaphroditic. His madness is also a phase of his intoxication, for he is pre-eminently the god of the vine. He goes dancing through Asia, surrounded by various companions, all insane with enthusiasm; they carry staffs headed with pine cones and entwined with ivy; they also clash cymbals, and in some legends are furnished with swords, or twined about with serpents. All the half-gods of the forest are the male companions of the Maenad women.*

> *...In the worship of Bacchus there was a representative of the god, and he was chosen for his quality as a young and virile, but effeminate man. In the course of the centuries, the worship naturally became degraded; other ideas joined themselves to the original form; and, partly because of the orgiastic character of the ritual, the idea of the Fool took definite shape.*

> *...In his right hand he bears the wand, tipped with a pyramid of white, of the All-Father. In his left hand he bears the flaming pine-cone, of similar significance, but more definitely indicating vegetable growth; and from his left shoulder hangs a bunch of purple grapes. Grapes represent fertility, sweetness, and the basis of ecstasy. This ecstasy is shown by the stem of the grapes developing into rainbow- hued spirals. The Form of the Universe. This suggests the Threefold Veil of the Negative manifesting, by his intervention, in divided light. Upon this spiral whorl are other attributions of godhead; the vulture of Maut, the dove of Venus (Isis or Mary), and the ivy sacred to his devotees.*

Much of what we know of the Bacchantes today comes from what is generally accepted as one of the greatest plays ever written: *The Bacchae* by Euripides, first performed in 405 BCE (that's over 500 years before the Bible) as an entry into the Dionysia drama competition in Athens shortly after the playwright's death. Euripides's play is notable for not only describing the worship of Bacchus in some detail, but also for its emphasis on the role of women, and its psychological depth - common themes in his work. The ritual following is mainly derived from excerpts from The Bacchae, edited into ceremonial form. As such it's not an original ritual text, though it is certainly contemporary and perfect for setting the scene that we need.

Maenad

The Bacchae contains many descriptions of how the Bacchantes, or Maenads as they were sometimes known, worshipped. For example, at one point this exchange takes place as the set up for a joke:

PENTHEUS   Is it by night or day thou performest these devotions?

DIONYSUS   By night mostly; darkness lends solemnity.

This gives us some useful background information, as well giving the audience a good laugh - the worship of Dionysus was anything but solemn!

The ritual below was originally compiled by Cathryn Orchard, to whom I am grateful for permission to include it here. It uses text taken from both Euripides and Crowley, to form a harmonic synthesis of ancient and modern.

The Bacchanal

Participants:	Minimum 4, but can have a Chorus of up to 50 or more
Time required:	About half an hour
Setup:	Moderate, though can be made more complex as required. An outdoors setting is preferred
Words:	Medium
Equipment:	

- Thyrsus - staves topped with a pine cone
- Noise makers - drums, cymbals, shakers, flutes, bull-roarers - whatever you can get your hands on and the members of your group are able to play convincingly
- Altar in the centre of the temple, with
  - A bowl of wine - something resembling a punch bowl filled with wine placed on it
  - Goblets for the Bacchantes to drink with
  - Incense and burner. Traditionally Syrian rue, also known as Aspand or Harmal (Peganum harmala). Note that this incense is an abortifacient, so do not use around any woman who may be pregnant!
  - Candle or flaming torch (lit)
  - Feast (may include milk, honey, olives, and venison or beef, preferably rare)
- Costumes
  - White robes
  - Fawn or goat skins tied around the waist, or something to resemble skins (optional)
  - Crowns woven from ivy, oak, or bindweed (not worn at start)
  - Hair should be worn loose
  - Serpent Crown
  - Flaming torches (unlit at start), candles would do if working inside

[Dionysus is concealed; behind a veil would do if working inside, or behind a tree or rock if working outdoors. The bowl of wine and goblets are on a pedestal in the centre of the space. The woven crowns and fawn skins (if used) are scattered about the perimeter of the space, ready for when needed. The Chorus gather together in the temple. All is in relative darkness.

During the rite the members of the Chorus should act out the instructions as recited by the Lead Chorus.]

Lead Chorus   From Asia o'er the holy ridge of Tmolus hasten to a pleasant task, a toil that brings no weariness, for Bromius' sake, in honour of the Bacchic god. Who loiters in the road? Who lingers 'neath the roof? Avaunt! I say, and let every lip be hushed in solemn silence;

[Tmolus is a mountain in Turkey. Bromius is another ancient god of wine, whose name is often also used to describe Dionysus.]

(All make the sign of Hoor-paar-kraat)

for I will raise a hymn to Dionysus, as custom aye ordains. O happy he! who to his joy is initiated in heavenly mysteries and leads a holy life, joining heart and soul in Bacchic revelry upon the hills, purified from every sin; observing the rites of Cybele, the mighty mother, and brandishing the thyrsus, with ivy-wreathed head, he worships Dionysus.

[Cybele was the grandmother of Dionysus, an Earth Mother goddess worshipped in caves and upon mountains. She rode a chariot pulled by lions, and may have been the original model for Babalon in the Bible. *Her worship was also notable for drinking, dancing, and wild music, so there is a strong connection with the Bacchic rites.]*

(She brandishes her thyrsus while saying:)

Go forth, go forth, ye Bacchanals, bring home the Bromian god Dionysus, child of a god, from the mountains of Phrygia to the spacious streets of Hellas, bring home the Bromian god!

[Phrygia is modern-day Turkey, Hellas is Greece.]

(Chorus begin to search for Dionysus as directed)

Whom on a day his mother in her sore travail brought forth untimely, yielding up her life beneath the lightning stroke of Zeus' winged bolt; but forthwith Zeus, the son of Cronos, found for him another womb wherein to rest, for he hid him in his thigh and fastened it with golden pins to conceal him from Hera.

[Zeus was the ancient Greek god of the sky and thunder, who deposed his father Chronos to become King of the Gods. He was married to Hera, yet had many other amorous dalliances, leading her to become extremely jealous of his other lovers and their children by him. Hence his hiding Dionysus from her.]

(Dionysus is revealed to the Bacchantes, standing in the sign called Vir. The hands, with clenched finger and thumbs thrust out forwards, are held to the temples; the head is then bowed and pushed out, as if to symbolize the butting of an horned beast.)

> **And when the Fates had fully formed the horned god, he brought him forth and crowned him with a coronal of snakes,**

(During the preceding speech, Dionysus is brought forward and crowned)

> **whence it is the thyrsus-bearing Maenads hunt the snake to twine about their hair.**

(Chorus put on their woven crowns as Lead Chorus says:)

> **Crown thyself with ivy; burst forth, burst forth with blossoms fair of green convolvulus, and with the boughs of oak and pine join in the Bacchic revelry; don thy coat of dappled fawn-skin, decking it with tufts of silvered hair; with reverent hand the sportive wand now wield. Anon shall the whole land be dancing, when Bromius leads his revellers to the hills, to the hills away!**

Dionysus: **What ho! my Bacchantes, ho! hear my call, oh! hear.**

[While there are lines for nine chorus members given here, if you have less people these lines may be distributed between them.]

Chorus I: **Who art thou?**

Chorus II: **What Evian cry is this that calls me?**

Chorus III: **Whence comes it?**

Dionysus: **What ho! Once more I call, I the son of Semele, the child of Zeus.**

Chorus IV:	**My master, O my master, hail!**
Chorus V:	**Come to our revel-band, O Bromian god.**
Chorus VI:	**He who makes the clustering vine to grow for man.**
Chorus VII:	**Thou solid earth!**
Chorus VIII:	**Within these walls the triumph-shout of Bromius himself will rise.**
Chorus IX:	**Kindle the blazing torch with lightning's fire**

(Light the torches)

Lead Chorus	**With milk and wine and streams of luscious honey flows the earth, and Syrian incense smokes. While the Bacchante holding in his hand a blazing torch of pine uplifted on his wand waves it, as he speeds along, rousing wandering votaries, and as he waves it cries aloud with wanton tresses tossing in the breeze; and thus to crown the revelry, he raises loud his voice...**

The Bromian god exults with cries of Evoe!

(The Chorus begin a chant of "Evoe" (pronounced Eh-vo-hey) each beating their thrysus on the ground or using a noise maker. The idea is to build a rhythm and volume so be as frantic as possible. All frenzy is sacred to Dionysus so try to raise the spirit of Dionysus in all the attendants. Dancing around and throwing back of hair to be positively encouraged. While the Chorus chant and dance the Lead Chorus recites:)

Lead Chorus	**Bacchus, divine and human! Bacchus, begotten on Semele of Zeus, the adulterous Lord of Thunder ravishing, brutally, his virginal victim! Bacchus, babe hidden from hate in the most holy of holies, the secret of thy sire, in the Channel of the Star-Spate, Whereof one Serpent is thy soul! Bacchus, twy-formed, man-woman, Bacchus, whose innocence tames the Tiger, while yet thy horns drip blood upon thy mouth, and sharpen the merriment of wine to the madness of murder! Bacchus, Thy thyrsus oozes sap;**

thine ivy clings to it; thy Lion-skin slips from thy sleek shoulders, slips from thy lissome loins; drunk on delight of the godly grape, thou knowest no more the burden of the body and the vexation of the spirit.

Come, Bacchus, come thou hither, come out of the East; come out of the East, astride the Ass of Priapus! Come with thy revel of dancers and singers! Who followeth thee, forbearing to laugh and to leap? Come, in thy name Dionysus, that maidens be mated to God-head! Come, in thy name Iacchus, with thy mystical fan to winnow the air, each gust of thy Spirit inspiring our Soul, that we bear to thee Sons in Thine Image!

[This section from Crowley "Notes for an Astral Atlas", from "Magick, Book 4"]

(When the noise and chanting reach critical mass, and the members of the Chorus are filled with Dionysian frenzy, each yells in turn:)

Chorus (All):   **Dionysus is within this house!**

Lead Chorus   **Do homage to him.**

Chorus (All):   **We do! I do!**

(All feast and drink by dipping their goblets in the central bowl of wine, and prophesy as the spirit of Dionysus moves them.)

[See Homer's Odyssey: *"For myself I declare that there is no greater fulfilment of delight than when joy possesses a whole people, and banqueters in the halls listen to a minstrel as they sit in order due, and by them tables are laden with bread and meat, and the cup-bearer draws wine from the bowl and bears it round and pours it into the cups."]*

(During this Dionysus recites:)

Dionysus: **I bring ye wine from above,**
From the vats of the storied sun;
For every one of ye love,
And life for every one.
Ye shall dance on hill and level;
Ye shall sing in hollow and height

In the festal mystical revel,
The rapturous Bacchanal rite!
The rocks and trees are yours,
And the waters under the hill,
By the might of that which endures,
The holy heaven of will!
I kindle a flame like a torrent
To rush from star to star;
Your hair as a comet's horrent,
Ye shall see things as they are!
I lift the mask of matter;
I open the heart of man;
For I am of force to shatter
The cast that hideth - Pan!
Your loves shall lap up slaughter,
And dabbled with roses of blood
Each desperate darling daughter
Shall swim in the fervid flood.
I bring ye laughter and tears,
The kisses that foam and bleed,
The joys of a million years,
The flowers that bear no seed.
My life is bitter and sterile,
Its flame is a wandering star.
Ye shall pass in pleasure and peril
Across the mystic bar
That is set for wrath and weeping
Against the children of earth;
But ye in singing and sleeping
Shall pass in measure and mirth!
I lift my wand and wave you
Through hill to hill of delight :
My rosy rivers lave you
In innermost lustral light..
I lead you, lord of the maze,
In the darkness free of the sun;
In spite of the spite that is day's
We are wed, we are wild, we are one.

[Poem by Crowley, also used in Crowley's Rite of Jupiter, part of the Rites of Eleusis.]

Chapter Eight
Roots of Thelema III - Goetia

It is found by experience (confirming the statement of Zoroaster) that the most potent conjurations are those in an ancient and perhaps forgotten language, or even those couched in a corrupt and possibly always meaningless jargon. Of these there are several main types. The "preliminary invocation" in the "Goetia" consists principally of corruptions of Greek and Egyptian names. For example, we find "Osorronnophris" for "Asor Un-Nefer".

The conjurations given by Dr. Dee (vide Equinox I, VIII) are in a language called Angelic, or Enochian. Its source has hitherto baffled research, but it is a language and not a jargon, for it possesses a structure of its own, and there are traces of grammar and syntax.

However this may be, it "works". Even the beginner finds that "things happen" when he uses it: and this is an advantage - or disadvantage! - shared by no other type of language. The rest need skill. This needs Prudence!

- Aleister Crowley, Magick

Mention magick to most people and chances are they'll think it's all about standing in a circle, and reciting strange phrases to call up demons from hell. Of course it very rarely is - unless you're working with Goetia. Goetia is pretty much classical medieval demon evocation at its finest. It's not the only example of such – there are many medieval grimoires still extant, of varying degrees of usefulness; but Goetia is generally considered the pinnacle of the art and science of evocation within the Western Esoteric tradition.

Many magicians wouldn't naturally associate Goetia with group working - for example the translation published by Crowley in 1904 doesn't specify anything about requiring more than one person. In fact, several modern commentators have stated that they think that Goetia should only be performed alone. Although it can be done by one person alone, it can also be very efficacious with more than one; even if you have a primary Magician doing the main evocations, just having someone else to act as Assistant to keep the incense burning, take notes, etc. can be extremely useful. Usually in medieval grimoires, the presence of one or more Assistants is assumed, so for most of its long history it most certainly has been performed as a group operation. Goetia is also a vital part of the original preparation of The Brazen Head ritual (see next chapter) which is very much a group working.

Goetia is traditionally associated with King Solomon, the supposedly wisest man in the world according to the Judeo-Christian Bible, but it seems highly unlikely that it was actually written by him. The earliest complete versions we know of date from the seventeenth century, well over two thousand years after Solomon died. Most likely it was attributed to him so people possessing a copy could say that it was a holy text, and thus save themselves from getting burnt at the stake for witchcraft. The list of demons given in the book is similar to the *Steganographia* of Trithemius, from around 1500 CE, and Johann Weyer's *Pseudomonarchia Daemonum* from 1563 CE, so it does seem to have been something that was frequently worked and passed down from magician to magician for quite some time.

The Crowley publication of *The Goetia* was translated by S. L. Mathers (one of the original founders of the Golden Dawn occult order) in 1903, based on Sloane manuscripts 2731 & 3648 in the British Library. In common with much of Mathers' other research it contained significant errors and omissions, but Crowley appears to have found it very effective and continued to use it throughout his life, although being Crowley it seems he simplified it greatly from its original complex structure.

A major innovation by Crowley was the use of the Enochian language of Dr. John Dee. I do not intend to go deeply into Enochian in this book as it's an exceedingly complex and involved magical system that could easily fill several books on its own. It is based on the use of the "language of the angels", a synthetic language derived from magical work done by Dee and his assistant Edward Kelly during the reign of Queen Elizabeth I of England. For more detailed information on Enochian I refer the reader to Lon Milo DuQuette's excellent book on the subject *Enochian Vision Magick*.

Crowley translated many of the evocations of Goetia into the Enochian language in his publication, and evidence suggests that eventually he even replaced the original Conjurations entirely with the First and Second Enochian Keys. For the version given here, I have followed this practice for the Conjurations, but kept the rest of the working in English. The original Conjurations, although very powerful in their own right, are based on language and events from the Old Testament of the Judeo-Christian

Bible, which of course had great meaning to Western European medieval magicians, but are unlikely to mean much to modern young Thelemites, who may never have even opened a Bible in their lives.

Most modern books on Goetia have tended to focus on "authenticity" in getting their subject matter as close as possible to the original manuscripts. While this is a laudable ideal, it often doesn't make for the most practical of systems. As we have seen above, Goetia has gone through many revisions since the 17th century as magicians have adapted it. For this book I have kept the basic structure of the rite very close to the original, but greatly streamlined the rather wordy text.

Most people have some awareness of "traditional" demonic theory - that there is a Heaven and Hell, and that the good guys go to Heaven and the bad guys go to Hell. Traditionally Goetic demons are supposed to be "fallen angels" (such as Belial), who rebelled against Jehovah and were banished to Hell; or sometimes they were older pagan Gods and Goddesses that were turned into demons when they were conquered by the early Jewish tribes (such as Bael or Asteroth). These demons resent their fallen state and will do anything to get back into Heaven - and that's where the magician comes in. By working with a magician who is close to God, the demons earn good karma, and get closer to redemption. As you ascend to the Divine, so do they if they are associated with you. So there is nothing "evil" about dealing with Goetia, it's actually quite the contrary. The Jewish Bible reveres Solomon as holy and wise, and even the Christian Bible quotes Jesus as controlling demons in the name of Beelzebub (*Matthew: 24-27*).

Of course all of the above is based on the view of Earth being some kind of kindergarten where God watches us and decides whether to reward us or punish us for all eternity when we finally die. Personally I don't hold with this belief and I'm sure many of my readers don't hold it either. So where does that leave demons? If there's no "Hell" where do they live? Honestly, I don't know; but I suspect they live in our unconscious minds. Crowley suspected something similar, and in the introductory section to his edition of the The Goetia added an essay named *The Initiated Interpretation of Magick* where he put forward the following theory:

- Our perception of reality is composed of changes in our brain chemistry
- Therefore our personal reality lies within the brain, not outside it
- Magical effects are illusory products of brain changes
- Many non-magical effects are also illusions of the brain
- Therefore magick is as real as many other everyday things that we perceive as reality

That deals with why magick works in general. Take a moment to think about this, then move on the next set of theorums, which deal with Goetia in particular:

- Goetic magick creates magical effects
- Magical effects exist within the brain
- Therefore Goetic Spirits are portions of the human brain
- Evoking a Spirit stimulates a specific area of the brain
  - General control of the brain (names of God)
  - Control over brain in detail (rank of Spirit)
  - Control of specific area of brain (name of Spirit)
- This area is also stimulated by sight (seal of the Spirit) & smell (incense)

I think Crowley may have been on to something here, but there are some problems with this interpretation, most notably that it assumes that magick is entirely happening inside one person's head only, and has no way of affecting the outside world directly. However experience shows us that Goetic magical working does have an effect on the outside world, so there's something missing in Crowley's theories.

Since Crowley's time however we have had the benefit of some excellent research done into the nature of consciousness and change by two of my favourite scientists: Julian Jaynes and Rupert Sheldrake. Using their work as a basis, I present an expanded interpretation of what might be happening (you can call it the Jaynes-Sheldrake-Orpheus model if you like):

- Certain areas of our brains are normally inaccessible to our consciousness (e.g. Wernicke's Area)
- By magical stimulation of these areas we are able to "speak" to the thought processes within them
- Through this communication we can access different modes of thought, and increase the brain's processing capability
- These areas can inspire new ideas and cause us to respond to our environment in different ways
- Changes in one person's consciousness can cause corresponding changes across the entire species

For more detail on this, I recommend the reader study *The Origin of Consciousness in the Breakdown of the Bicameral Mind* by Julian Jaynes, and *A New Science of Life* by Rupert Sheldrake. Be warned that they aren't easy reading, especially Jaynes' book.

Note that you IN-voke (call from outside into you) a god or goddess, but E-voke (call out from within you) a demon.

Practically speaking however, it's really irrelevant whether you believe in demons with pitchforks that come from Hell, or whether you believe it's just part of your own unconscious mind. What is important is that these spirits are as real as anything else in the world, have their own personalities, and are entirely capable of acting independently of you; and that's what makes them so useful. Instead of you having to worry about every little detail of stuff, you can instruct the Spirits to handle it for you, and go on about your life, knowing that the Spirits are doing the dirty work for you.

However it's important to remember that just because demons may be part of your own unconscious doesn't mean that you can dispense with the required parts of the ritual given here - you'd be surprised how little you really know about the subtle workings of the inside of your own head.

So how do we do this evocation then?

Preliminaries

What is the theory implied in such rituals as those of the Goetia? What does the Magician do? He applies himself to invoke a God, and this God compels the appearance of a spirit whose function is to perform the Will of the magician at the moment. There is no trace of what may be called machinery in the method. The exorcist hardly takes the pains of preparing a material basis for the spirit to incarnate except the bare connection of himself with his sigil. It is apparently assumed that the spirit already possesses the means of working on matter. The conception seems to be that of a schoolboy who asks his father to tell the butler to do something for him.

- Aleister Crowley, *Magick*

There are 72 Goetic spirits, each one with particular specialties in the work they do. Which one we decide to evoke will depend greatly on what we're trying to achieve. So before going any further you need to sit down and write down exactly what it is you need. And I do mean exactly. Demons thrive on vagueness and ambiguity. They are lazy workers who will take any opportunity to wiggle out of having to do something. And they are incredible rules lawyers - they'll happily argue for hours over what a certain thing says, if it means they can get away with not doing some work. So don't leave them any wiggle room - figure out in detail precisely what you need done, and precisely when it needs to be done. Dot every i and cross every t, down to the last word and the last minute.

Demons are not your friends, and don't ever catch yourself thinking that. They are more like business partners, who are happy to do whatever needs to be done providing it's in the contract. But a contract is only good as long as it is based on mutual respect. If you want these Goetic forces to obey you, your principles should be noble and correct at all times. Yes, you could use Goetia to go out and mess with people you don't like, but you're not likely to get much respect from the demons you send to do the job. They might not have much of a moral sense, but they expect you to have one. So at all times, remember your basic Thelemic principles: every man and every woman is a star, and love is the law, love under will. If you go against principles such these, your Goetic magick is likely to get seriously messed up. I strongly advise against doing anything to force other people to bend to your desires; that means that generally it's a bad idea to ask demons to make someone fall in love with you, or to kill someone, or any similar practice. It's perfectly legitimate to use Goetia to aid you, but not at someone else's expense. This goes double for the use of Goetia against fellow initiates of your magical group – that's a recipe for disaster, for you as well as them.

You need to write down what it is you want to achieve, and the practical steps necessary to achieve it. Note that "Make me rich" isn't really very detailed, and would be a perfect example of a very bad thing to write down. Better would be something like "Help me get a job that pays well doing something that I love" would be better, but still leaves lots of room for confusion - that's the kind of request that a demon would look at and immediately think "Ah, she wants to be a porn star, let's make that happen!" So learn to specify *what it is you really need*.

Note that I say what you *need*, not what you want, since these are often two completely different things. You might think you want free beer for the rest of your life, but you may realise you were wrong a few years later when you're laying in hospital waiting for a new liver. So try to think ahead about what it is your life really requires, and work towards that.

If you're doing Goetia as a group endeavor, it's also important that everyone in the group be informed of the purpose of the rite, and to be in agreement with it. You don't want to be asking the demon to do something, only to have someone say "Hang on, I'm not so sure about that..." So do take care that everyone is in absolute agreement.

Another important thing to remember is to put in a time limit for the demon to do the work. This should be reasonably realistic, but not so far away that it gets too vague. Also demons don't wear watches, so try to use times they can understand: "one solar day" is better than "24 hours", and "one lunar month" better than 4 weeks. For example, if you're doing your ritual at the time of the Full Moon, then something like "by the next time the Moon is Full" is a perfect way to express the time limit. What makes a good time frame depends on the situation, but a maximum of three months is probably as far as you want to extend anything. If the thing you want requires a longer time frame to come to pass, try to break it up into chunks so you can track how it progresses.

Choosing your Demon

Once you've figured out precisely what you want, you need to figure out which demon will be most effective in delivering that aim. There are 72 to choose from, each with various talents and abilities. Some of these medieval talents may seem rather quaint and outdated today - for example Leraje's talent for making arrow wounds putrefy may not be particularly useful to most readers of this book. However it's important to remember that in many cases their talents are still relevant when translated into modern day usage. So examine the descriptions given of each Spirit closely to see which one seems closest to the thing you need.

Demonic society appears to be rather hierarchical, and each of the Spirits of Goetia is somewhat of an aristocrat in that society - these aren't your common or garden demons. They have titles and often command entire demonic legions of their own. It's important to check what rank is held by the demon that you choose. Their titles and attributions are (in approximate order of rank from top to bottom):

- King: Sol (Gold)
- Prince or Prelate: Jupiter (Tin)
- Duke: Venus (Copper)
- Marquis: Luna (Silver)
- Earl: Mars (Iron)
- President: Mercury (alloy containing Silver)
- Knight: Saturn (Lead)

Generally speaking the lower in rank they are the easier they should be to command, so you might not want to start with a King or Prince. Aim for something lower in the hierarchy first. However remember that even a Knight or a President is not exactly working-class. These guys won't be doing the work themselves, most of them have entire legions of servitors under their command. Conversely, even the highest demonic power is still subservient to the angels, who in turn rank below the gods. That's a vital principle to remember - in a classic operation of evocation you first connect with the divine powers, and then in the name of the gods you command angels who in turn command demonic princes, who in turn command the lesser servitors.

For all evocations the moon should be 2, 4, 6, 8, 10, 12, or 14 days old (i.e. waxing, not waning). From the time of the Full Moon to the time of the New Moon you should not perform Goetic evocation. It's never specified why, in the original text, but I assume it's because traditionally the time of the waxing Moon is a more positive time for doing magick.

The time of day at which you will do your evocation depends on which rank your demon holds:

- King: 09.00-Noon & 15.00-Sunset

- Prince or Prelate: any time

- Duke: Sunrise-Noon in clear weather

- Marquis: 15.00-21.00 & 21.00-Sunrise

- Earl: any time, as long as the place has no people or noise (e.g. deep in the woods)

- President: any time except Twilight & Night (unless you are also invoking his King)

- Knight: Dawn-Sunrise & 16.00-Sunset

Procedure

If you take a look at a traditional book on Goetia you'll see a huge amount of text that basically tends to go on and on. But let's look beyond all the flowery language and look at the basic structure of Goetia. It's a very formal system, and it's important that when you come to do it that you follow the structure very clearly and precisely. Briefly it works as follows:

1. Set up the temple
2. Ritual bath & purification
3. Preliminary Invocation (prayers according to your work)
4. Conjuration(s)
5. Constraint (if necessary)
6. Deliver command to Spirit
7. License to depart
8. Prayer of thanks

Let's start with point 1, setting up the temple. Every Goetic temple needs the following equipment:

1. Magick circle
2. Triangle of Art
3. Crystal ball, magick mirror, or bowl of water
4. Seal of the Spirit (& container for later)
5. Robe
6. Hexagram
7. Pentagram
8. Wand
9. Ring
10. Incense & burner
11. Vessel of Brass

The magick circle is traditionally three metres in diameter. You can make one by painting a circle on the floor or on a piece of carpet that you can roll up later; or just use a long cord spread around you to make a circle you can stand within. Inside the perimeter of the circle you need to inscribe "the Holy Names of God". These can be any gods or goddesses that you feel an affinity with - if you've been doing some of the other rituals in this book you may already have built up a relationship with some of the deities you've invoked. If so, use them, they will be your magical protectors during your evocations. You'll be staying inside this circle all the way through the evocation.

Outside the circle lies the Triangle of Art. This is the place where the Spirit will appear when evoked. It's an equilateral triangle, with each side normally about a meter in length. It should have more divine names around the outside (though I usually don't bother with this), and the names of your protector angel in the inner corners. The traditional Triangle of Art has the name MI-CHA-EL written around the inside. You may wish to substitute the name of your own Holy Guardian Angel (if known) or perhaps AIWASS, the Angel that delivered the Book of the Law, would be fitting for a Thelemic magician. Another good option would be to use the name MEI-TH-RAS instead, since the archangel Michael was basically a Judeo-Christian re-interpretation of Mithras anyway.

Within the Triangle draw another smaller circle, preferably in green, this is your "target zone" for evocation. Needless to say, you do not stand in this Triangle, it's where the Spirit goes, not you. Within this circle you should place a magick mirror (traditionally a concave black mirror, but any small mirror should do), a bowl of water, or perhaps a crystal ball. This serves to give the demon something to manifest through during the evocation.

Each of the Spirits of the Goetia has its own Seal. You need to draw this out on "virgin parchment" - which simply means paper that hasn't been used before, nothing to do with real virgins, I assure you! You'll be using this as a

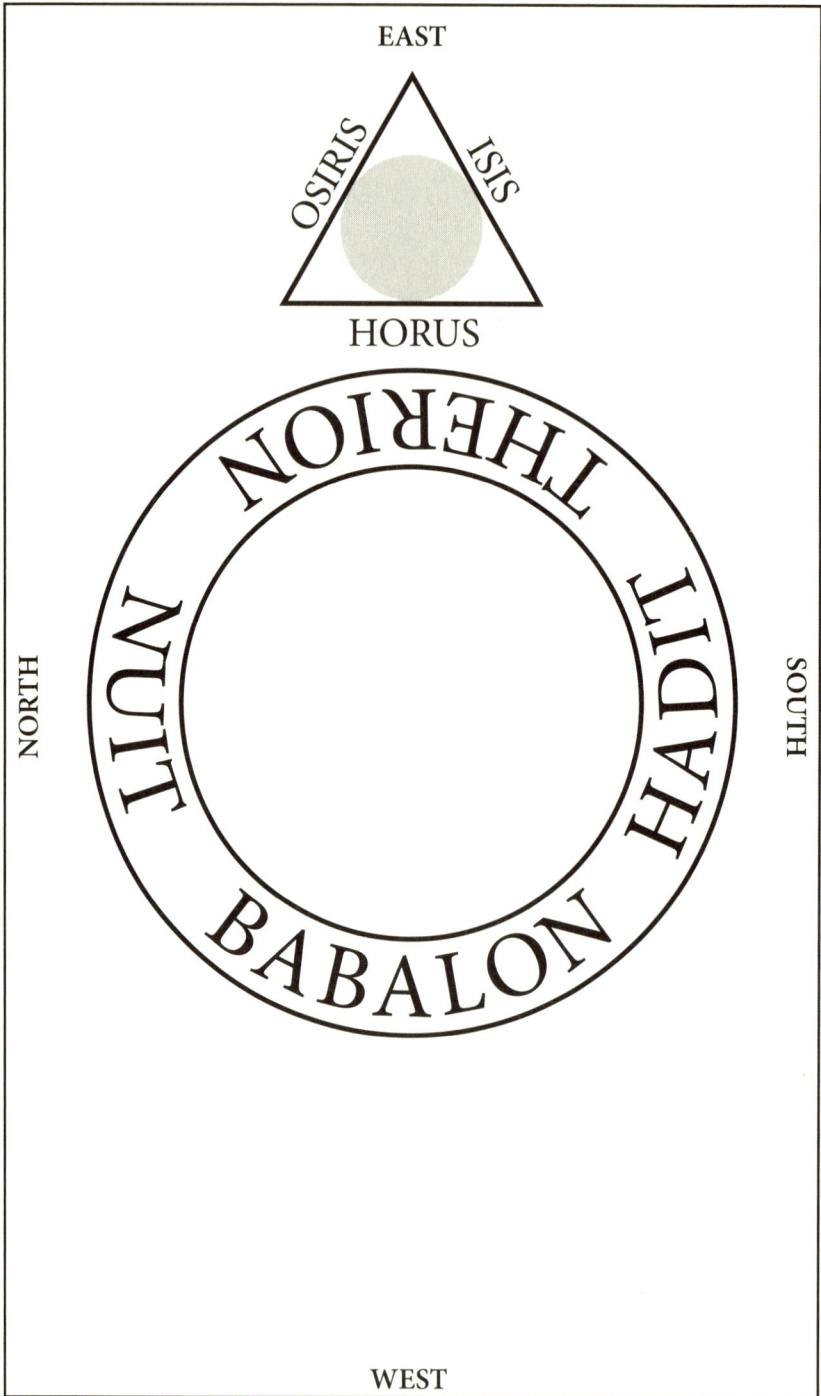

EAST

OSIRIS

ISIS

HORUS

THERION

NUIT

HADIT

BABALON

NORTH

SOUTH

WEST

visualisation tool during the ritual itself, and afterwards if you need to call the Spirit again. So you'll need to prepare something to keep the Seal in after the rite, you don't want it getting damaged accidentally. In a very real sense, it's the representation of the Spirit in your world, so look after it.

The traditional magical robe is just a plain white over-the-head garment. Linen was originally specified in most medieval books, but you have to remember that they didn't have a lot of other light material to work with in Europe back then; today we have a lot more choice in textiles. You can make one yourself, or just go to your local Arab dress emporium and buy a very nice one for very little money. If you are a member of a magical order, for example if you're an initiate of O.T.O. you could wear the robe of your Degree. The advantage of this it that it helps to show your authority as a magician, and demons respect that they are dealing with a "professional".

The Hexagram, composed of two interlocking triangles, is the representation of the union of man and divine. Again, it serves to show the authority of the magician, and your connection with the gods. It may be embroidered on to the robe, or simply drawn on paper and pinned to it. The original text says it should be fastened to the "skirt" of the robe, which can be anywhere from the chest down really. Initiates of the III Degree of O.T.O. will not require this.

The Pentagram is to be engraved on a small disk traditionally made of silver or gold. However you could also use the metal attributed to the Spirit you will be evoking, which might be iron, copper, lead etc. On one side of the disk engrave a simple pentagram shape, on the other side engrave the sigil of the Spirit again. If you can't engrave, you could paint it - however I do recommend the purchase of a cheap electric engraving tool, you'll be amazed at how much fun you can have with one of these things! Attach a ribbon to the disk when you're done, you'll be wearing it during the evocation.

The Wand is the symbol of your Will. Traditionally it should be the length of your forearm, measured from the tips of your fingers to the elbow. You can easily make one of these yourself, or just go buy a length of dowel rod from your local hardware store. Rub some oil into it to keep it in good condition.

The Ring was traditionally made of iron, possibly with brass engraving. It had a pentagram engraved upon it, possibly with the name of God written around it or inside it. Again you could use whatever god name is most appropriate to your personal system. If in doubt, a powerful commanding god would be most advisable, for example Ra-Hoor-Khuit. The ring is used to control recalcitrant demons - note that during the ritual you are told to stretch out your hand when commanding the spirit, so presumably the ring would be on your hand while doing so.

For any kind of evocation you'll need incense - and I don't mean a couple of joss sticks. You'll probably need something very strong and heavy for the full medieval feel. Abramelin incense is ideal, or Frankincense at a pinch. Order a goodly amount from your local occult/new age supply store, and some charcoal disks to go with it. The quality of Abramelin incense sold by many occult supply stores does vary considerably however, so you may have to shop around. Get an incense burner that's a decent size and that's well insulated so that it isn't going to burn a hole in your table when you set it down. For the rite some people like to put the incense and burner in the Triangle, but if the smoke runs out during the ritual you can't get back at it to add some more incense; so you might prefer to keep your burner in the circle with you instead (just don't leave it on the floor where you can step on it!).

The "Vessel of Brass" is one of the more unusual items - it's used to threaten and, if need be, punish a recalcitrant Spirit. In design it's supposed to be a small brass bottle with a lead cap that can be melted to seal it shut. The idea is that if the Spirit does not do what it's supposed to do, you'll put its Seal inside the bottle, melt the lead cap to close it permanently, and then, I guess, never touch it again; something like the "Genie in the Bottle" story of The Book of the One Thousand and One Nights fame. Frankly I've always found that simply threatening to burn the Seal and never contact the Spirit again is usually more than enough to get things moving, but your mileage may vary.

The Operation

Preparation

[So, time for the Operation itself. Get all the things you require together well in advance of the time appointed for the rite. Then go take a nice hot bath or shower. That might not seem so important, but back in the 17th century taking a bath was a pretty big deal. So make your own ritual bath a big deal too. Take your time, and as you clean yourself, prepare yourself mentally for the Work ahead. The Goetia gives phrases to recite while bathing and putting on your robes - I like to recite the first phrase as a mantra all the way through the cleansing process.]

While bathing:

Thou shalt sprinkle me with hyssop, O Lord! and I shall be clean: Thou shalt wash me, and I shall be whiter than snow.

[You can use this in Latin if you prefer, it's more sonorous: Asperges me, Domine, hyssopo, et mundabor: Lavabis me, et super nivem dealbabor. This phrase comes from Psalm 51:7 of the Bible, although the use of hyssop dates all the way back to

the priests in first Temple of Solomon (see Leviticus Chapter 14). Hyssop is a herb still used widely, most notably in Roman Catholic sprinkling sticks; but also as an ingredient in Green Chartreuse and Absinthe.]

While putting on vestments:

In the mystery of these vestures of the Holy Ones, I gird up my power in the girdles of righteousness and truth in the power of the Most High: Ancor: Amacor: Amides: Theodonias: Anitor: let be mighty my power: let it endure for ever: in the power of Adonai, to whom the praise and the glory shall be; whose end cannot be.

[These names "of the Most High" originally appear in the Heptameron of Peter de Abano, published in Venice in 1496. I have no idea what they mean, but they seem to work. If you prefer something more Thelemic, I suppose you could substitute names of more Thelemic deities instead, such as Nuit, Hadit, Ra-Hoor-Khuit, Therion, Babalon; or whatever you think of as the Most High powers in your work.

Once you are vested, check that the temple is fully prepared, and enter your circle.]

Optional: Pentagram Ritual

[Although the original medieval grimoires did not specify the use of a so-called "Banishing Ritual" before and after the Working, the Golden Dawn added it, and Crowley continues the practice in his edition of The Goetia. It's really up to you to decide if you want to or not. It certainly can't do any harm to do so, and might help to prepare you and the ritual space you are in. Use the Rite of the Infinite Stars, Mark of the Beast Ritual, or other Pentagram Ritual that suits. If used, repeat the Pentagram Ritual at the very end of the whole working, after the Spirit has been given license to depart.]

[The next section does not form part of the original medieval texts, but was added by Crowley in his edition. However it works extremely well to get the energy of the Magician flowing. It was derived from 'Fragment of a Graeco-Egyptian Work upon Magic from a Papyrus in the British Museum' translated by Charles Wycliffe Goodwin, published by Oxford Press in 1852; but heavily amended by Crowely from the original. Twenty years later Crowley altered it again and published it as Liber Samekh - personally I prefer this version.]

Preliminary Invocation

Thee I invoke, the Bornless one.
Thee, that didst create the Earth and the Heavens:
Thee, that didst create the Night and the day.

Thee, that didst create the darkness and the Light.
Thou art Osorronophris: Whom no man hath seen at any time.
Thou art Jäbas:
Thou art Iäpos:
Thou has distinguished between the just and the Unjust.
Thou didst make the Female and the Male.
Thou didst produce the Seed and the Fruit.
Thou didst form Men to love one another, and to hate one another.

I am [your name] Thy Prophet, unto Whom Thou didst commit Thy Mysteries, the Ceremonies of Thelema.
Thou didst produce the moist and the dry, and that which nourisheth all created Life.
Hear Thou Me, for I am the Angel of Paphrö Osorronophris: this is Thy True Name, handed down to the Prophets of Thelema.

Hear Me: --
Ar: Thiao: Rheibet: Atheleberseth:
A: Blata: Abeu: Ebeu: Phi:
Thitasoe: Ib: Thiao.

Hear Me, and make all Spirits subject unto Me: so that every Spirit of the Firmament and of the Ether: upon the Earth and under the Earth: on Dry Land and in the Water: of Whirling Air, and of rushing Fire: and every Spell and Scourge of God may be obedient unto Me.

I invoke Thee, the Terrible and Invisible God: Who dwellest in the Void Place of the Spirit: -- Arogogorobrao: Sothou:
Modorio: Phalarthao: Döö: Apé, The Bornless One:

Hear Me, and make all Spirits subject unto Me: so that every Spirit of the Firmament and of the Ether: upon the Earth and under the Earth: on Dry Land and in the Water: of Whirling Air, and of rushing Fire: and every Spell and Scourge of God may be obedient unto Me.

Hear me: --
Roubriao: Mariobam: Balbnabaoth: Assalonai: Aphniao: I: Thoteth: Abrasar: Aëoöü: Ischure, Mighty and Bornless One!

Hear Me, and make all Spirits subject unto Me: so that every Spirit of the Firmament and of the Ether: upon the Earth and under the Earth: on Dry

Land and in the Water: of Whirling Air, and of rushing Fire: and every
Spell and Scourge of God may be obedient unto Me.

I invoke Thee: --
Ma: Barraio: Ioel: Kotha:
Athorebalo: Abraoth:

Hear Me, and make all Spirits subject unto Me: so that every Spirit of the
Firmament and of the Ether: upon the Earth and under the Earth: on Dry
Land and in the Water: of Whirling Air, and of rushing Fire: and every
Spell and Scourge of God may be obedient unto Me.

Hear Me!
Aoth: Abaoth: Basum: Isak:
Sabaoth: Iao: This is the Lord of the Gods:
This is the Lord of the Universe:
This is He Whom the Winds fear.
This is He, Who having made Voice by His Commandment, is Lord of All
Things; King, Ruler and Helper.

Hear Me, and make all Spirits subject unto Me: so that every Spirit of the
Firmament and of the Ether: upon the Earth and under the Earth: on Dry
Land and in the Water: of Whirling Air, and of rushing Fire: and every
Spell and Scourge of God may be obedient unto Me.

Hear Me: --
Ieou: Pur: Jou: Pur: Iaot: Iaeo: Ioou: Abrasar: Sabriam: Do: Uu: Adonaie:
Ede: Edu: Angelos ton Theon: Anlala Lai: Gaia: Ape: Diathana Thorun.

I Am He! the Bornless Spirit! having sight in the Feet: Strong, and the
Immortal Fire!
I Am He! The Truth!
I Am He! Who hate that evil should be wrought in the World!

I am He, that lighteneth and thundereth.
I am He, from whom is the Shower of the Life of Earth:
I am He, whose mouth ever flameth:
I am He, the Begetter and Manifester unto the Light:
I am He, the Grace of the World:
"The Heart Girt with a Serpent" is My Name!

Come Thou forth, and follow Me: and make all Spirits subject unto Me so that every Spirit of the Firmament, and of the Ether: upon the Earth and under the Earth: on dry land, or in the Water: of whirling Air or of rushing Fire: and every Spell and Scourge of God, may be obedient unto Me!
Iao: Sabao:
Such are the Words!

The Conjurations

[The original text of the Goetia has two Conjurations, each derived from the Old Testament from the Bible. Evidence suggests that Crowley himself did not use these, instead substituting the First and Second Enochian Keys. I've followed this practice, as the Bible means nothing to most Thelemites today.

At this point take the Seal of the Spirit to be evoked in your hand, gaze at it and commit it to your memory, then recite the following two Enochian Keys. The English translation is provided solely for reference purposes, you should just recite the Enochian parts.]

All letters are pronounced as in English with the following exceptions:

  · *A: ah as in "fAther"*

  · *C: k as in "Cook"*

  · *E: eh as in "grEy"*

  · *I: ee as in "mEEt"*

  · *O: long o as in "jOke"*

  · *Q: k as in "Qabalah",*

  · *U: long u as in "fOOl"]*

The First Key

Ol sonuf vaoresaji, gohu IAD Balata, elanusaha caelazod: sobrazod-ol Roray i ta nazodapesad, Giraa ta maelpereji, das hoel-qo qaa notahoa zodimezod, od comemahe ta nobeloha zodien; soba tahil ginonupe pereje aladi, das vaurebes obolehe giresam. Causarem ohorela caba Pire: das zodonurenusagi cab: erem Iadanahe. Pilahe farezodem zodenurezoda adana gono Iadapiel das home-tohe: soba ipame lu ipamis: das sobolo vepe zodomeda poamal, od bogira aai ta piape Piamoel od Vaoan! Zodacare, eca, od zodameranu! odo cicale Qaa; zodoreje, lape zodiredo Noco Mada, Hoathahe I A I D A!

[Translation: I reign over you, sayeth the God of Justice, in power exalted above the firmaments of wrath: in whose hands the Sun is as a sword and the Moon

as a through thrusting fire: which measureth your garments in the midst of my vestures, and trussed you together as the palms of my hands: whose seats I garnished with the fire of gathering, and beautified your garments with admiration. To whom I made a law to govern the holy ones and delivered you a rod with the ark of knowledge. Moreover you lifted up your voices and swear obedience and faith to him that liveth and triumph whose beginning is not, nor end can not be, which shineth as a flame in the midst of your palace, and reigneth amongst you as the balance of righteousness and truth. Move, therefore, and show yourselves: open the Mysteries of your Creation: Be friendly unto me: for I am the servant of the same your God, the true worshiper of the Highest.]

The Second Key

Adagita vau-pa-ahe zodonugonu fa-a-ipe salada! Vi-i-vau el! Sobame ial-pereji i-zoda-zodazod pi-adapehe casarema aberameji ta ta-labo paracaleda qo-ta lores-el-qo turebesa ooge balatohe! Gjui cahisa lusada oreri od micalapape cahisa bia ozodonugonu! lape noanu tarofe coresa tage o-quo maninu IA-I-DON. Torezodu! gohe-el, zodacare eca ca-no-quoda! zodameranu micalazodo od ozodazodame vaurelar; lape zodir IOIAD!

[Translation: Can the wings of the winds understand your voices of wonder, O you the second of the first, whom the burning flames have framed within the depth of my Jaws; whom I have prepared as Cups for a Wedding, or as the flowers in their beauty for the Chamber of righteousness. Stronger are your feet than the barren stone, and mightier are your voices than the manifold winds. For you are become a building such as is not, but in the mind of the All-powerful. Arise, sayeth the First! Move therefore unto his Servants! Shew yourselves in power! And make me a strong Seething: for I am of him that liveth for ever.

You might want to recite the name of the Spirit as a mantra after performing these Conjurations.]

(If he come not yet at the rehearsal of these two first conjurations (but without doubt he will), say on as followeth; it being a constraint:)

[Can you see the contradiction in terms here? If there's no doubt that the Spirit will come, then there's no need for a constraint... If you are not entirely satisfied with the results you get after reciting the two Enochian Keys, then recite the following:]

The constraint

I Do conjure thee, O thou Spirit N., by all the most glorious and efficacious names of the **Most Great and Incomprehensible Lord God of Hosts**, that thou comest quickly and without delay from all parts and places of the earth and world wherever thou mayest be, to make rational answers unto my demands, and that visibly and affably, speaking with a voice intelligible unto mine understanding as aforesaid. I conjure and constrain thee, O thou Spirit N., by all the names aforesaid; and in addition by these seven great names wherewith Solomon the Wise bound thee and thy companions in a Vessel of Brass, **Adonai, Preyai or Prerai, Tetragrammaton, Anaphaxeton or Anepheneton, Inessenfatoal or Inessenfatall, Pathtumon or Pathatumon, and Itemon**; that thou appearest, here before this Circle to fulfil my will in all things that seem good unto me. And if thou be still so disobedient, and refusest still to come, I will in the power and by the power of the name of the **Supreme and everlasting Lord God**, who created both thee and me and all the world in six days, and what is contained therein, **Eie, Saraye**, and by the power of this name **Primeumaton** which commandeth the whole host of Heaven, curse thee, and deprive thee of thine office, joy, and place, and bind thee in the depths of the Bottomless Pit or Abyss, there to remain unto the Day of the Last Judgment. And I will bind thee in the Eternal Fire, and into the Lake of Flame and of Brimstone, unless thou comest quickly and appearest here before this Circle to do my will. Therefore, come thou! In and by the holy names **Adonai, Zabaoth, Adonai, Amioran**. Come thou! for it is **Adonai** who commandest thee.

[The original text says you should repeat these conjurations and constraints if the Spirit still does not appear, along with more and more fearful curses. Renowed Goetic scholar David Rankine compares this to the ringing of a telephone - sometimes the person you are calling will be right by the phone, but more often you'll need to ring a few times before they pick up. So don't worry if you have to repeat it a few times. As a last resort you can threaten the Spirit that you will burn his seal in the fire, and never again attempt to conjure him - that you will cut him out of your universe entirely. There's nothing Spirits hate more than to be ignored, and this is one of the most powerful threats imaginable to them. If he still doesn't come after that - then burn the Seal of the Spirit and never again work with him. You still have 71 others to go, and they will be a lot happier to do your bidding if they know you are willing and able to carry out your threats.]

The welcome unto the spirit

Welcome Spirit N. (name of demon), O most noble king!

[Substitute Prince, Duke, etc. depending on the rank of the Spirit.]

I say thou art welcome unto me, because I have called thee through Him who has created Heaven, and Earth, and Hell, and all that is in them contained, and because also thou hast obeyed. By that same power by which I have called thee forth, I bind thee, that thou remain affably and visibly here before this Circle and in this triangle so constant and so long as I shall have occasion for thy presence; and not to depart without my license until thou hast duly and faithfully performed my will without any falsity.

The charge to the spirit

(Then standing in the midst of the Circle, thou shall stretch forth thine hand in a gesture of command and say:)

By the pentacle of Solomon have I called Thee! Give unto me a true answer.

(Then let the exorcist state his desires and requests. And when the evocation is finished thou shalt license the Spirit to depart thus:)

The license to depart

O thou Spirit N. (name of demon), because thou hast diligently answered unto my demands, and hast been very ready and willing to come at my call, I do here license thee to depart unto thy proper place; without causing harm or danger unto man or beast. Depart, then, I say, and be thou very ready to come at my call, being duly exorcised and conjured by the sacred rites of magic. I charge thee to withdraw peaceably and quietly, and the peace of GOD be ever continued between thee and me. AMEN!

(After thou hast given the Spirit license to depart, thou art not to go out of the circle until he or they be gone, and until thou shalt have made prayers and rendered thanks unto God for the great blessings He hath bestowed upon thee in granting thy desires, and delivering thee from all the malice of the enemy the devil.)

[A prayer of thanks to the gods and goddesses you have used to protect you during the ritual is very appropriate here, and I do recommend it. It doesn't have to be anything complex, just a simple thank you. If you have begun the Operation with a Pentagram Ritual you should also now repeat it here to finish off.]

(Also note! Thou mayest command these spirits into the Vessel of Brass in the same manner as thou dost into the triangle, by saying: "**that thou dost forthwith appear before this Circle, in this Vessel of Brass, in a fair and comely shape,**" *etc., as hath been shown in the foregoing conjurations.)*

[That the Spirit may be commanded into a Vessel of Brass is expanded further in the next chapter on The Brazen Head.]

Chapter Nine
The Brazen Head

One of the traditional powers of magicians throughout the ages has been the animation of inanimate objects and the creation of artificial life. The most notorious example of this in popular culture must be Mickey Mouse's problems as a Sorcerer's Apprentice in the Walt Disney cartoon *Fantasia*. Needless to say, don't try this at home kids. For one thing, making brooms sweep the floor by themselves might still be a touch too difficult for your powers.

A simpler form of this type of animation was the creation of a talking head in order to advise magicians and be a focus of their power. One of the charges levelled against the Knights Templar was that they had created an idol called Baphomet that they worshipped in the form of a head. In *The Temple and the Lodge* Baigent & Leigh state:

> *...when the officers of the French king burst into the Paris Temple on 13 October 1307, there was found a silver reliquary in the shape of a head, containing the skull of a woman. It bore a label denoting it as 'Caput LVIIIm' – 'Head 58m'. This might at first seem a mere grisly coincidence. But in the list of charges drawn up by the Inquisition against the Templars on 12 August 1308, there appears the following:*

> - *Item, that in each province they had idols, namely heads...*
> - *Item, that they adored these heads...*
> - *Item, that they said the head could save them.*
> - *Item, that [it could] make riches...*
> - *Item, that it made the trees flower.*
> - *Item, that [it made] the land germinate...*

In the *Chinon Parchment*, the authentic record of the Templar trials recently rediscovered in the Vatican Secret Archives, it appears that the Templar Knight Hugo de Pérraud claimed to have seen the head of an idol in the possession of Brother Peter Alemandin, Preceptor of Montpellier, while on a visit there.

The legendary head of John the Baptist, severed at the whim of Salome, was often rumoured to have been later animated (whether by its own power or by another) and used as an oracle - Grant Morrison's graphic novel *The Invisibles* contains an hilarious modern take on this story. Jewish mysticism has long had its tradition of the Golem, a creature of dust animated to serve its master, an obvious reference to the creation of Adam in the biblical book of Genesis. At the turn of the first millennium (in the Christian calendar) the occultist Pope Sylvester II was reputed to have possession of a brazen head which would give him oracular advice.

Aleister Crowley was clearly influenced by many of these myths in his writing of The Brazen Head. In this ritual an image is graven to provide a focus for the group and to be used as an oracle. The creation of such a focus object, or egregore, can be an extremely useful way for a new group to direct their energies, or for an already existing group to re-direct themselves. Also the head can be used as an oracle and provide guidance in situations where the members of the group may be unsure of their way forward.

Crowley's rite of The Brazen Head isn't so much a ritual itself as the structure for a rite, but that's a good thing in this case. In many ways the magical energy is in the creation and animation of the head itself, and once that's done, all that is needed is to create the correct ritual environment for it to speak to the group.

Crowley uses as an animating spirit in his ritual the Goetic demon Belial. You've already come across traditional Goetia in the preceding chapter, but this ritual is based on a peculiar passage in the text, as follows:

> *These be the 72 Mighty Kings and Princes which King Solomon Commanded into a Vessel of Brass, together with their Legions. Of whom BELIAL, BILETH, ASMODAY, and GAAP, were Chief. And it is to be noted that Solomon did this because of their pride, for he never declared other reason why he thus bound them. And when he had thus bound them up and sealed the Vessel, he by Divine Power did chase them all into a deep Lake or Hole in Babylon. And they of Babylon, wondering to see such a thing, they did then go wholly into the Lake, to break the Vessel open, expecting to find great store of Treasure therein. But when they had broken it open, out flew the Chief Spirits immediately, with their Legions following them; and they were all restored to their former places except BELIAL, who entered into a certain Image, and thence gave answers unto those who did offer Sacrifices unto him, and did worship the Image as their God, etc.*

You'll also remember that the Goetia specifically states near the end that Spirits can not only be evoked into the Triangle of Art, but also into a Vessel of Brass. That Vessel is usually portrayed as a type of bottle, but there's no reason why it has to be - a Vessel to contain Spirits can be of almost any size or shape. We can see from the passage above that the Vessel Belial entered into was an Image, or statue. This ritual of The Brazen Head (brazen meaning *made of brass*) is designed to mimic that event, and have a Spirit enter permanently into an Image created by you and your magical group, there to act as an oracle and helper.

Clearly Belial is appropriate to a rite of this nature, having done this sort of thing before. Feel free to use him as well - note that even if someone else may have him trapped in a Vessel before, you can still do the same thing. That may seem a little illogical - if he's already "trapped" somewhere else, how can he come to serve you too? In reality when we entrap a spirit in this way it's not like imprisoning a material creature, it's rather more like constraining the relationship between us, the Spirit, and the universe we inhabit.

There's no reason why you can't use any other spirit, Goetic or otherwise - the important thing is to find one that is suitable for your particular group. You've already got a working version of the Goetia in this book, so have a look through the description of the spirits in the appendix. You could also think about planetary spirits, or nature spirits associated with a particular geographical region where you reside. If your group is situated near an area with some ancient magical history then using that *genus loci* (spirit of the place) is often an excellent choice.

A group I worked with had as its spiritual guardian the Goetic demon Halphas and had embodied him within the broken blade of a dagger contributed by one of the members (who had previously been attacked with it in a bar brawl and broken it off while it was in his assailant's hand, but that's another story). The reason that our group picked Halphas was because we were trying to build up a new local body in a new location and Halphas has as his speciality the building up of towers and warriors, so it seemed fitting.

Before your group starts this process of choosing an animating spirit, a useful prerequisite is a discussion of what your group's goals and ideals are, what you all want to achieve, and why. I think it's important that the entire group take part in this, even if the leader/founder has a very clear idea beforehand what their direction should be. And it's vital that such a discussion stick to clear simple principles and doesn't get distracted by trivial details.

It's easy for such a discussion to become an argument or lead to resentment if there are minor disagreements – don't let this happen! Remember that you're all there for a purpose that supersedes tiny trivial disagreements, and to keep that over-riding purpose in mind. If your group is a part of a bigger organization then it can be very helpful to consult the founding documents, constitution etc. of your Order, since your purpose needs to be in complete harmony with those documents before you even think of anything else. Take your time over this process, it's really worth making sure that the entire group is moving in the same direction before and during the creation of your head.

Crowley's rite uses a bronze head (hence the title), cast from a wax mould in traditional style. If a member of the group is capable of doing this, or willing to expend the effort to learn, you are likely to end up with an extremely pleasing and impressive bust. However many groups aren't going to be capable of such a feat, but alternatives are possible, such as using papier mache or even modelling clay - with the right treatment they can be surprisingly imposing, although may need careful handling. You could also use a ready-made bust or statuette - I've seen people use a standard small statue of Baphomet bought in a store as a fairly effective egregore in the past.

I would recommend the creation of a head though if possible, since the process of creation itself will tend to make a stronger connection with the group, symbolizing the creation of the group as an entity itself.

If one person in the group will sculpt it, then it would be perhaps useful for each member to contribute something that can be contained within it during the process of creation. Each member could contribute a small piece of paper with their (magical) name written on it, or with one word or sentence that sums up their aspirations for the group, which could then be encased in the head, or ceremonially burnt and the ashes mixed in with the sculpting material. Another option would be for each member to contribute spit, blood, hair, or other part of their vitality to help animate the head. Or to contribute a piece of earth from outside their home etc. - there are many possibilities. Note that these are all only suggestions, you could just use a ready-made object with strong symbolic value to the group and proceed from there. One group I know used a small statue that mysteriously appeared in the street outside their temple after a celebration, and seemed connected with their workings.

Once the head has been created, polished, painted, or otherwise made ready, it needs to be consecrated to its purpose. This purpose would normally be something like being an oracle or servitor for the group. This should be done using some form of evocation such as the mechanism shown in the previous chapter on Goetia: put the head into the Triangle of Art and evoke the spirit into it, then command the spirit to re-appear within the head in the future when called. You could also easily adapt any other evocatory rite, such as that of Bartzabel which we'll come to in a later section of this book.

Once the head is consecrated its job is not over - in fact it is just beginning. The group may want to make a regular weekly or monthly ritual to reconsecrate the head, or to use it as an oracle, or as a repository of power that the members of the group can draw upon - the possibilities are endless. I'd suggest using Crowley's rite as a foundation of all subsequent ritual meetings to do with the egregore, and add extra features as appropriate to the subject at hand. The group could simply sit in silent communion with the head for 20 minutes, or music could be played. The sounds of traditional religious instruments such as bullroarers, singing bowls, and sistrums can provide a good carrier for messages from the head's indwelling consciousness.

Crowley specifies that the head should have two membranes, corresponding to the ear and the mouth, one for "hearing" the requests of the group, and one for replying. This seems to imply that Crowley's original Head was designed to be fitted with a two-way radio, so that "the High Pontifex" could be outside the temple and hear and reply to what was going on within the temple, as the voice of the Head. This idea of giving a high priest some kind of access to speak as the god or demon was supposedly a standard device of ancient temples. It can be very effective within the highly charged atmosphere of a magical ritual, even if the Postulants know consciously what's going on. If you play role-playing games, think of the way that a Game Master takes on the voices of major Non-Player Characters in order to advance the plot, and you'll be heading in the right direction.

Another possibility is to have the head equipped with some kind of automatic sound making apparatus, that can "speak" with the voice of the spirit inside. Now, no-one is expecting that the head will actually form English sentences in the air around it, but it can be amazingly effective if it is capable of creating sounds of some sort, no matter how odd those sounds might be. I have heard of the creation of heads in an outdoor shrine with membranes and tubes that were agitated by the wind and created eerie sounds that under ritual conditions really did appear to be the voices of the gods. A similar effect can be produced indoors by placing it near an air conditioner or fan. Groups with more geeky members might try to experiment with embedded electronic tone generators that can produce low level pink noise or other pseudo-random sounds (or even lights). If need be you can easily create random white noise by simply playing a radio or television set on a channel where there is no signal broadcast. If you do this, keep it at a low volume level, since high levels of white noise can be extremely unpleasant (and even dangerous) over time. If your noise generator has tone controls, turn down the high frequency tones, and boost the bass a little to make the noise more "pink". Some people find that noise such as this creates a very powerful effect; whereas others find it extremely irritating and confusing.

The third possibility is the simplest one: that the Head produces no physical sound at all, and thus the "voice" of the spirit is simply a direct telepathic communication with the Priestess and/or the Postulants. This is certainly the easiest system to start with and requires no special technical preparation; definitely the way I'd recommend for most groups.

The ritual specifies "a Virgin Priestess dedicated to the Service of the DAIMON". This is reminiscent of a similar line introducing the Priestess in Crowley's *Liber XV* – The Gnostic Mass. In that ritual it says that the Priestess "should be actually Virgo Intacta or specially dedicated to the service of the Great Order", which these days is usually taken to mean that she has been initiated to the Degree of a Dame Knight of the East & West within O.T.O. However in the case of this operation I think any female member of the group who wished to volunteer for the office is acceptable. Perhaps some small ritual and oath of dedication could be performed before the group when she fully accepts the office. Actual physical virginity need not be a fixed requirement.

The Priestess may also act as a Pythoness, or voice of the Spirit. She may interpret what the Spirit tells her and communicate this message to the Postulants. Care must be taken that she does not allow her own prejudices to get in the way, but transmit clearly what the Spirit is saying. To this end, she should spend as much time as possible with the Head, learning to communicate with the Spirit and building a relationship with it over time. She should also not know what questions the Postulants are asking - so I suggest that all questions are written down secretly by the Postulants before the rite begins, and the contents not shared with anyone else in the group.

The other officer is the role of the Warder of the Portal, played by a "young boy". This need not actually be played by a male child, but can be played successfully by an adult man in his role as the personification of innocence. It is highly advisable that children below the Age of Majority (usually 18 years old) are not used in this or any other rite, it can lead to serious legal issues. Do carefully check local laws on this before inviting any child into a magical temple for any reason.

The ritual text implies that the Priestess receives gifts and sacrifices on behalf of the Head. The diagram shows that there's a black Offertory cloth between the place of the Postulant and the altar, but there's nothing to say how exactly it's to be used, except that it is be to used for Offerings. Sacrifices being rather messy things generally, I suppose it's reasonable to assume that the Virgin Priestess has some sort of bowl or dish to receive them on, rather than placing them directly on to cloth. Probably it's best if the Priestess herself should perform any sacrifice needed, not the Postulants.

Offerings acceptable to such a Head would depend on its nature – standard types of offerings might be food or drink, especially corn or wine and fruits of the earth; or perhaps appropriate flowers such as sunflowers for a Solar spirit or roses for a Venusian one. Crowley's diagram gives as examples of offerings gold and jewels, and that may also be reasonable depending on the particular spirit in the Head (though perhaps a little expensive).

Sacrifices are different to offerings, and tend to require life energy from higher in the food chain, particularly of blood, so a cut of meat from a butcher, or a small amount of blood from the members of the group might be appropriate. A raw egg is also an easy and effective sacrifice of this type. Note that some kind of metaphorical "sacrifice" (as in "I'm sacrificing my time and energy here") is not acceptable. It needs to be something material that literally embodies life.

Many people living in the Western World have moral objections to blood sacrifice, but it's been a standard part of magical and religious practice since time immemorial. Personally I have no issue with it, and have attended rituals where animal sacrifice was performed. Ironically I was once lectured on how horrible killing an animal like this was by someone who was eating a hamburger at the time, and who failed entirely to see the irony (I'm a vegetarian).

If you do intend to actually sacrifice an animal (which I do not recommend unless you have a very good idea of what you're doing), please do treat it with respect and make sure no suffering is involved. Also be aware that in many places it may be against the law to slay an animal without an appropriate license. If in doubt, use the ideas above regarding butcher's blood or eggs.

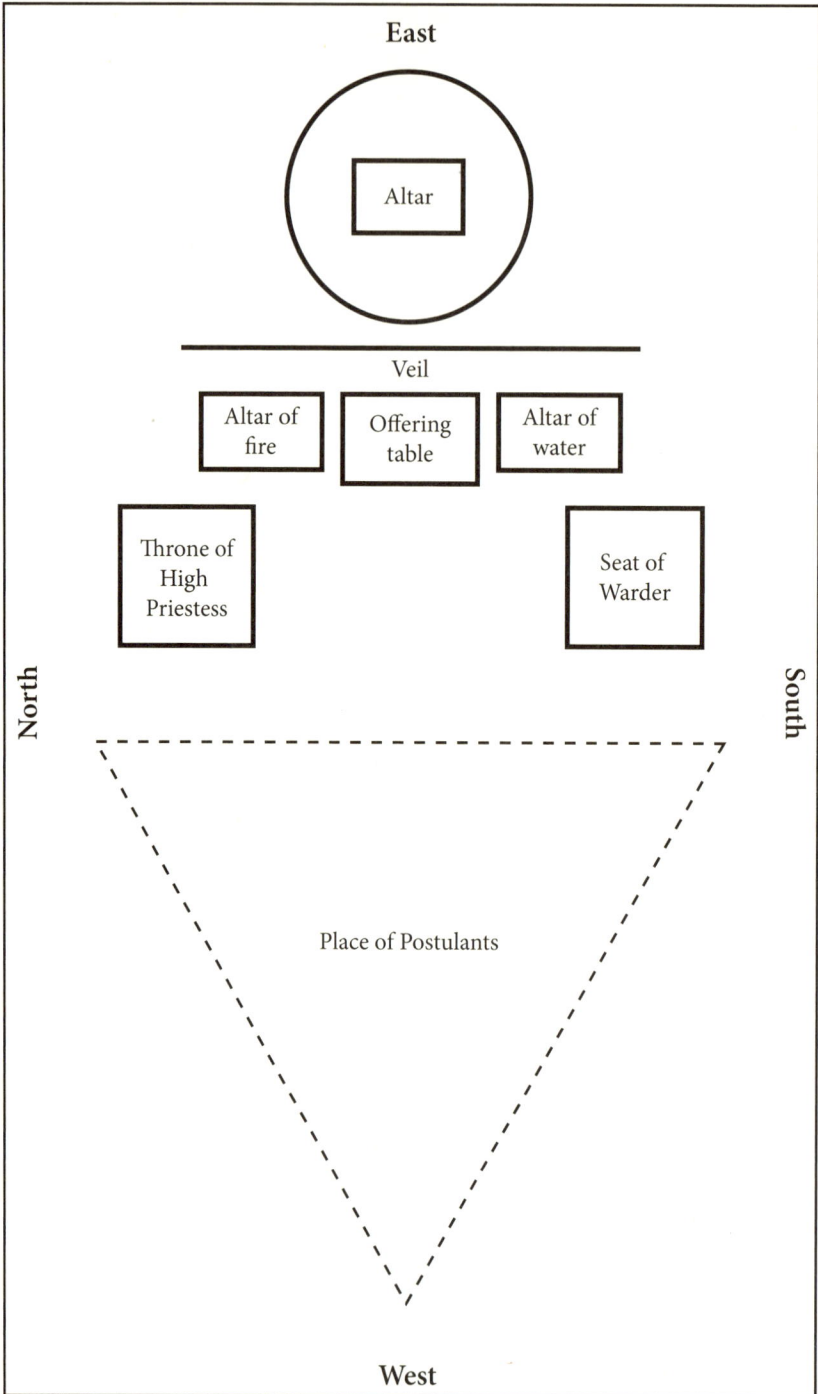

East

Altar

Veil

| Altar of fire | Offering table | Altar of water |

Throne of High Priestess

Seat of Warder

North

South

Place of Postulants

West

The Brazen Head

Participants:	Minimum three: a Priestess, a Warder of the Portal, and Postulants. The rite works well with a medium size group.
Time required:	Requires considerable preparation the first time. After that, 20 minutes to perform.
Setup:	Fairly complex.
Words:	Minimal.
Equipment:	• Artificial head or materials to construct one
	• Altar
	• Veil (optional)
	• Censer & incense, and candle
	• Vessel & water
	• Black cloth and (optionally) bowl or dish to receive offerings
	• Throne (for Priestess)
	• Seat (for Warder of the Portal)
	• White robes for Priestess and Warder

See *Goetia* p. 31 paragraph 2. Belial entered into an Image of Brass and gave answers unto them that did sacrifice unto Him, and did worship the Image as their God.

> [Crowley is referring to the passage I've already reproduced in the introduction above - no need to go looking for it.]

> *Belial is the 68th Spirit: a King mighty and powerful, created next after Lucifer, as they pretended; yet evidently before God, since His Nature is to deny God.*

> *He appeareth in the form of Two Beautiful Angels seated in a Chariot of Fire. He speaketh with a Comely Voice, saying that he "fell" first from among the worthier sort, that were before Michael and other heavenly Angels. Id est: He was the leader of the "Old Nobility" who resisted the usurpation of the upstart Jehovah. His office is to distribute presentations, Senatorships etc. and to cause favour of friends and of foes.*

> *He giveth excellent familiars, and governeth 80 legions of Spirits. He demands offerings, sacrifices and gifts, and he will not speak the truth. Nor even so, unless constrained by the Will of the Exorcist.*

[Note here that Crowley is fully aware that Belial does not speak the truth except when fully constrained. So if you're going to use Belial as your own animating spirit, you'd better bear in mind that many of the messages the group receives from him may be falsehoods! And don't fall into the trap of then assuming that if he says one thing and is a liar, then the opposite of what he says must be true. Goetic demons are tricky spirits and will attempt to deceive you in exactly this kind of way. Just assume that unless you take great precautions whatever someone like Belial says is wrong, and the opposite is also wrong.

Then why would Crowley or indeed anyone else want to use Belial? Well, for one thing because the text of The Goetia specifically points out that in the past he did "enter into an Image of Brass" and give answers to the people who sacrificed to him - so he's got experience in this field at the very least. He is also very powerful – he can really make things happen and make you look good in the process. If that's what your group needs, then use him. If your group does not contain some experienced magicians (and I do mean really experienced magicians, not some 25 year old guy wearing a long black coat who's trying to impress you with his elite black magick skillz he learnt from a Kenneth Grant book) you might be better off with a different spirit. Consult the list of spirits and see if there's one that might be more suited to your purposes.]

His Sigil is this:

His number is 73, that of a Magus. In many other respects, also, He is mine own especial DAIMON. Let me therefore cause men to pay honour to Him, as unto a Great King!

[Crowley here calls Belial his "especial DAIMON" or Guardian. Of course in later life the angel Aiwass would come to supplant Belial in most of this kind of working for Crowley, and that is perhaps one possibility for a Thelemic group to use instead. It might be aiming a little high though!]

The Considerations concerning this Procedure of Art Magick aforesaid

1. Let there be a Temple wrought in Ninefold Disposition, as Luna is in the House of Sol, and He combineth those Natures.

    [Nine is the number of the Moon, and Crowley advises a temple where everything is based around the number nine for Belial. This strikes me as a rather strange setup, since Belial isn't really particularly lunar or solar that I can see, despite Crowley's note.

    If your particular egregore spirit was more Mercurial for example, you might want to set the temple up based on the number eight, or if Venusian, the number seven, and so on. You could do this by having an appropriate number of candles, for example. See Liber 777 or the appendices of Book 4 for more details on the planetary numbers. To be honest, I think this to be a little more complex than really necessary. Personally I'd just use enough candles to light the temple.]

2. There shall be therein a Magical Circle for the Image of Brass wherein He may enter and abide, receiving Offerings, and giving Answers; Sacrifices, and bestowing Favours.

    [Crowley's use of English might be slightly confusing at first glance here: what he is saying is that the Spirit resides within the Head, which in turn sits upon an altar; the altar is placed within a large Magick Circle drawn on the floor of the temple. This Head receives Offerings and gives Answers in return; or receives Sacrifices and bestows Favours. So if you just want information, make an offering. However if you want the Head to actually do something that has a material effect, a sacrifice is called for.]

3. There shall be a Magical Triangle wherein the Worshipper or Postulant may kneel, when as he would adore and consult or beseech Him.

    [The triangle shown in Crowley's original diagram has a somewhat nebulous form, so it clearly isn't designed to have the same purpose as a classical magical triangle in a temple. I think it's more intended to just denote the place where the people may congregate, and as such I didn't think it necessarily would even need to be a triangle at all. Also I'm personally not a big fan of kneeling to spirits, I'd recommend a more confident approach – standing or sitting might be more appropriate.]

4. Within the Circle shall be an Altar of open brass work, but its top a plate of thin Iron.

[That's a tall order for an altar - I think you can happily make do with something simpler if need be. I'm sure the Spirit won't mind. A simple solution is a standard wooden altar with an iron trivet on top. A trivet is small metal tripod with a round plate on top, used for placing pots on, and easily obtainable from any hardware store. Note that the iron & brass combination mentioned is the same as that of the Ring used to command the demons in Goetia.]

5.   Upon this Iron shall be deeply engraven the Sigillum of Belial, with the Names, Forms, Numbers, and other Symbols thereunto appropriate.

[Obviously this sigil would be different if you're using a different spirit. See the illustrations of the demonic sigils in the Goetia for examples of these. If you don't have a metal plate to top the altar with you could paint this on wood or card, but as mentioned earlier, iron is traditionally used for commanding spirits.]

6.   Into the lines of this Graving aforesaid shall be fitted the Base of the Image of this No-God Belial.

[The term No-God that Crowley uses here is quite fascinating. I think he is trying to make us wary of allowing the spirit in the Head to be taken as being some kind of divinity. We must treat it with respect, but not allow it to command us. It's an easy trap to fall into, that of assuming that if something gives us knowledge or success, that it must be superior to us, or able to rule over our own internal divinity. Be vigilant that you don't fall into such a trap. The Spirit serves you, not the other way round.]

7.   This Image shall be of molten Bronze after the fashion of the Head of a Man, such as the Magus TO MEGA THERION shall by His Art devise, design, model, and execute in Red and Yellow Wax.

[This is another easy line to get confused - Crowley isn't saying make a Head that looks like TO MEGA THERION! He's just referring to himself in the third person as the artist sculpting a head of his own design. So the line actually means that you should make a Head that looks like a human person of whatever type you can personally devise.
   Crowley uses his own magical motto of Magus TO MEGA THERION here, since he was originally writing this ritual for his own use.
   The Red and Yellow wax is used to create a mould for casting the bronze, using the Lost-wax method (see any good bronze casting textbook for more details on this process). I have no idea why the wax needs to be red and yellow - maybe that's all that Crowley had available at the time. If you're using a different method of creating a Head, then just ignore these instructions.]

8.   Within the circle, as a Veil upon the Brass Work of the Altar, shall be a certain membrane invisibly virtuous in this kind that the High Pontifex of the DAIMON albeit distant by a league and leagues and

half a league from the Imago, shall hear clearly all sounds within the Circle. And within the Imago itself shall be contrived by the Art Magick of Reginaldus de Gouraldus an Organ of Speech, so that the Magus or Pontifex may be able to reply to the Postulant, or to direct that which shall be done before the Circle.

[See introductory note on the Head's sound transmission abilities. I assume that Reginaldus de Gouraldus is simply a Latinised version of the name of an engineer that Crowley figured could build this thing. It appears that Crowley's idea was for the altar to contain a hidden microphone to transmit sound to a Magus sitting in another room outside the temple, plus an amplifier and speaker to transmit speech from him back into the temple.]

9.   Upon the Circle shall be a Censer and Offertory together with a Vessel of Pure Water.

[The Vessel and Censer are used to respectively purify and consecrate the Postulants. They may be placed on the main altar or on two small tables in front of it. The Offertory is the place where the offerings are to be placed during the rite, either on the main altar before the Head, or on a special table near the Postulants - see below.]

10.   The Temple shall be directed by a Virgin Priestess dedicated to the Service of the DAIMON. She shall in her Office receive gifts and sacrifices, purify and consecrate the Postulant, shewing forth unto him how rightly he may attain to that which he seeketh. To aid Her, a young boy as Warder of the Portal.

[From this point on Crowley doesn't clarify what the actual procedure of the rite should be. One possible method is as follows:]

The Priestess and Warder of the Portal are within the temple.

1.   The Postulants outside the temple write down the questions they wish to ask and things they wish done on pieces of paper, and fold them. They knock when they are ready to be admitted

2.   The Warder of the Portal admits the Postulants to the temple.

3.   As they enter, they give their Offerings to the enthroned Priestess, who places them on the black Offertory cloth.

4.   The Warder performs the opening ceremony, and opens the Veil before the Head.

5.   The Priestess proceeds to purify each Postulant in turn with water from the Vessel, and consecrate each in turn with the smoke of the incense in the Censer. A formula similar to that in the Gnostic Mass could be used, with the Priestess making three crosses over the bodies of the Postulants. The Warder should attend the Priestess ready to pass her the implements as she requires them.

6.   The Priestess takes the folded papers with the questions from the Postulants. The Postulants take their seats.

7.   The Priestess asks the Postulants to concentrate on their questions. She takes the folded pieces of paper and burns them in the flame.

8.   She seats herself on her throne, and listens to the voice of the Spirit for the answers to the questions posed. As the Spirit moves her, she may answer or prophesy to the Postulants, or the Spirit may communicate directly with them.

9.   When all is done, the Postulants offer up their thanks to the Spirit. The Warder sprinkles water on the forehead of the Priestess, to ensure her consciousness is fully returned to her.

10.   The Warder closes the temple and ushers out the Postulants.

[Opening and closing the temple may be done by any standard Pentagram ritual, or simply by using words such as "I declare this Temple (open/closed) in the name of Heru-Ra-Ha, for the work of magical communication with the Spirit (name of spirit) embodied herein."]

11.   And so may all go to the Establishment of the Law of Thelema, and of the Kingdom of Heru-Ra-Ha!

[This was the original end note in Crowley's typescript. It could be used to end the ritual as part of the closing (see previous note).]

Chapter Ten
An Evocation of Bartzabel
The Spirit of Mars

The Formulae of the Magick of Light, let them be puissant in the Evocation of the Spirit Bartzabel

The Evocation of Bartzabel was first performed on the 9th of May 1910 by Aleister Crowley and several other members of the A.A. and is historically an interesting rite in many ways. It shows Crowley very much in a transitional phase as regards to ritual working. Whereas it is based on traditional, long-winded evocation techniques, being similar to what Crowley had learned from *The Goetia* and in the Golden Dawn, the ritual also included innovations that were fairly unique at the time within the Western esoteric tradition. As Crowley later wrote in Chapter 67 of his *Confessions*:

> In the Triangle was Frater Omnia Vincam, to serve as a material basis through which the spirit might manifest. Here was a startling innovation in tradition. I wrote, moreover, a ritual on entirely new principles. I retained the Cabbalistic names and formulae, but wrote most of the invocation in poetry. The idea was to work up the magical enthusiasm through the exhilaration induced by music.

The use of a material basis to evoke a spirit into is hardly new. From time immemorial magicians have been evoking spirits into talismans and fetishes, or using blood or incense to draw spirits down to earth. Crowley went one step further, and decided to use a human being. Instead of evoking a spirit into an inanimate object, or evoking it to visible appearance in a cloud of incense smoke, Crowley decided that the best thing to do was to give the spirit a real body (at least temporarily), and then talk to it and get answers to his questions from the spirit while it was inside that body.

Invoking gods and goddesses into human beings isn't unusual of course - in a sense that's what powers almost every form of magick. But generally it was always considered vaguely dangerous to have anything "lower" than deities inside a human form. However when you actually look at what's going on here, there are two important points to note.

As mentioned in previous chapters, one way of looking at ritual is that we invoke gods from the universe outside us into ourselves, whereas we evoke spirits from our unconscious minds out into the universe in material form. As such, they are already inside us, but hidden. So we're not really putting something into our heads that isn't there already in some form. We may be calling up deep-rooted complexes into our consciousness, which can be psychologically dangerous (at least in the short term), but can also be very therapeutic. Of course we need to do this in a carefully controlled way, in a fully controlled environment - which is what a ritual essentially is.

Also of course, many so-called spirits or demons are actually just the gods and goddesses of older religions that have been "transmuted" or denigrated by later religious belief - such as the "demon" Astaroth in the Goetia, which was clearly originally based on Astarte, the fertility goddess of the Phoenicians, herself derived from the Mesopotamian goddess Ishtar. The early Biblical writers turned her into a female demon of lust because her unbridled female sexuality didn't really sit well with their conception of one big angry male god punishing everyone. The Bible tries to hide the fact that Solomon, supposedly the wisest of all men, and a great Biblical hero, actually worshipped Ashtoreth and built sacred groves to her. Fortunately for us, the writers of the Bible did not do a very good job of hiding this information - for example in 2 Kings we read that one of Solomon's successors as King of Israel wasn't too happy about what Solomon had achieved and smashed the shrines he had built:

13. And the high places that were before Jerusalem, which were on the right hand of the mount of corruption, which Solomon the king of Israel had builded for Ashtoreth... did the king defile.

14. And he brake in pieces the images, and cut down the groves, and filled their places with the bones of men.

The "mount of corruption" mentioned is the Mount of Olives near Jerusalem, where Solomon built temples to various pagan gods and goddesses. The most notable of these shrines was probably the Garden of Gethsemane, later made famous as the place where the legendary Jesus of Nazareth supposedly spent his last night before the crucifixion. Why Jesus spent his last night on Earth in a pagan goddess shrine is not explained, but this is the kind of background stuff they don't teach at Christian Sunday Schools, and you can probably figure out why...

One might ask then, how come Astoreth can be both an ancient pagan goddess and a medieval Judeo-Christian demon? Which one is she really?

I guess the answer to that is both, given the particular cultural matrix that most of the readers of this book have been brought up within. We've been brought up in a society where the "background reality" is that unbridled lust is "sinful" and belongs to the Devil (whoever he may be); and even though we may have consciously rejected that ridiculous idea of sin, unconsciously our brains are often still hard-wired into a Judeo-Christian mindset. Most of our basic emotions and reactions are learned responses that are programmed into us in the first few years of our lives, and these programmed responses rarely, if ever, change, regardless of how much we might wish it. Magick is actually one of the (very) few methods we can use to change this basic brain wiring, but even then it's not easy and requires a lot of time and work. So I suppose the difference between invoking the Goddess form of Asteroth, and evoking the "demonic" form is really a matter of how we are approaching the interface between our interior selves and our exterior reality.

That was a fairly long digression from the main plot, but I think it's important to show that what many would consider to be "traditional magical wisdom" can often actually be little more than superstitious belief, passed down without question from generation to generation. It's important that we examine these things closely, through the twin lenses of logic and history, so that we can understand what's really going on beneath the surface.

So for the reasons given above, evocation of a spirit into a person, despite being "untraditional", is not really as dangerous and strange as it might at first appear. However it's certainly still not something that should be attempted lightly, and it requires a great deal of trust in the ability and sincerity of the adepts performing the ritual. For this reason I do not recommend trying this ritual as it is written unless you are absolutely sure that your group can really handle it (and in 30 years of doing magick I can count on my fingers the number of people I've met that I'd trust that much). It is quite easy to adapt this ritual so that instead of a person as a Material Basis you can use a talisman if you want the spirit's power permanently embodied in something; or use a bowl of water or a magick mirror (as in Goetia) if you just want the spirit to appear for a short time while you talk to it, ask it questions, or ask it to perform a task for you.

The other great innovation that Aleister Crowley claimed for this rite was in the use of poetry. It did certainly show a departure from the Golden Dawn way of working that Crowley had been taught – the Golden Dawn was an Order wherein they never used one word when twenty-five would do. Medieval grimoire writers had always enjoyed verbosity, and the Golden Dawn followed the time-honoured principle that if a lot of words is good, then double the words must be twice as good. Here we see Crowley starting to realise that it wasn't the amount of words that was important, but the amount of spiritual intensity raised by the participants. This realisation would come to its full fruition a couple of years later when he was visited by Theodor Reuss, Outer Head of O.T.O. and became a full member of that Order. From that moment on Crowley set about simplifying and clarifying ritual technique, which led to the masterpieces of succinct ritual that are the O.T.O. initiation rituals and the Gnostic Mass.

Crowley writes about this process he was going through later in *Magick* (referring to himself in the third person):

> *Various considerations impelled Him to attempt conjurations in the English language. There already existed one example, the charm of the witches in Macbeth; although this was perhaps not meant seriously, its effect is indubitable.*

> *He has found iambic tetrameters enriched with many rimes both internal and external very useful. "The Wizard Way"* (Equinox I,I) *gives a good idea of the sort of thing. So does the Evocation of Bartzabel in* Equinox I,IX.

In a way it's amazing that Crowley didn't realise this sooner, since he had already been a poet for many years, but he had tended to separate his poetic works and his magical works. I think at least part of the influence here was Leila Waddell, an Australian violinist living in Britain that Crowley had become besotted with around this time. Music was an innate part of her magical technique, and it was slowly becoming clear to Crowley that ritual music, dance, and verse was highly effective. Unfortunately, I don't think that the poetry Crowley composed for this rite was anywhere near his best, but when recited with the correct intent it is definitely powerful.

Another innovation that we can see in hindsight is that this is one of Crowley's earliest attempts to "Thelemicise" traditional magical workings. Although *The Book of the Law* had been written in 1904, it had taken several years for Crowley to really begin to accept its principles himself, particularly its problematic and violent Third Chapter dedicated to Ra-Hoor-Khuit. In this ritual I think we can see Crowley unconsciously attempting to magically close the distance between himself and this current of Force and Fire.

When Aleister Crowley did this working, the purpose was for divination. Once the spirit had appeared, questions were asked of it. Divination by spirit in this way can often be very useful, but it can also often be rather tricky. In this case the latter seems to have applied. The answers that the original adepts got were particularly obscure, and Crowley scholars are still puzzling over them trying to make some sense of what was said. However some of the answers are quite enlightening from a technical ritual perspective. For example at one point it seems that Victor Neuburg, the person acting as Material Basis in this working, doesn't look very happy and Crowley (the Chief Magus) asks:

Speak. Hast thou not suffered torments from Graphiel? Speak plain.

To which the spirit replies:

I don't want to be imprisoned in this form. What dost thou want?

Continuing on, the spirit says a few random things, then finally admits he has lied. After that, he is clearly reluctant to speak, and tries really hard to get out of giving any answers at all. Crowley keeps asking more and more obscure questions about magick and the spirit doesn't seem to want to answer them, or perhaps is unable to, being only a fairly lowly spirit of Mars. The only clear answer that was given was right at the end of the ritual when one of the other participants, Commander Marston of the British Royal Navy (called AFK in the text) asks:

AFK.	*Shall nations of Earth rise up against one another?*
B.	*When?*
AFK.	*Soon.*
B.	*Yes.*
CM.	*When?*
B.	*Within 5 years. Turkey or Germany.*

Given that this rite was performed in 1910, and both Turkey and Germany went to war against Britain in 1914, that's certainly remarkably accurate. I think it's important to remember that Bartzabel is a Martial spirit, and clearly felt a great deal more comfortable answering questions about war than about anything else. Asking him questions about advanced magical doctrine was akin to asking a plumber to pontificate about nuclear physics. Despite this, Crowley pronounced the ritual a great success.

On the subject of divination, perhaps it would be appropriate here to quote a little more of what Crowley had to say on the subject:

I may here remark that I have always been able to foretell the future by various methods of divination. Some give more satisfactory results than others, some are better suited to one class of inquiry, some to another. In all cases, constant practice, constant checking up of one's results,

*critical study of the conditions, elimination of one's personal bias, and
so on, increase one's accuracy. I am always experimenting and have
taught myself to get absolutely reliable results from several methods...
but there is some sort of curse on me as there was on Cassandra. I can
foretell the issue of any given situation, and feel the utmost confidence
in the correctness of my conclusion, but though I can and do act on
these indications, when they concern my own conduct I cannot use my
power to benefit myself in any of the obvious ways.*

You would do well to remember this in any working of divination you
may do.

Many years later, one of the truly great Thelemites, Jack Parsons, made
a much more effective use of this ritual on July 5, 1945, when he evoked
Bartzabel to get his revenge on L. Ron Hubbard (yes, that L. Ron Hubbard,
founder of Scientology). Some time before he invented Scientology Hubbard
had been living with Jack Parsons in Pasadena, where Agape Lodge O.T.O.
was based, although Hubbard never actually became a member of the Order.
The two men quarrelled and Hubbard ended up taking a boat that partly
belonged to Parsons and sailing off on it. Parsons retaliated by using a solo
version of this ritual to evoke Bartzabel and employ it to force Hubbard to
return with the boat - and apparently succeeded admirably according to a
letter he wrote to Crowley about the incident:

*Hubbard attempted to escape me by sailing at 5 p.m. and I performed
a full invocation to Bartzabel within the circle at 8 p.m... At the same
time, so far as I can check, his ship was struck by a sudden squall off
the coast, which ripped off his sails and forced him back to port, where
I took the boat in custody.*

Near the end of her life I discussed this incident with Parson's widow,
Marjorie Cameron Parsons, who had lived and worked with both men. Her
opinion on the whole thing was:

Ron? Let me tell you about Ron... Ron was an asshole. But he was a
smart *asshole.*

Parsons was a smart magician too. He realised the value of using Bartzabel
for the kind of purpose he was most fitted to i.e. anger, fighting, force, and
causing trouble. A much more fitting task for Bartzabel than sitting around
talking about the future. So bear that in mind during your magical workings:
use the correct tool for the task you want to accomplish!

An Evocation of Bartzabel the Spirit of Mars

Participants:	3-4
Time required:	About an hour
Setup:	Fairly complex
Words:	A goodly amount
Equipment:	• Circle on floor, with pentagon and Tau within

- Circle on floor, with pentagon and Tau within
- Five candles in pentagrams
- Triangle of Art
- Altar in the centre, with
  - Square of Mars and Seal of Mars
  - Statue of Ra-Hoor-Khuit (optional)
  - Rope
  - Burin (sharp engraving tool)
  - Anointing Oil
  - Lamen of Mars (on ribbon or cord for hanging round neck)
  - Torch (a lighter or matches)
  - Book & Pen (or preferably a digital recording device)
- Statue of Isis (outside the circle in the East - optional)
- Statue of Khem (outside the circle in the West - optional)
- Censer & incense (inside the circle in the South)
- Cup (inside the circle in the North)
- Chief Magus
  - Robe
  - Uraeus crown and nemmes (Egyptian style headress - optional)
  - Lamen of the Heireus (optional)
  - 1st Talisman of Mars
  - Spear
  - Sword
  - Bell
- Assistant Magus (sometime referred to as 2nd Magus)
  - Robe
  - Nemmes (optional)
  - 3rd Talisman of Mars
- Magus Adjuvant (sometimes referred to as 3rd Magus)
  - Robe
  - Nemmes (optional)
  - 5th Talisman of Mars

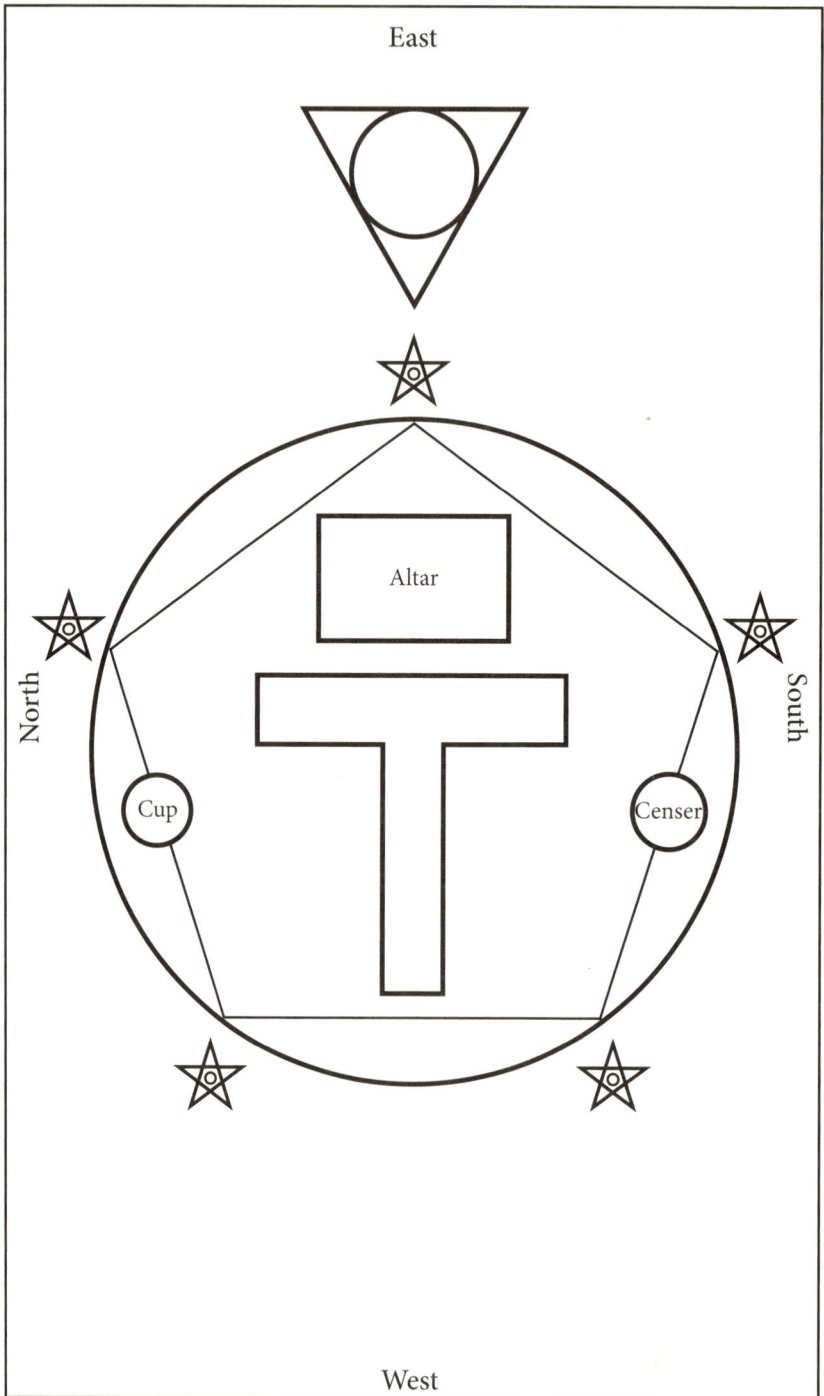

East

Altar

Cup

Censer

North

South

West

- If using human Material Basis
  - Mask
  - Red robe
  - Lamen of Mars

The Ceremony consists of Five Parts:
1. The Banishings and Consecrations.
2. The Special Preparation of the Material Basis.
3. The Particular Invocations of the Forces of Mars.
4. The Dealings with Bartzabel, that mighty Spirit.
5. The Closing.

Gloria Deo Altissimo
Ra Hoor Khuit
in nomine Abrahadabra et in hoc signo

[Glory to the Most High God Ra Hoor Khuit in his name Abrahadabra and in his sign]

The Circle has an inscribed Pentagon, and a Tau within that.

[This is the magick circle on the floor of the temple. It has a pentagon inscribed within it, five points for Mars - this would be a different geometrical figure if you're using a different planetary spirit. Note that it is a pentagon, not a pentagram i.e. it is a solid shape with five sides, not a five-pointed star. The Tau is the shape of a large capital T. Although not specified, it's probably easiest to have the long end of the T at the Western edge of the circle, with the crossbar about 2/3 of the way to the Eastern edge, and the altar at the Eastern edge of the circle. This leaves plenty of room for the three Magi to move around without crashing into things and each other; their stations are also marked out by the points of the Tau.]

Without are 5 pentagrams with 5 ruby lamps. There is an Altar with the Square of Mars and the Seal of Mars. The triangle has the names Primeumaton, Anaphaxeton, Anapheneton and Mi-ca-el within. Also the Sigil of Bartzabel, and his name. About the Circle is the name ALHIM.

[I.e. There should be five small pentagrams drawn on the floor around the outside of the circle, each with one candle in the middle - five since Bartzabel is a spirit of Mars. The number of candles can be varied depending on the spirit to be evoked.

Note that the sigil and name of Bartzabel is within the triangle, not on the altar.

This whole setup is the classic medieval Goetia design for evocation - see the Goetia chapter for more details on this. It may be modified as given there to suit a more Thelemic outlook.]

The Chief Magus wears the robe of a Major Adept, and the Uraeus crown and nemmes. He bears the Lamen of the Hiereus and the 1st Talisman of Mars. He bears as weapons the Spear and Sword, also the Bell.

[Since this ritual was originally performed by members of the A.A. magical Order, the robes described are the robes of that Order. Of course, unless you are a member of A.A. there is no reason to wear these exact robes. If you're a member of O.T.O. your Degree robe in that Order would be suitable, or of any other Order you may happen to be in. If in no Order, a plain black or white robe is always a reliable substitute.

The Lamen of the Hiereus is originally derived from Golden Dawn sources. It is a pendant in the shape of a circle containing an upward pointing triangle in white on a black background, suspended from a scarlet ribbon; it is basically there to show the authority of the Chief Magus. If you hold a similar position in another magical Order you can wear the badge of your rank in that Order, or simply dispense with this item altogether, it's not vital. The First Talisman of Mars from the Key of Solomon is reproduced below. It includes the sigil of Mars, and the names of the four Martial angels Madimiel, Bartzachiah, Eschiel, and Ithuriel written around the rim. "It is proper for invoking spirits of the nature of Mars, especially those which are written in the pentacle."]

The Assistant Magus wears the Robe of a Probationer and a nemmes of white and gold. He attends to the suffumigations of Art. He bears the 3rd Talisman of Mars (from the *Key of Solomon*), and the consecrated Torch.

[The robe of a Probationer is white with gold trim around the sleeves, hem, and collar, with a pentagram on the chest and a hexagram and Tau design on the back. See The Equinox, *Volume 4, Number 1: The Vision & the Voice for a colour picture of this robe. Again this may be replaced with the robe of your Degree in whatever magical group you belong to. The Torch is used to light the incense and keep it going throughout the ritual - it should actually be a cigarette lighter or lighted taper, or similar. The 3rd Talisman of Mars is reproduced below. The verse is probably from the Bible, Psalm 77 verse 13: "non est fortis sicut Deus noster", roughly meaning "there is none as powerful as our God". Although the text here states that he carries the Torch, this is a mistake - the Torch begins the ritual on the altar.]*

The Magus Adjuvant is robed as his brother, but wears the 5th Talisman of Mars. He attends to the Lustrations of Art. He bears the Book and Pen.

[The Book & Pen are of course used to write down whatever happens during the rite - again they actually begin the ritual placed on the altar and are given to the Magus Adjuvant during the rite. Lustrations of Art means dealing with the watery parts of the ritual. The 5th Talisman of Mars is reproduced below. "Write thou this pentacle upon virgin parchment or paper, because it is terrible unto the demons, and at its sight and aspect they will obey thee, for they cannot resist its presence." The writing on the rim is "Super aspidem et basiliscum ambulabis et; conculcabis leonem et draconem" which means "'Thou shalt go upon the lion and adder, the young lion and the dragon shalt thou tread under thy feet."]

Upon the Altar is the Image of Ra Hoor Khuit, Isis is the East his Mother, Khem is the West facing him. In the South is the Censer, in the North the Cup.
   [If you can't get hold of statues of these gods, you could always just use pictures of them.]

The Material Basis is masked, and robed in red.

[If you are using a talisman as a Material Basis, then leave it on the altar covered with a red cloth at the beginning instead.]

On the Altar are also the rope, the burin, the oil, and the Lamen of Mars for the Material Basis.

[The Spear also needs to be on the altar at the beginning of the ritual. A burin, or graver, is a tool normally used in making woodcuts. It has a rounded wooden handle and a thin steel shaft with a very sharp cutting tip. If you're going to use one of these, please be extremely careful!]

The Lamps are all alight.

Part 1

(Chief Magus: At altar, kneeling in humility.
Second Magus: With sword of Chief Magus
Third Magus: In other chamber with M.B.
Chief Magus knocks once
Second Magus: Performs Banishing Rituals of Pentagram and Hexagram around whole room, and replaces Sword on Altar.)

[Whereas I'm no fan of the "Banishing Ritual" idea in general in this case a good strong Pentagram Ritual performed carefully both before and after this ritual might not go amiss, especially if you intend to use a human Material Basis. The Ritual of the Mark of the Beast would be ideal.

The Banishing Ritual of the Hexagram would be the Golden Dawn Hexagram rite as given in Crowley's Liber O vel Manus et Sagittae *(see appendix). I've never bothered with this Hexagram ritual personally, and I've never noticed that it makes the slightest difference once you've done a decent Pentagram rite; but if you wish to do it here too, please go ahead. I don't think it essential though.]*

(Third Magus: Washes Material Basis with pure water, saying:)

> **Asperge eam (eum) Domine hyssopo et mundabitur; lavabis eam (eum) et super nivem dealbabitur.**

[The classic purification formula as we saw before in The Goetia: "Thou shalt sprinkle me with hyssop, O Lord! and I shall be clean: Thou shalt wash me, and I shall be whiter than snow." Eam is feminine, and eum masculine.]

(He masks her/him with the mask and robe of Mars, saying:)

> **By the figurative mystery of these holy vestures of concealment, doth the Lord cloak thee in the Shroud of Mystery in the strength of the Most High ANCOR AMACOR AMIDES THEODONIAS ANITOR that our desired end may be effected through thy strength, Adonai, unto whom be the Glory in Saecula saeculorum AMEN.**

[These preceding purifications have been done in the other chamber. When complete, Third Magus opens the door and enters the temple leading the Material Basis.]

(He leads her/him to her/his place in the Triangle.)

The Chief Magus now rises from his knees, and takes the Spear from the Altar.

Chief Magus: **Hail unto Thee, Ra Hoor Khuit, who art the Lord of the Aeon!**
Be this consecrated Spear
A thing of cheer, a thing of fear!
Cheer to me who wield it! ---
My heart, its vigour shield it!

Fear to them who face it ---
Their force, let fear disgrace it!
Be a ray from the Most High
A glance of His unsleeping eye!
Arm me, arm me, in the fray
That shall be fought this dreadful day!

(He hands Spear to 2nd Magus to hold. The Chief Magus takes the Sword.)

Chief Magus: Hail unto Thee, Ra Hoor Khuit, who art the Lord
of the Aeon!
Be this consecrated Sword
Not abhorred before the Lord!
A guard of Steel, a tongue of flame
Writing in adamant His Name!
Puissant against the Hosts of Evil!
A mighty fence against the Devil!
A snake of lightning to destroy
Them that work Mischief and Annoy!
Arm me, arm me, in the fray
That shall be fought this dreadful day!

(He hands Sword to 3rd Magus to hold. The Chief Magus raises his hands
above the Altar.)

Chief Magus: Hail unto Thee, Ra Hoor Khuit, who art the Lord
of the Aeon!
Be this consecrated Altar
A sign of sure stability!
Will and Courage never falter,
Thought dissolve in Deity!
Let thy smile divinely curving,
Isis, bless our dark device!
Holy Hawk, our deed unswerving
Be thy favoured sacrifice!
Holy Khem, our vigour nerving,
We have paid the priestly price.
Hail, Ra Hoor, thy ray forth-rolling
Consecrate the instruments,
Thine Almighty power controlling
To the Event the day's events!
Arm me, arm me, in the fray
That shall be fought this dreadful day!

(Chief Magus takes Spear from Second Magus and gives him the Censer and Torch; Sword from Third Magus and gives him the Cup, Book and Pen.

[i.e. the Chief Magus takes the Spear and lays it on the Altar, then gives Censer and Torch to Second Magus. When that is done, Chief Magus takes the Sword and lays it on the Altar, then gives Cup, Book and Pen to Third Magus.]

Chief Magus goes to apex of triangle. The others support him at the base. He takes the cord from the altar.)

Chief Magus: **Frater N! As thou art blindfolded save for that light and sight which I can give thee, so do I now bind thee, so that thou mayst be for a space subject to my will and mine alone.**

(Ties hands and feet.)

[He ties the hands of the Material Basis in front of his body.]

(Takes Spear from altar.)

[During the next sections the Chief Magus needs to walk back and forth between the Altar and Triangle, picking up and laying down each needed instrument in turn.]

                 And since thou art without the circle in the place of the triangle, with this Spear do I invoke upon thee the protection of Ra Hoor Khuit, so that no force either of Heaven or of Earth, or from under the earth, may act upon thee, save only that force that I shall invoke within thee.

[Chief Magus points the Spear at M.B.]

                 Bahlasti! Ompehda!

[Chief Magus replaces Spear on Altar and picks up the vial of Oil.]

                 So then, I being armed and exalted to the Power of the Most High, place upon thy head this drop of consecrated oil, so that the ray of Godhead may illumine thee.

                 And I place this holy kiss upon thy neck, so that thy mind may be favourable unto us, open to our words, sensible of the power of our conjurations.

[This kiss should probably be at the back of the neck, the place where traditionally spirits enter the body during possession. Chief Magus replaces Oil, picks up Burin and goes to stand in front of M.B.]

> And with this burin do I draw from thy breast five drops of blood, so that thy body may be the Temple of Mars.

[The usual caveats about drawing blood apply here as always. This part can be left out if desired.]

> Wherefore also I command thee to repeat after me: I submit myself to thee and to this operation; I invoke the Powers of Mars to manifest within me.

(MB repeats this affirmation.)

[Chief Magus replaces Burin and picks up the Lamen of Mars.]

(Chief Magus places about his neck the Lamen of Mars.)

[That is, puts the Lamen about the neck of the Material Basis.]

(Magi return to circle, face east.)

Chief Magus: Now, Brethren, since we are about to engage in a Work of so great danger, it is fitting that we make unto ourselves a fortress of defence in the name of the Most High, Elohim. Frater Adjuvant Magus, I command thee to purify the place with water.

(Third Magus sprinkles thrice around circle walking widdershins.)

[When he has finished this, he sets the Cup back in its place in the North.] .

Chief Magus: Thus, therefore, first the Priest who governeth the works of Fire, must sprinkle with the waters of the loud-resounding sea. Frater Assistant Magus, I command thee to consecrate the place with Fire.

(Second Magus censes the circle thrice around, walking widdershins.)

[When he has finished this, he sets the Censer back in its place in the South.]

Chief Magus: So when all the phantoms are vanished, and through the Universe darts and flashes that holy and formless Fire --- Hear Thou the Voice of Fire!

[From the Chaldean Oracles.*]*

(Chief Magus takes Sword.)

> The Lord is my fortress and my deliverer; my God in whom I will trust, I will walk upon the lion and adder; the young lion and the scorpion will I tread under my feet. Because he hath set his Love upon me, therefore will I deliver him:
> I will set him on high, because he hath known My Name.

[From the Bible, Psalm 91.*]*

(Chief Magus circumnambulates thrice widdershins with sword.)

[Recites the following prayer to Ra Hoor Khuit while circumnambulating.]

> Hail unto Thee, Ra Hoor Khuit, who art the Lord
> of the Aeon!
> Be this consecrated Tower
> A place of power this fearful hour!
> May the Names of God that gird us
> Be our sign that he hath heard us!
> By the five unsleeping Stars
> Ward us from the wrath of Mars!
> By the rood of God erect
> Be He perfect to protect!
> rm me, arm me, in the fray
> That shall be fought this dreadful day!

(He now conjures the Dog of Evil.)

[Returns to the centre of the circle and addresses the Material Basis, pointing the Sword at him, during the following Conjuration:]

> Arise, Dog of Evil, that I may instruct thee in thy
> present duties.
> In the name of Horus, I say unto thee, Arise.
> Thou art imprisoned.
> Confess thou that it is so.

I have done this in the name and in the might of Horus.
Except thou set thy face in my defence, thou art blind,
and dumb, and paralysed: but thou shalt hear the curses
of thy Creator, and thou shalt feel the torments of my
avenging wrath.
Therefore be thou obedient unto me, as a guard against
them that hate me.
Let thy jaws be terrible as the storm-parted sky.
Let thy face be as a whirlwind of wrath and fury against
the enemy.
Arise, I say, and aid and guard me in this Work of Art.
O thou! whose head is of coal-black fire!
Thou, whose eyes are as columns of smoke and flame!
Thou, from whose nostrils goeth forth the breath
of destruction!
Thou whose body is of iron and brass, bound with
exceeding strength: girt with the power of awful blind
avenging force --- under my control, and mine alone!
Thou, whose claws are as shafts of whirling steel to rip
the very bowels of my adversaries.
Thee, thee, I summon to mine aid!
In the name of Horus: rise: move: appear:
And aid and guard me in this Work of Art!
Rise, Dog of Evil, to guard the Abyss of Height!
Rise, I say, to guard the Four Quarters: the Abyss of the
North; the Abyss of the South; the Abyss of the East;
the Abyss of the West.
Rise, I say, to guard the Abyss of the Great Deep.
Horus it is that hath given this commandment.
Be thou terrible against all them that hate me!
Be thou mighty to defend me from the Evil Ones!
At the confines of Matter: at the Threshold of the
Invisible: be thou my Watcher and my Guardian! Before
the face of the Dwellers of the Abodes of Night!
As a flaming sword turning every way to keep the gates
of my Universe: let thy teeth flash forth!
Nothing shall stop thee while thou settest thyself in
my defence.
In the name of Horus: Rise, Move, and Appear: Be thou
obedient unto me: for I am the Master of the Forces of
Matter: the Servant of the Same thy God is my Name:
true Worshipper of the Highest.

(Much incense is now burnt, and there is a pause.)

The Invocations

(Chief Magus first performs the Invoking Ritual of Mars.)

[This may be a reference to the Golden Dawn Invoking Hexagram of Mars. It may be performed or omitted as desired.]

(The Adepts stand at the points of the Tau.)

Chief Magus: Even as of old there came three Magi from the ends of the earth to adore the Fivefold Star, so come we, O Lord, armed for the holy work of an Evocation of Bartzabel the spirit of Mars, that is obedient unto the Intelligence Graphiel, chosen from the Seraphim who follow Kamael the Great Archangel that serveth God under his name of Elohim Gibor, a spark from Thine intolerable light, Ra Hoor Khuit! Therefore hear Thou the Oath of the Obligation that we assume before Thee.

(The Chief Magus points the Sword downward upon the apex of the Triangle of Ra Hoor Khuit and the other Magi place their hands upon the hilt.)

[The Triangle mentioned here is the one formed by the three Magi as they stand at the points of the Tau - the downward pointing triangle of Ra Hoor Khuit. In other words, the Chief Magus actually stands still and points the sword at his feet, and the other two Magi reach across to him to touch it.]

We, Perdurabo, a Neophyte of the A∴ A∴, All For Knowledge, a Probationer of A∴ A∴, and AGATHA, a Probationer of A∴ A∴,

[These were the magical mottoes of the adepts who originally performed the ritual. Perdurabo was Aleister Crowley, All For Knowledge was Commander Marston, and AGATHA was Leila Waddell. During your own performance this section should be changed to the magical names and grades of the people performing the rite.]

swear unto Thee, O Lord God, by Thine own almighty power, by Thy force and fire, by Thy glittering Hawk's eye and Thy mighty sweeping wings: that we all here in this place and now at this time do utterly devote ourselves, mind, body, and estate, at all times and in all places soever to the establishment of Thy holy Kingdom.

> And if we fail herein, may we be burnt and consumed by the Red Eye of Mars!

(Magi return to stations.)

[Chief Magus replaces Sword on altar.]

> And this our purpose is fivefold:
> Firstly, that the Kingdom of Ra Hoor Khuit may be established in the Aeon.
> Secondly, that we may succeed in that particular design of which it is not lawful to speak, even before Thee.
> Thirdly, that we may have power to help the weak.
> Fourthly, that we may be filled with the Courage and Energy of Mars for the Prosecution of the Great Work.
> And, lastly, that we may obtain the service of Bartzabel that he may be obedient unto us thy servants, that between him and us there may be peace, and that he may always be ready to come whensoever he is invoked and called forth.

[The purposes mentioned here were the original ones used by Crowley and his assistants. You should change these to your own purposes when you perform the ritual for yourself.]

> Now because in such a work it is not possible for us to do anything at all of ourselves, we have humble recourse unto Thine Almighty power, beseeching upon our knees Thy favour and Thine aid.

[I've never been too keen on this line, I don't think "beseeching upon our knees" is the correct posture for a magician to take in a case such as this. The Stele of Revealing shows the magician approaching Ra-Hoor-Khuit on his feet, not on his knees. Personally I would alter this line appropriately.]

(The Magi kneel at three sides of altar, all clasping Spear in the proper manner.)

[The "proper manner" is not specified. I would suggest that the Chief Magus pick up the Spear from the altar, kneel and hold it upright with both hands, right hand over left. Then the other two Magi also grip the body of the Spear with both hands, so all three are kneeling, holding it upright.]

I adore Thee in the Song:
I am the Lord of Thebes, and I
The inspired forth-speaker of Mentu;
For me unveils the veiled sky,
The self-slain Ankh-f-n-Khonsu
Whose words are truth. I invoke, I greet
Thy presence, O Ra Hoor Khuit!

Unity uttermost shewed!
I adore the might of Thy breath,
Supreme and terrible God
Who makest the Gods and death
To tremble before Thee:
I, I adore Thee!

Appear on the throne of Ra!
Open the ways of the Khu!
Lighten the ways of the Ka!
The ways of the Khabs run through
To stir me or still me!
Aum! let it fill me!

(All say, repeatedly:)

A Ka dua
Tuf ur biu
Bi a'a chefu
Dudu ner af an nuteru!

[Unity uttermost showed!
I adore the might of Thy breath,
Supreme and terrible God,
Who makest the gods and death
To tremble before Thee:-
I, I adore thee!]

(When the Chief Magus is satisfied with the Descent of the God, let all rise and let Chief Magus say:)

[The Chief Magus needs to be satisfied that the God is present, since the divine energy must be present in order to have the authority to command Bartzabel.]

So that Thy light is in me; and its red flame is as a sword in my hand to push thy order. There is a secret door that I shall make to establish thy way in all the quarters... as it is said:

The light is mine; its rays consume
Me: I have made a secret door
Into the house of Ra and Tum,
Of Khephra, and of Ahathoor.
I am thy Theban, O Mentu,
The prophet Ankh-f-n-Khonsu!

By Bes-na-Maut my breast I beat;
By wise Ta-Nech I weave my spell.
Show thy star-splendour, O Nuit!
Bid me within thine House to dwell,
O winged snake of light, Hadit!
Abide with me, Ra Hoor Khuit!

(Magus faces triangle, and others support him.)

Hail! Hail! Hail! Hail! Hail!

Send forth a spark of thine illimitable light and force, we beseech Thee, that it may appear in the Heaven of Mars as the God Elohim Gibor.

O winged glory of gold! O plumes of justice and stern brows of majesty!
O warrior armed with spear and shield! O virgin strength and splendour as of spring! That ridest in thy Chariot of Iron above the Storm upon the Sea! Who shootest forth the Arrows of the Moon! Who wieldest the Four Magick Weapons! Who art the Master of the Pentagram and of the blazing fury of the Sun!

Come unto me, thou great God Elohim Gibor, and send thy Angel Kamael, even Kamael the mighty, the Leader of thine Armies the fiery Serpents, the Seraphim, that he may answer my behests.

O purple flame that is like unto the whirling
wheel of Life!

O strong shoulders and virginal breasts and
dancing limbs!

Kamael! Kamael! Kamael! Kamael!

I see thee before me, O thou great Archangel!
Art thou not the Leader of the armies of the Lord?
Of the grey snakes upon whose heads are triple crowns
of spiritual light, and whose tongues are triply forked
with judgment? Whose bodies are like the Sun in his
strength, whose scales are of the adamant of Vulcan,
who are slim and splendid and virginal as they rush
flaming over the lashed sea?

Come unto me, Kamael, thou archangel almighty,
and send to me Graphiel that great intelligence of thine,
that he may answer my behest.

O moon, that sailest on the shoulders of the Sun!
Whose warrior body is like white-hot steel!
Whose virgin limbs and golden wings move like
ripe corn at the caress of the thunderstorm!

O thou that wieldest the Sword and Balances of Power!

Graphiel! Graphiel! Graphiel! Graphiel! Graphiel!
Graphiel!
Come unto us, thou bright intelligence of Mars, and
answer my behest. In the name of Kamael thy Lord,
I say: Compel the spirit Bartzabel that is under thy
dominion to manifest within this triangle of Art, within
the Ruach of the material basis that is consecrated to
this work, within this pure and beautiful human form
that is prepared for his habitation.

And now I see thee, O thou dull deceitful head,
that I shall fill with wit and truth; thou proud heart
that I shall humble and make pure; thou cold body
that I shall fashion into a living flame of amethyst.

Thou sexless being of whom I shall make the perfect
child of Hermes and Aphrodite that is God; thou dull
ox that I shall turn into the Bull of Earth; thou house of
idleness wherein I shall set up the Throne of Justice.

Bartzabel! Bartzabel! Bartzabel! Bartzabel! Bartzabel!
Bartzabel!

Come forth, and manifest beyond the bars!

Forth from the palace of seraphic stars!
Come, O thou Bartzabel, the sprite of Mars!

Come: I unbind thee from the chains of Hell,
Come: I enclose thee in the invisible
To be my slave, thou spirit Bartzabel!
By the spear, the sword, the spell,
Come unto me, Bartzabel!
By the word that openeth Hell!
Come unto me, Bartzabel!

By the power o' th' panther's pell,
Come unto me, Bartzabel!
By the circling citadel,
Come unto me, Bartzabel!
By this mind of miracle
Come unto me, Bartzabel!

By Ra Hoor Khuit, by Elohim Gibor,
By Kamael and the Seraphim; by Hoor,
Khem, and Mentu, and all the Gods of War,
Ares and Mars and Hachiman and Thor,
And by thy master, Graphiel,
Come unto me, Bartzabel!

(And if he come not, let the Chief Magus and his assistants humble themselves
mightily, and repeat these holy invocations, even unto thrice.

And if still he be obdurate and disobedient unto the Words of Power, the
Chief Magus shall assume the dignity of Khem, and conjure him and curse
him as his own ingenium shall direct.)

[*That is, the Magus should stand in the traditional posture of the Egyptian god Khem (see Mark of the Beast ritual), and use his divine power to force Bartzabel to appear.*]

(Yet, if the rites have been duly performed, he will assuredly have manifested before this. And these will probably be the tokens of the manifestation:

A ruddy light will play about the form of the Material Basis; or even a dark lustre beetle-brown or black. And the Face thereof will be suffused with blood, and the Heart beat violently, and its words will be swift and thick and violent. The voice thereof must be entirely changed; it may grow deep and hoarse, or at least strained and jerky, and it may be that it will suffer the torment of burning. On the appearance of the Spirit much incense is thrown upon the Censer.)

The Charge

[*Chief Magus replaces Spear on altar and takes up Sword. Magus Adjuvant picks up Book and Pen (or other recording device) and gets ready to record any answers given by the Spirit.*]

> Hail, Bartzabel, and welcome, thou mighty spirit of Madim!
>
> Welcome unto us art thou who comest in the name of Graphiel and of Kamael and of Elohim Gibor, and of Ra Hoor Khuit the Lord of the Aeon. I charge thee to answer and obey.
>
> 1. How shall the Kingdom of the Aeon be established?
> 2. Will success attend that particular design of which it is not lawful to speak?
> 3. We shall obtain power to aid the weak; in what manner? Give us a sign.
> 4. Give us a sign of the Courage and Energy of Mars that floweth and shall ever flow through us by virtue of this ceremony.

[*These were the original questions put when the rite was first performed in 1910. Obviously in your working you will ask different questions of the spirit, or ask it to assist you in the particular manner you require - but make sure your questions harmonize with the intent stated at the beginning of the rite. Don't pester the spirit with all the questions at once either - give it time to answer and converse on each one before moving to the next. See the introduction to the Goetia chapter for how you should go about this.*]

5. Lastly, O thou Spirit Bartzabel, lay thine hands
upon this sword, whose point I then place upon thine
head, and swear faith and obedience unto me by
Ra Hoor Khuit, the Lord of the Aeon, saying after me:

*[Chief Magus extends Sword beyond the circle, places it carefully on the head of
the Material Basis, who raises his hands and puts them on the blade. Once he is in
this position, he should repeat the following Oath:]*

I, Bartzabel, the Spirit of Mars, do swear by the glory
of Him that is Lord of the Aeon, and by the Might of
Elohim Gibor, and by the Fear of Kamael and the Hosts
of Fiery Serpents, and by Graphiel whose hand is heavy
upon me --- before which names I tremble every day
--- that I will punctually fulfil this present charge, not
perverting the sense thereof, but obedient to the inmost
thought of the Chief Magus; that I will be ever the
willing servant of thee and thy companions, a spirit of
Truth in Force and Fire; that in departing I will do no
hurt to any personor thing, and in particular that the
Material Basis shall not suffer through this ceremony,
but shall be purified and fortified thereby; that I will
be at peace with thee and seek never to injure thee, but
to defend thee against all thine enemies, and to work
eternally for thy welfare; finally, that I will be ready to
come unto thee to serve thee whensoever I am invoked
and called forth, whether by a word, or a will, or by this
great and potent conjuration of Magick Art.

*[On no account should you leave this section out, especially if you have a human
Material Basis!]*

AMEN.

The Benediction

[Chief Magus returns to his station.]

Let Ra Hoor Khuit bless thee!
Let His light shine perpetually in thy darkness!
Let His force eternally brace up thy weakness!

Let His blessing be upon thee for ever and for ever!
Yea, verily and Amen, let His blessing be upon thee
for ever and ever!

The License To Depart

Now, O thou Spirit Bartzabel, since thou didst come
at my behest and swear faith and fealty unto me by
the Lord of the Aeon, I license thee to depart in peace
with the blessing of the Lord until such time as I have
need of thee.

The Closing

(Let the Chief Magus perform the Banishing Ritual of Mars, give great
Thanks unto the Lord of the Aeon, and perform the Lesser Rituals of the
Pentagram and Hexagram)

*[The Pentagram and Hexagram rituals performed at the end should be the same
rituals used at the beginning, in order to preserve symmetry. Since the Second
Magus performed the Lesser Rituals of the Pentagram and Hexagram at the
beginning of the rite, I would recommend that he also perform them at the end.*

*I assume that what is meant by the Banishing Ritual of Mars is a Hexagram ritual
using the hexagram of Mars - however I think that three banishing rituals at the end
might be slightly overkill. One good strong one should be more than enough.]*

Chapter Eleven
The Supreme Ritual

A feast for the Supreme Ritual.
To him is the winged secret flame, and to her the stooping starlight.
                                                              - Liber Legis

In an earlier chapter we dealt with A Ritual to Invoke HICE, one of *Two Fragments of Ritual* that Aleister Crowley published in 1913. The Supreme Ritual is the other fragment. In this rite we see Crowley fully manifesting his theory of the use of poetry to create spiritual intoxication that had been one of the features of the Evocation of Bartzabel - The Supreme Ritual goes a step further, and is basically one long poem in action.

Crowley wrote about his change in attitude towards ritual in a letter to Jack Parsons in February 1946 (quoted in Martin Starr's excellent biographical work *The Unknown God*):

> *...To follow out fully all the formulae of technical ceremonial is really too much like hard work, though for that very reason of course it is enormously valuable. At the same time one must consider that the whole tempo of the world has changed since the 15th century or thereabouts... These considerations alone made me very happy when I was initiated into a method which produced equally good results without all this how-d'you-do.*

It is easy to see in the following ritual the huge leap in technique that Crowley had made in just a short few months of being initiated into the highest Degrees of O.T.O..

The ritual is also notable for its distinct lack of paraphernalia. Here Crowley strips everything down to its absolute basics: the interaction between two people, who between them raise divine energy. In a sense it is based on the tried and trusted Dionysian formula of "wine, woman, and song." This obviously implies that there may also be a sexual component to the ritual, although this is never expressed openly. I leave it to you, the reader, to make up your own mind on that question.

Although it is not specified directly in the text, I think it safe to assume that the ritual is designed for one female officer and one male. If you wish to replace this with a ritual featuring two members of the same gender you may have to make appropriate adjustments.

At two points in the ritual the female officer may play music. This indicates that the ritual was probably originally written with the violinist Leila Waddell in mind for the female role, and presumably Crowley himself in the male role. It is true that many magicians are also fairly accomplished musicians, but not necessarily so. If you aren't a skilled musician, or if your chosen musical instrument is the tuba, it might be hard to create the desired ambiance required. Music is required however, being one of the three sacraments mentioned in the ritual itself. You could always use a very simple musical instrument, such as a sistrum - it's hard to play that wrong (though some magicians I know do have difficulty even with that). Another viable and easy solution is to simply use pre-recorded music, which has the added advantage of leaving your hands free for other things.

It seems likely Crowley wrote this not long after being initiated to the secrets of the IX° of O.T.O. and it contains one of his few public allusions to that Degree.

Note that there is no specific magical intention given within the text of the rite - it appears to be solely for the purpose of "intoxicating the soul". However there is no doubt that significant magical energy could be raised from the interplay of the forces during this opus, and so it could thus perhaps be adapted for particular material purposes.

The Supreme Ritual

Participants:	Two
Time required:	About an hour
Setup:	Simple
Words:	Medium
Equipment:	• Feast
	• Altar
	• Vessel of wine
	• Robes (optional)
	• Incense (optional)
	• A device for playing music
	• A small dagger
	• Anointing oil

Let a feast be made by the Officers of the Temple. This Temple, into which they then retire, may be any convenient place. An altar is necessary; also a vessel of wine; otherwise as may be appointed by them: e.g. the robes, etc., as said in *Liber Legis*.

> [Robes etc. would appear to be a reference to Chapter I, verse 61 of the Book of the Law: "...if under the night stars in the desert thou presently burnest mine incense before me ...ye shall wear rich jewels ...I charge you earnestly to come before me in a single robe, and covered with a rich headdress. I love you! I yearn to you! Pale or purple, veiled or voluptuous..." All of these phrases might be taken as appropriate instructions for optional additions.]

The officers are two in number, and seek Nuit and Hadit through Babalon and the Beast. To conceal themselves, they are disguised as Isis and Osiris.

> [Nuit and Hadit are the ultimate female and male deities. Babalon and the Beast are equally a duo of female and male divine forces, but in a less exalted form. We can see the conception as being that the two officers invoke Babalon and the Beast first, then through their intercession achieve a connection to the Most High.
>
> The reference to them being "disguised as Isis and Osiris" is misleading, I think intentionally so. This doesn't mean that you dress up as these Egyptian deities. Rather it refers to the O and I used throughout the text. In this case the letters are not actually abbreviations for the names of Osiris and Isis - rather they refer to the negative and positive principles, rather like binary 0 and 1, or the O and I symbols used on off/on switches; O being the female officer and I being the male officer.]

(The officers meet and clasp hands above the altar. Any preliminary operations, such as opening, banishing, etc., are now done by I., who returns, and they again greet, but as initiates.)

> [These preliminary operations are optional, but I think a Mark of Beast ritual could work very well as an opening here - since it is an excellent ritual for the raising of power, as well as for banishing. Note that the first greeting they make is a simple clasping of hands, whereas after the preliminaries they greet "as initiates", which I assume means they use the signs of the grade they possess within the group. O.T.O. initiates should use the signs of the highest shared Degree they have.]

(O. and I. face to face.)

O.   What is the hour?

I.   When time hath no power.

O.   What is the place?

I.   At the limits of space.

O.   What God do we wake?

I.   The Lord of the Snake!

O.   With what do we serve?

I.   Blood, Muscle, and Nerve!

O.   The shrine in the gloom?

(Gives the Sign of a Babe of the Abyss, which I. destroys by the Sign of Men Tu the God.)

> [The sign of the Babe of the Abyss is also known as Puella (Girl). The Sign of Men Tu is also known as Puer (Boy). See the Mark of the Beast ritual where they are also used.]

I.   Is the Mouth Of Thy Womb

O.   And the Priest in the Shrine?

I.   Is this Member Of Mine!

(I. repeats Sign of Men Tu and O. gives Sign of Baphomet.)

[The Sign of Baphomet is the one also known as Mulier (Woman). The conception appears to be that the Member makes Puella into Mulier.]

O.   And the wonder above?

I.   **The Quintessence of Love.**

O.   There are sacraments?

I.   **Nine.**
         There are music and wine
         And the delicate dance -

[Despite this reference to nine sacraments, only three are specified by name in the ritual: music, wine, and dance. It is possible that the missing six refers to the Hexagram, being the conjunction of the material and the divine, but I cannot be certain on this point.]

O.   To accomplish?

I.   **The trance.**

[We are here told the purpose of the three sacraments: to achieve a trance state. This implies that there should be enough of each of these in order to actually bring the participants into an altered state of consciousness. So you do need lots of music, and lots of dancing. Some people may have a tendency to overdo the wine at the expense of the other two - be careful of this. You need to retain enough consciousness and motor function control to actually complete the ritual!]

O.   And are these three enough?

I.   **They are servants of Love.**

O.   And the sacrifice?

I.   **I.**

O.   And the priestess?

I.   **Is thou.**
         I am willing to die
         At thy hands - even now.

O.   Worship me first!

(I. seats O. upon the Altar.)

I.   Mistress, I thirst.

(O. gives wine. They drink.)

O.   My mouth is on fire
          To my lord's desire.

(They exchange the holy greeting by a kiss.)

I.   I kneel at thy feet,
          And the honey is sweet.

(O. plays music while I. worships in silence.)

O.   Exhausted, I sink.

I.   I am dead, on the brink.

O.   Let us dance!

I.   Let us dance!

O. and I.   The Lord give us power
                 To be lost in the trance.
                 For an hour - for an hour!

(They dance together. A pause of perfect stillness and silence follows: until
O., sua sponte, advances and places I. upon the altar.)

   [sua sponte = of her own accord]

O.   Exhaust me!

I.   Nay, drink!

O.   Ere I sink!

I.   I shall sink!

O.   Drink wine! oh, drink wine!

I.   I am thine!

O.   I am thine!

(They drink and greet as before.)

   [i.e. with a kiss.]

I.   Art thou armed?

O.   With a knife.

(O. draws the dagger from her hair.)

   [Keeping a dagger sharp enough to cut flesh in your hair is possibly not the safest practice. I do not recommend this! I suggest either keeping the dagger to one side where it can be picked up, or simply using a small symbolic magical dagger (a letter opener is ideal) that can be safely wound in the hair. The other option I suppose is to simply use something like a hairpin as the "dagger".]

I.   Love is better than life.

(O. cuts a upright Tau Cross, or if possible, the sigil of N.O.X., on I's breast.)

   [The Tau Cross is in the shape of a capital letter T; when Crowley calls it "upright" like this he may be referring to it having the horizontal crossbar at the bottom, and the vertical bar above it, i.e. like a T upside down. The sigil of N.O.X. is an X within a circle. The usual caveats about blood-letting apply. If in doubt, simply trace the design lightly on the skin with the edge of the dagger. Note that if you are going to pierce the skin, cutting a Tau cross of two straight lines is infinitely easier than cutting a circle; so unless you are a professional surgeon or tattooist, I strongly recommend choosing the Tau option.]

O.   Let us dance!

I.   (giving wine.)

        To the trance!

(They drink, then dance.)

O.   Back to the throne!

(I. returns, and takes seat thereon.)

O.   I adore thee alone!

[This line was attributed to I. in the original text. However given the next line where it
says "O. does so", referring to the adoration being performed by her, it would seem
that the original attribution appears to have been an error. I have changed it to O.
instead, and it makes a lot more sense within the context of the rite now.]

(O. does so, plays music if so inclined, and continues as necessity or
inclination may dictate.)

O.   It is ended, the play:
        I am ready to slay.
        Anoint me!

I.   I rise
        To the fire of thine eyes.
        I anoint thee, thy priest,
        Babalon - and The Beast!

[The poetic metre here can be confusing. Note that the meaning of these two lines
is "I, the Priest, anoint thee as Babalon - and myself as The Beast". A small vial of
anointing oil could be used here - though be extremely careful if you use something
like Oil of Abramelin, because it can badly burn sensitive skin tissue!]

        And I ask of Thee now:
        Who art Thou?

O.   Omari tessala marax
        tessala dodi phornepax.
        amri radara poliax
        armana piliu.
        amri radara piliu son';
        mari narya barbiton
        madara anaphax sarpedon
        andala hriliu

[This is in the so-called lunar language given in Liber 418, The Vision & The Voice,
2nd Aethyr, which deals with the goddess Babalon (see Chapter 15 of this book for
more information). I suggest that when O is reciting it she keeps the meaning of
the translation below strongly in her mind. She may also try using the whole verse
as a repeated mantra.]

I am the harlot that shaketh death
This shaking giveth the Peace of Satiate Lust
Immortality jetteth forth from my skull
And music from my vulva.
Immortality jetteth forth from my vulva also
For my Whoredom is a sweet scent like a seven-stringed instrument
Played unto God the Invisible, the all-ruler,
That goeth along giving the shrill scream of orgasm.]

The Ritual of the S.... of R.... is in silence accomplished.

[The missing words would appear to be "Star of Ruby". The Thelemic Holy Book called Liber Stellae Rubeae may shed some light on this. See appendix.]

IX°

[A reference to a ritual technique available to initiates of the Ninth Degree of O.T.O. I could not possibly comment on the exact details of what this might be, but I can point out that in several public O.T.O. documents it is made clear that the Order teaches the secret of sexual magic.]

Closing

I.   Mouth to mouth and heart to heart!

O.   For the moment we must part.

I.   Time and space renew the illusion.

O.   Love is swallowed in confusion.

I.   Love sustains us eminent
            Till the hour of Sacrament.

O.   I love you, and you love me.

I.   Now and ever may it be!

I. and O.   Hand in hand is heart to heart
                   Love be with us, though we part.

(They greet, as before, and depart.)

Chapter Twelve
The Ritual of Consecration of an High Priest of L.I.L.

One of the great advantages of [dramatic ritual] is that a large number of persons may take part, so that there is consequently more force available; but it is important that they should all be initiates of the same mysteries, bound by the same oaths, and filled with the same aspirations.

- Aleister Crowley, *Magick*

The following is one of Crowley's earliest attempts at formal group ritual, being an initiation rite for an abortive new magical Order called the Lamp of Invisible Light, or L.I.L., that he had hoped to set up in Mexico around 1901. In his *Confessions* Crowley records:

I hired part of a house overlooking the Alameda, a magnificent park intended for pleasure and protected from the police. I engaged a young Indian girl to look after me and settled down to steady work at Magick. I had an introduction to an old man named Don Jesus de Medina, a descendant of the great duke of Armada fame, and one of the highest chiefs of Scottish rite free-masonry. My Cabbalistic knowledge being already profound by current standards, he thought me worthy of the highest initiation in his power to confer; special powers were obtained in view of my limited sojourn, and I was pushed rapidly through and admitted to the thirty-third and last degree before I left the country.

I had also a certain amount of latitude granted by Mathers to initiate suitable people in partibus. I, therefore, established an entirely new Order of my own, called L.I.L.: the 'Lamp of the Invisible Light'. Don Jesus became its first High Priest. In the Order L.I.L., the letters L.P.D. are the monograms of the mysteries. An explanation of these letters is given by Dumas in the prologues of his Memoirs of a Physician, *and Eliphas Levi discusses them at some length. I, however, remembered them directly from my incarnation as Cagliostro. It would be improper to communicate their significance to the profane, but I may say that the political interpretation given by Dumas is superficial, and the ethical suggestions of Levi puerile and perverse; or, more correctly, intentionally misleading. They conceal a number of magical formulae of minor importance but major practical value, and the curious should conduct such research as they feel impelled to make in the light of the Cabbala. Their numerical values, Yetziratic attributions, and the arcana of the Atus of Tahuti, supply an adequate clue to such intelligences as are enlightened by sympathy and sincerity.*

The general idea was to have an ever-burning lamp in a temple furnished with talismans appropriate to the elemental, planetary and zodiacal forces of nature. Daily invocations were to be performed with the object of making the light itself a consecrated centre or focus of spiritual energy. This light would then radiate and automatically enlighten such minds as were ready to receive it.

Even today, the experiment seems to me interesting and the conception sublime. I am rather sorry that I lost touch with Don Jesus; I should like very much to know how it turned out.

Since this ritual precedes the writing of the *Book of the Law* in 1904, it has nothing Thelemic about it at all, being much closer to Masonic and Golden Dawn workings of the time. Much of the symbolism is derived from passages taken from the Judeo-Christian *Bible*, as was (and still is) common in Masonic initiation. It's notable that many of the biblical passages are drawn from the *Book of Revelations*. It appears Crowley was already much influenced by notions of the Apocalypse. However Crowley also adds Egyptian touches similar to what he was familiar with from his own Golden Dawn initiations.

As Crowley mentions in the *Confessions*, the letters LPD play an important role in the ceremony. These letters were originally found inscribed near to the Seal of Cagliostro (whom Crowley claimed as an earlier incarnation), pictured below. Eliphas Levi describes the Seal in his *History of Magick*:

"As explained by the cabalistic letters of the names Acharat and Althotas, it expresses the chief characteristics of the Great Arcanum and the Great Work. It is a serpent pierced by an arrow, thus representing the letter Aleph, an image of the union between active and passive, spirit and life, will and light. The arrow is that of the antique Apollo, while the serpent is the python of fable, the green dragon of Hermetic philosophy. The letter Aleph represents equilibrated unity. This pantacle is reproduced under various forms in the talismans of old magic.... The arrow signifies the

Seal of Cagliostro

active principle, will, magical action, the coagulation of the dissolvent, the fixation of the volatile by projection and the penetration of earth by fire. The union of the two is the universal balance, the Great Arcanum, the Great Work, the equilibrium of Jachin and Boaz. The initials L.P.D., which accompany this figure, signify Liberty, Power, Duty, and also Light, Proportion, Density; Law, Principle and Right. The Freemasons have changed the order of these initials, and in the form of L.·.D.·.P.: . they render them as Liberte de Penser, *Liberty of Thought, inscribing these on a symbolical bridge, but for those who are not initiated they substitute* Liberte de Passer, *Liberty of Passage. In the records of the prosecution of Cagliostro it is said that his examination elicited another meaning as follows:* Lilia destrue pedibus: *Trample the lilies under foot; and in support of this version may be cited a Masonic medal of the sixteenth or seventeenth century, depicting a branch of lilies severed by sword, having these words on the exergue:* Talem dabit ultio messem - *Revenge shall give this harvest.*

Crowley was heavily influenced by Levi's work at this time (he would later come to believe that he was Levi's reincarnation as well), as can be seen by the addition of several passages from Levi's work in this ritual; most notably the Elemental Prayers. These Elemental Prayers serve as invocations to the spirits of the elements during the ritual, inviting the salamanders (fire), undines (water), slyphs (air), and gnomes (earth) to participate in consecrating the candidate.

Unfortunately it appears that Crowley's experiment in setting up L.I.L. never worked out. A few years later he set up the A.A. in which the letters LPD took on even more significance (see Crowley's Probationer Oath form reprinted in *The Law is for All* and other places); and later still he joined O.T.O. These two orders formed the great bulk of his work for the rest of his life. Since then this initiation rite has become something of an orphan without a home, and as such, open to us to study and perform.

As an initiation ritual, this piece is somewhat different from the others I've given in the book. It has a very different purpose for one thing - it's designed to initiate and consecrate a candidate into working in a group. The word initiation is derived from Latin roots meaning to begin something new and to participate in secret rites, and initiation is an almost essential prerequisite to good magical group working. Initiation helps bind the new candidate to the group, and serves to transmit in a tightly focused manner the essential beliefs and principles that the group adheres to. In turn that means that an initiation ritual needs to be very well designed and performed by those already in the group.

A good initiation rite needs to contain all of the following:
- A candidate for initiation (obviously)
- Initiation officers who are confirmed members of the group already, and aware of its principles
- A strong dramatic setting
- Some kind of ordeal that the candidate must pass through
- A secret that is passed to the candidate during the ritual
- Moral or ethical teaching that the group espouses
- Oaths of loyalty to the group and its principles
- Fulfilment or enlightenment of the candidate

Building a ritual that contains all of these things in a coherent form is no easy task, and I don't recommend that you try. Even before you can start you need to figure out exactly what the principles of the group are, and of course you have the problem of who has the authority to perform the initiation in the first place.

I strongly recommend that readers apply for initiation in an established, successful, long-running Order - I joined O.T.O. myself over twenty years ago and I'm very happy I did, it changed my life utterly in an extremely positive way. If the group you are working with is already part of an established magical Order such as O.T.O. then there's really no need to work this rite. However I do understand that some people would rather work with their own small group, so if you are forming your own group you could use this rite as a template for your own initiation ritual with only small changes required. Alternately, if you are considering initiation into an established group then this should give you some idea of what initiation is about.

The ritual as written requires just one officer plus the candidate. However I recommend that there be two officers, the second officer leading the candidate around the temple and acting to prompt the candidate on his answers during the initiation. This makes the ritual a lot more fluid in practice. The candidate will certainly require prompting at several points, so when doing this, do be sure to prompt her clearly - don't whisper, but give answers in a slow, clear voice. During initiation candidates tend to be rather nervous and won't pick up whispers too well.

Once you have used the ritual a few times to initiate people into your group, those initiates can of course attend new initiations as spectators, so you might end up with several people in the temple during an initiation. If so, one of them could also be deputised to read the Elemental Prayers during the rite.

This rite makes the candidate "an High Priest". There is evidence to suggest that in later life Aleister Crowley would probably not have used this title quite so freely; in a letter to Frater Achad in 1919 in reference to the Gnostic Catholic Church (Ecclesia Gnostica Catholica) Crowley says:

> *...you can't elect a priest... I am ordained priest and consecrated Bishop and Archbishop by the laying on of hands. Nothing else is valid.*

Since this laying on of hands occurred some years after Crowley wrote this ritual of L.I.L., even by his own reckoning he did not have the spiritual authority to consecrate someone as an High Priest at the time he was putting this ritual together. Crowley was still fairly young and inexperienced when he first wrote this ritual (he was in his mid-Twenties) and to be honest I don't think he fully understood the concept of priesthood at that time - it probably just sounded fairly impressive to him, so he stuck it in. The fact that the initiation didn't seem to have the effect he originally intended would seem to bear out the theory that his decision in this case may have been flawed.

By the same logic if you do decide to use this rite for your group you might want to replace "High Priest" with "New Initiate" instead. It's a much more accurate term in the context of the ritual, so I'd definitely advise such a substitution.

"High Priest" in the original Biblical sense of the word meant someone who performs sacrifices to the gods, particularly animal sacrifice, and there is a reference to this custom within the rite. Although modern Christianity tries to whitewash it, early Jewish religion was heavily based on animal sacrifice - the Biblical story of Cain and Abel is all about the fact that Jehovah prefers animal sacrifice to vegetable sacrifice. I personally have nothing morally against animal sacrifice; it's no different than eating a hamburger after all - and it could be argued that sacrificial animals are at least treated respectfully while they are alive. However I certainly don't encourage readers to go out and start biting the heads off chickens after having undergone this rite. Animal sacrifice requires a great deal of training and skill, not to mention that in many places there are laws against it. The sacrifice performed during this ritual itself is a good example of modern Western sacrificial practice - the new initiate sacrifices the life energy embodied within the flower, salt and other items on the altar to the Gods.

I've excised one section near the end where the Adept talks a couple of paragraphs of Qabalistic nonsense - it's not useful in the context of the rite, and serves no real practical purpose. For reference the excised section is:

> The secret meaning of the first is "the Blood of the Lamb". For the Greek Letters L P D combined give W D M in Coptic, and these again give the Hebrew Word "Dam", blood, which by Temurah yield Car = Lamb. L.V.X. is the mystic expansion of the Cross or Hebrew Tau and if this letter is inserted in the midst of Car we have KThR, Kether the Crown.

> The Age of the Priesthood is 114 years, from L.P.D. and it refers to the mourning of Isis over the Slain Osiris, that is, to the lamentation of the priesthood over their country. For Daleth Mem Ayin means "tear". The Corresponding Sign of Greeting: The Priests weep or sigh heavily. The Answer is 65 and the elder Priest is glad, saying "Adonai hath shone in His Palace", the other is glad also, and replies "Keep Silence".

If you really like it you can add it back in; I'd recommend that you give it on paper to the Candidates as part of their studies after the ritual is over.

The Ritual of Consecration of an High Priest of L.I.L.

Participants: Minimum three
Time required: About an hour
Setup: Relatively complex
Words: Quite a lot
Equipment:
- Coffin (a simple chest or blanket box would do so long as you can put someone in it and close the lid. Do make sure there is adequate ventilation, and do not lock the box! The candidate needs to be able to get out in case of emergencies.)
- Candle or flaming bowl
- Sword
- Bowl of alcohol (I recommend surgical spirit kept in the fridge beforehand. It will feel cold to the touch but it will also evaporate quickly causing a cold sensation immediately after taking the hand out of the liquid.)
- Altar with:
  - Lamp
  - Salt
  - Fire (an unlit candle to be lit by the candidate during the ritual)
  - Rose
  - Water
  - Lighter
- For Candidate
  - Robe
  - Hoodwink & hand bindings
  - Oath for candidate to study and sign beforehand
  - Crown
  - Wand

The Opening

Let the forces of Jupiter be invoked by the hexagram in a temple purified by the elements. Let the Spirit be also invoked.

> [This would be the Golden Dawn Hexagram rite from Liber O. I see no real need for it here to be honest; it seems rather overly complex for opening an initiation rite. Perhaps substituting the group Mark of the Beast ritual as a temple opening would be preferable. In some of Crowley's later initiation rites as well as things like the Gnostic Mass he dispenses with extraneous formalities such as these.]

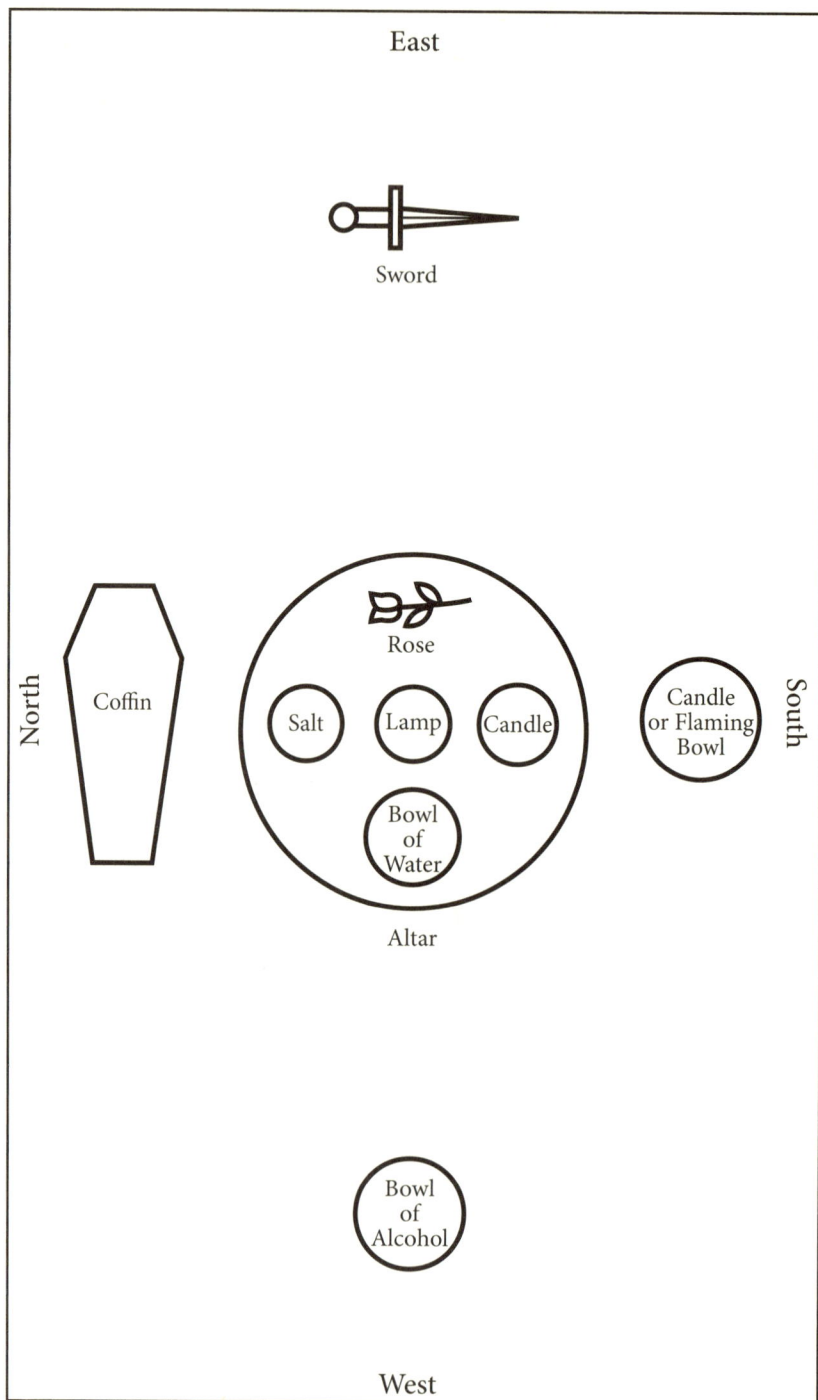

East

Sword

North

Coffin

Rose

Salt Lamp Candle

Candle
or Flaming
Bowl

South

Bowl
of
Water

Altar

Bowl
of
Alcohol

West

The temple has: in the North, a Coffin: in the South, a candle or flaming bowl; in the East, a Sword; in the West, a bowl of bitterly cold alcohol. In the centre, an altar with the Star of Magick Light: N,S,E,W are salt, fire, rose, water.

[The Star of Magick Light is presumably an electric lamp. The attribution of the equipment to the four quarters appears to be wrong in several places in the original manuscript - I have altered the text to fix this.]

The opening being finished, let the doors be opened; and let the Introducing Adept admit the Candidate, his hands bound and his eyes blinded. Follows the Ritual.

[Introducing Adept would normally be Second Officer, but may be another initiate if there are enough people. The Candidate should have spent some time in another room meditating before being bound and hoodwinked and brought to the temple.]

Ritual

Adept: **Who art thou?**

Candidate: **_____ [candidate's name/magical name], in darkness and slavery which I have voluntarily taken myself; that I may bring Light and Liberty to others.**

[In each case, the Candidate should be prompted with the correct answer by the Second Officer.]

Adept: **Whence comest thou?**

Candidate: **From the Place of the Meditations.**

Adept: **Whither goest thou?**

Candidate: **To the Place of the Tryings.**

Adept: **Art thou furnished for the journey?**

Candidate: **I am naked, and poor, and miserable.**

Adept: **Hast thou nought to sacrifice unto the guardians of the Ways?**

Candidate: The Breath of my Nostrils, the Flesh of my Body, the
                    Tears of mine Eyes and the Blood of my Heart.

Adept: Add thou thereto the Silence of Thy Tongue. Let the
                    Purification be performed.

(Ritual J is solemnly recited of Candidate.)

   [Ritual J was the Oath of Obligation used in the early Golden Dawn Neophyte
   initiation. It contained clauses in which the candidate promised to keep secret the
   Order's rituals and the names of its members; and promised not to use the powers
   given for evil purposes etc. See appendix for the original text. Your group might want
   to create something similar to fit here.]

Adept: Thou hast signed the Oath of thine Obligation: art thou
                    now ready to confirm its provision in this Presence?

   [This sentence implies that it should be printed on paper and given to the Candidate
   before the ritual to be studied and signed. Note that this is not common practice in
   O.T.O. and other Thelemic Orders today. It could be given to the Candidate at this
   point to be signed if you think that would work better.]

Candidate: I am.

   [Do not prompt the Candidate here, he must agree of his own free Will.]

(Candidate is led to foot of Altar and kneels. His hands are unbound; they
are placed around the lamp in the centre, as if ready to support it. The Oath
is then taken.)

Adept: Knowest thou the Force of the name I H V H ?

   [Usually pronounced Yod Heh Vav Heh, or Jehovah.]

                    At this name the Elements are moved. Thy Name is the
                    Child of the Children of the Elements: In This Name
                    Tetragrammaton dost thou trust?

Candidate: It is written: It is better to trust in Tetragrammaton
                    than to put confidence in Princes.

   [The candidate should again be prompted here]

Adept: The River Kishon swept them away: that ancient river, the River Kishon. The Lord is a Man of War: the Lord of Hosts is his name.

The Dukes of Edom were amazed: trembling took hold of the Mighty in Moab. Lord, when thou wentest out of Seir; when thou marchedst out of the field of Edom! He bowed the Heavens also and came down, and Darkness was under His feet; at the Brightness that was before Him the thick clouds passed: hailstones and coals of fire! Tetragrammaton thundered through the Heavens and the Mighty One gave forth His Voice. He sent out his arrows and scattered then; He hurled forth His lightnings and destroyed them. At Thy Rebuke, Oh Lord! At the blast of the Breath of Thy Nostrils! The Voice of Thy Thunder was in the Heavens: the Lightnings lightened the World: the Earth trembled and shook!

Oh Lord I have heard thy Speech and was afraid. The Voice of the Lord is upon the Waters! The God of Glory thundereth! The Lord is upon many waters! The Voice of the Lord is powerful! The Voice of the Lord is full of Majesty! The Voice of the Lord breaketh the cedars: yea, the Lord breaketh the cedars of Lebanon. The Voice of the Lord is full of Majesty! The Voice of the Lord divideth the Flames of Fire! The Voice of the Lord shaketh the Wilderness! Yea! the Lord shaketh the Wilderness of Kedar.

Before Him went the Pestilence: and Flaming Fire went forth at his feet. He stood and measured the Earth! He beheld and drove asunder the Nations. And the Everlasting Mountains were scattered: the Perpetual Hills did bow!

Ateh Gibor le-Olahm, Adonai. Let Power be ascribed unto the name I H V H.

[This is a compilation of various verses from the Old Testament of the Bible, including sections from Judges and Exodus. This particular version is taken from Part III of the Golden Dawn Philosophus initiation ritual.]

(Candidate is led to South and his right hand moved towards the Fire.)

[Needless to say, you need to be careful here! Do NOT actually BURN the candidate! Simply move his hand near enough to the flame so that the heat can be felt without any injury. Do NOT hold or force the candidate's hand into danger! Also be wary of the candidate's sleeve - it's very easy to set someone on fire if you are not careful! In this, as in all rituals containing open flames, have a fire extinguisher nearby and make sure everyone knows how to use it.]

> I said: Is not the Fire mine, and the Inhabitants thereof? Hear then the Voice of the Fire.

(Recite Prayer of Salamanders)

> Immortal, Eternal, Ineffable and Uncreated Father of all, borne upon the Chariot of Worlds which ever roll in ceaseless motion. Ruler over the Etherial Vastness where the Throne of Thy Power is raised from the summit of which Thine Eyes behold all and Thy Pure and Holy Ears hear all – help us, thy children, whom Thou hast loved since the birth of the Ages of Time! Thy Majesty, Golden, Vast and Eternal, shineth above the Heaven of Stars. Above them art Thou exalted.

> O Thou Flashing Fire, there Thou illuminatest all things with Thine Insupportable Glory, whence flow the Ceaseless Streams of Splendour which nourish Thine Infinite Spirit. This Infinite Spirit nourishest all and maketh that inexhausible Treasure of Generation which ever encompasseth Thee replete with the numberless forms wherewith Thou hast filled it from the Beginning. From this Spirit arise those most holy Kings who are around Thy Throne, and who compose Thy Court.

> O Universal Father, One and Alone! Father alike of Immortals and Mortals. Thou hast especially created Powers similar unto thy Thought Eternal and unto Thy Venerable Essence. Thou hast established them above the Angels who announce Thy Will to the world. Lastly, thou hast created us as a third Order in our Elemental Empire.

There our continual exercise is to praise and to adore Thy Desires; there we ceaselessy burn with Eternal Aspirations unto Thee, O Father! O Mother of Mothers! O Archetype Eternal of Maternity and Love! O Son, the Flower of all Sons! Form of all Forms! Soul, Spirit, Harmony, and Numeral of all things! Amen!

(Candidate to West and his left hand placed in freezing mixture)

[Again, do not force the candidate into danger. The mixture needs only to be cold, not freezing, and the candidate's hand should should only be placed in the cold mixture and not HELD there].

It is written: Who shall abide His frost?

(Recite Prayer of Undines.)

Terrible King of the Sea, Thou who holdest the Keys of the Cataracts of Heaven, and who enclosest the subterraean Waters in the cavernous hollows of Earth. King of the Deluge and of the Rains of Spring. Thou who openest the sources of the rivers and of the fountains; thou who commandest moisture which is, as it were, the Blood of the Earth, to become the sap of the plants. We adore Thee and we invoke Thee. Speak Thou unto us, Thy Mobile and changeful creatures, in the Great Tempests, and we shall tremble before Thee. Speak to us also in the murmer of the limpid Waters, and we shall desire Thy love.

O Vastness! wherein all the rivers of Being seek to lose themselves – which renew themselves ever in Thee! O Thou Ocean of Infinite Perfection! O Height which reflectest Thyself in the Depth! O Depth which exhalest into the Height! Lead us unto the true life through intelligence, through love! Lead us into immortality through sacrifice, that we may be found worthy to offer one day unto Thee, the Water, the Blood and the Tears, for the Remission of Sins! Amen.

(Candidate is taken to the East and blood drawn from heart.)

*[No sharp blades or pointed weapons should be allowed in an initiation temple -
blunt weapons ONLY. You do not need to draw physical blood here! Symbolically
holding the flat of the blade of a blunt sword to the candidate's heart is enough.]*

The Word of Tetragrammaton is a sharp sword: the
Breath of the Lord divideth the reins of men.

(Recite Prayer of Sylphs.)

SPIRIT OF LIFE! Spirit of Wisdom! Whose breath
giveth forth and withdraweth the form of all things:
THOU before whom the life of beings is but a shadow
which changeth, and a vapour which passeth;
THOU who mountest upon the clouds, and who walkest
upon the Wings of the Wind;
THOU who breathest forth Thy breath, and endless space
is peopled;
THOU who drawest in Thy breath, and all that cometh
from Thee returneth unto Thee!
CEASELESS MOTION in Eternal Stability, be Thou
eternally blessed!

We praise Thee and we bless Thee in the Changeless
Empire of Created Light, of Shades, of Reflections, and
of Images, and we aspire without cessation unto Thy
immutable and imperishable brilliance. Let the ray of
Thy intelligence and the warmth of Thy love penetrate
even unto us! Then that which is Volatile shall be Fixed;
the Shadow shall be a Body; the Spirit of Air shall be a
Soul; the Dream shall be a Thought. And no more shall
we be swept away by the Tempest, but we shall hold the
Bridles of the Winged Steeds of Dawn. And we shall
direct the course of the Evening Breeze to fly before Thee!
O Spirit of Spirits! O Eternal Soul of Souls! O imperishable
Breath of Life! O creative sigh! O Mouth which breathest
forth and withdrawest the life of all beings, in the flux
and reflux of Thine Eternal Word, which is the Divine
Ocean of Movement and of Truth! Amen.

(Candidate is taken to North, placed in coffin and closed up.)

As for man, his days are as grass, as a flower he flourisheth: dust thou art, and to dust shalt thou return.

(Recite Prayer of Gnomes.)

O Invisible King, who, taking the Earth for Foundation, didst hollow its depths to fill them with Thy Almighty Power. Thou whose Name shaketh the Arches of the World, Thou who causest the Seven Metals to flow in the veins of the rocks, King of the Seven Lights, Rewarder of the subterranean workers, lead us into the desirable Air and into the Realm of Splendour. We watch and we labour unceasingly, we seek and we hope, by the twelve stones of the Holy City, by the buried Talismans, by the Axis of the Lodestone which passes through the centre of the Earth – O Lord, O Lord, O Lord! Have pity upon those who suffer. Expand our hearts, unbind and upraise our minds, enlarge our natures.

O Stability and Motion! O Darkness veiled in Brilliance! O Day clothed in Night! O Master who never doest withhold the wages of Thy workmen! O Silver Whiteness – O Golden Splendour! O Crown of Living and Harmonious Diamond! Thou who wearest the Heavens on Thy Finger like a ring of Sapphire! Thou who hidest beneath the Earth in the Kingdom of Gems, the marvellous Seed of the Stars! Live, reign, and be Thou the Eternal Dispenser of the Treasures whereof Thou hast made us the wardens. Amen.

[Pause.]

And I heard a Great Voice out of Heaven saying: It is the Word of Tetragrammaton: it is the speech of I H V H. Seal up the Book: for the Name is written and the Word vibrated. And I said: "What is the Name?" And a great thunder rose up and roared and in its echo was the Name of Death.

(Knock once)

[Adept gives one hard knock on the lid of the coffin while Candidate is inside]

And I saw in the Midst as it were a Lamb slain, having seven horns and seven eyes, which are the seven spirits of God sent forth unto all the world. And the Four Beasts and the Four and Twenty Elders fell down, saying "Thou art worthy to take the Book, and to open the Seals thereof: for Thou hast redeemed us to God by thy blood out of every kindred people and nation and hast made us unto our God Kings and Priests!" Let the dead rise from their tombs!

For as in Adam all die, even so in Christ shall all be made alive! The first man is of the earth, earthy: the Second Man is the Lord from Heaven! The first man Adam was made a loving soul: the last Adam a quickening spirit

Let the dead rise from their tombs!
I AM, the Resurrection and the Life! I am He that liveth and was dead: and behold I am alive for evermore AMEN and have the Keys of Hell and of Death.

Let the dead rise from their tombs.

In the name of Osiris, I say unto Thee, Arise!
In the name of Osiris, I say unto Thee, Arise!
In the name of Osiris, I say unto Thee, Arise!

[Candidate is taken out of the coffin.]

(Candidate is assisted to kneel at altar.)

Awake thou that sleepest and rise from among the dead; and Christ shall give thee Light.

(Unbandage Candidate's eyes.)

Lux Umbra Kristi
Phos Logos Uiou

L.P.D.: L.V.X.: the Flaming Star of Light!

[The Initiator may wish to give the signs of L.V.X. here.]

I now clothe thee with the Robe and Crown of the High Priest: I bestow on Thee the consecrated Wand.

[For a female candidate change Priest to Priestess, obviously - or just use the phrase New Initiate, and solve that problem easily.]

The Grand Word is L.P.D. answered by L.V.X.

[I've taken out a bunch of Qabalistic babble here as having no real relevance or usefulness. See note above.]

But the Sign of True Esotericism is thus given.
The first priest looks to heaven saying "I watch".
The second, holding his hands as if to shield a flame: "I work".
The first, looking to earth, "I weep".
The second, pointing to heaven, "It beams".
The first, as shielding a flame, "It burns!"

[The Initiator should demonstrate these signs as he explains them, and the Candidate should repeat them to make sure he understands them.]

(Both Priests then give the grip: each places his arms around the neck of the other, arms straight, thus forming a hexagram; both look to heaven: they slowly lower their eyes and when they meet, the arms are crossed on the breast, and both bow profoundly.)

[When both bow here, do be careful that you don't bang your heads together! And yes, I have seen it happen...]

The Pass-Word is changed annually; it is at present _____.

[If you use passwords for your group, insert yours here. Otherwise just leave this line out.]

By virtue of which mystic Words and Signs I now declare thee fitted to sacrifice before the Most High: for in the name of Jeheshua art thou admitted to the mysteries hereof. Sacrifice thou therefore the four into the One. Cast the salt into the bowl; light the flame and place the rose therein!

[Jeheshua is the original Hebrew pronounciation of Jesus]

(Done.)

Let the Spirit of the Gods descend!

(Candidate kneels).

> I finally invoke upon Thee the Light Divine in the divine Name Jeheshua Jehovashah - and lo! I saw you to the end!
>
> By the virtue of the Name Osiris, in the Divine Name I A O , I say "Receive Thou the Holy Ghost! Whatsoever thou shalt loose on earth, shall be loosed in heaven: whatsoeverthou shalt bind on earth shall be bound in heaven!"
>
> Arise, High Priest of _____ [name of your group] for by this Name I call thee. Hail unto ye, O ye Great Gods of Heaven! Give me your hands, for this One is made as ye! Who is this that hath passed under the power of the Name? Who is he that cometh triumphant from the trials? Hail unto thee, O Thoth! Is not his name written in thy book of Life?

(High Priest led to East.)

[i.e. the candidate.]

> This is thy blood, the symbol of thy life. It shall be for a sign, that thou hast shed it willingly for men; or, if thou failest in thine oath, it shall be a practical and material link whereby the Chiefs of the Order shall the more speedily and easily execute vengeance upon Thee - yea - unto the Uttermost.

[The implication seems to be that the candidate is shown his own blood on the blade of the sword in the East, or that somehow it is preserved in a vial or something similar. I suggest that you just show the candidate the sword blade at this point, and keep the whole thing on a symbolic level.]

These kind of magical threats were commonplace in the past in initiation rituals. I am not a huge fan of them, and they should be taken as symbolic threats at most. At no time should anyone ever be magically attacked for disagreeing with the group or wanting to leave. Candidates who break their Oaths punish themselves through their own dishonour, there's no need for vengeance to be wreaked upon them by someone else.]

> Return then to the Altar and kneel in humble prayer unto the Gods, that they may hold thee in their hands to keep thee in all thy ways.

(Done, while Initiator chants:)

> O Lord, deliver me from hell's great fear and gloom!
> Loose thou my spirit from the larvae of the tomb!
> I seek them in their dread abodes without affright:
> On them will I impose my will, the law of light.
> I bid the night conceive the glittering hemisphere.
> Arise, O sun, arise! O moon, shine white and clear!
> I seek them in their dread abodes without affright:
> On them will I impose my will, the law of light.
> Their faces and their shapes are terrible and strange.
> These devils by my might to angels I will change.
> These nameless horrors I address without affright:
> On them will I impose my will, the law of light.
> These are the phantoms pale of mine astonied view,
> Yet none but I their blasted beauty can renew;
> For to the abyss of hell I plunge without affright:
> On them will I impose my will, the law of light.

> Est, sit, esto, fiat!
> Ad Virginis Fructifictionem
> Ad Gloriam Roseae Crucis
> Ad Matris Amorem
> Ad Patris Vitam
> Ad Lucem; ad Gloriam
> Tui Nominis Ineffabilis
> AMOUN

[The first line means something like "it is, it is, it is, it is" expressed in different ways
To the fructified Virgin
To the Glory of the Rosy Cross
To Love of the Mother
To the Life of the Father
To the Light; to the Glory
of Your Ineffable Name

AMOUN is a creator god of Egypt, here used to seal the prayer as AMEN is used in
Christian worship.]

Chapter Thirteen
The Ritual of Initiation
of a Thelemite

(A reworking of the Consecration of an High Priest of L.I.L.)

As mentioned in the last chapter, the foundation of the Lamp of Invisible Light magical order pre-dated the writing of the *Book of the Law* by several years, and thus the consecration rite of An High Priest of L.I.L. is not in any way Thelemic in its language, being largely based on Biblical sources. A hundred years ago this Biblical language and its context was familiar to everyone and considered the height of mystical expression. However to many young people coming into Thelemic magick today, the *Bible* is little more than meaningless drivel. We're living in a New Aeon where the lofty phrases mentioned in the original rite no longer hold power over the people we're trying to initiate.

So in order to make the ritual a little more relevant I thought I'd try to build a new version of this ritual, somewhat in the manner which Crowley might have done if he'd been writing it ten or twenty years later. We've already seen how Crowley's attitude towards ritual changed throughout his life after his experience with Rose in Cairo, and again after the Evocation of Bartzabel and his subsequent involvement with O.T.O. When Crowley originally joined O.T.O. its initiation rituals were extremely close to those of traditional Freemasonry; recognising that they had great power in their structure, but were full of irrelevant Biblical references, Crowley rewrote them to harmonise fully with the principles and language of the *Book of the Law*.

Crowley never bothered to update the L.I.L. ritual, since by that time L.I.L. was completely moribund; so I've completed the job by putting it through a process of "Thelemicisation" in a similar way to which Crowley altered and improved the O.T.O. rituals. I've taken out all of the Judeo-Christian elements, and replaced the Biblical quotes with sections from *Liber Tzaddi*, one of the Thelemic Holy Books that particularly deals with the process of initiation. I've also replaced kneeling with standing in many places, as more fitting to the subject matter of *Liber Tzaddi*, and tweaked and simplified a few other small bits as well. The result is an almost entirely new ritual based on Crowley's original framework, and still using words written by him; but focused now on dealing with the direct initiation of a candidate into a working Thelemic group. If you are forming a new magical group, you could still use the original version of this ritual as your main initiation rite, as mentioned in the last chapter; but I would recommend using this version instead.

I've also taken out the concept that the ritual is a consecration of "an High Priest". As mentioned in the last chapter, after becoming a Bishop of the Gnostic Catholic Church (E.G.C.) Crowley's opinion on priesthood seems to have changed significantly from the opinions of his youth. Crowley reorganised E.G.C. along Thelemic lines, writing the Gnostic Mass and aligning the Church more closely with O.T.O. practice. The consecration of an E.G.C. Bishop became part of the O.T.O. Seventh Degree ritual, and the ordination of a Priest or Priestess now occurs within the O.T.O. Degree of Knight of the East and West.

So to avert possible confusion I have modified this rite to work better as a general purpose initiation ritual without getting into any considerations of priesthood. It certainly doesn't lose anything in the process, quite the opposite I think; concentrating it on being solely an initation ritual makes it much more focused on its original purpose.

You may wish to change the Sign of True Esotericism to a private recognition sign better suited to your own group's purpose. Examples of such signs are the L.V.X. signs of the Golden Dawn or Crowley's N.O.X. signs as used in the Mark of the Beast ritual.

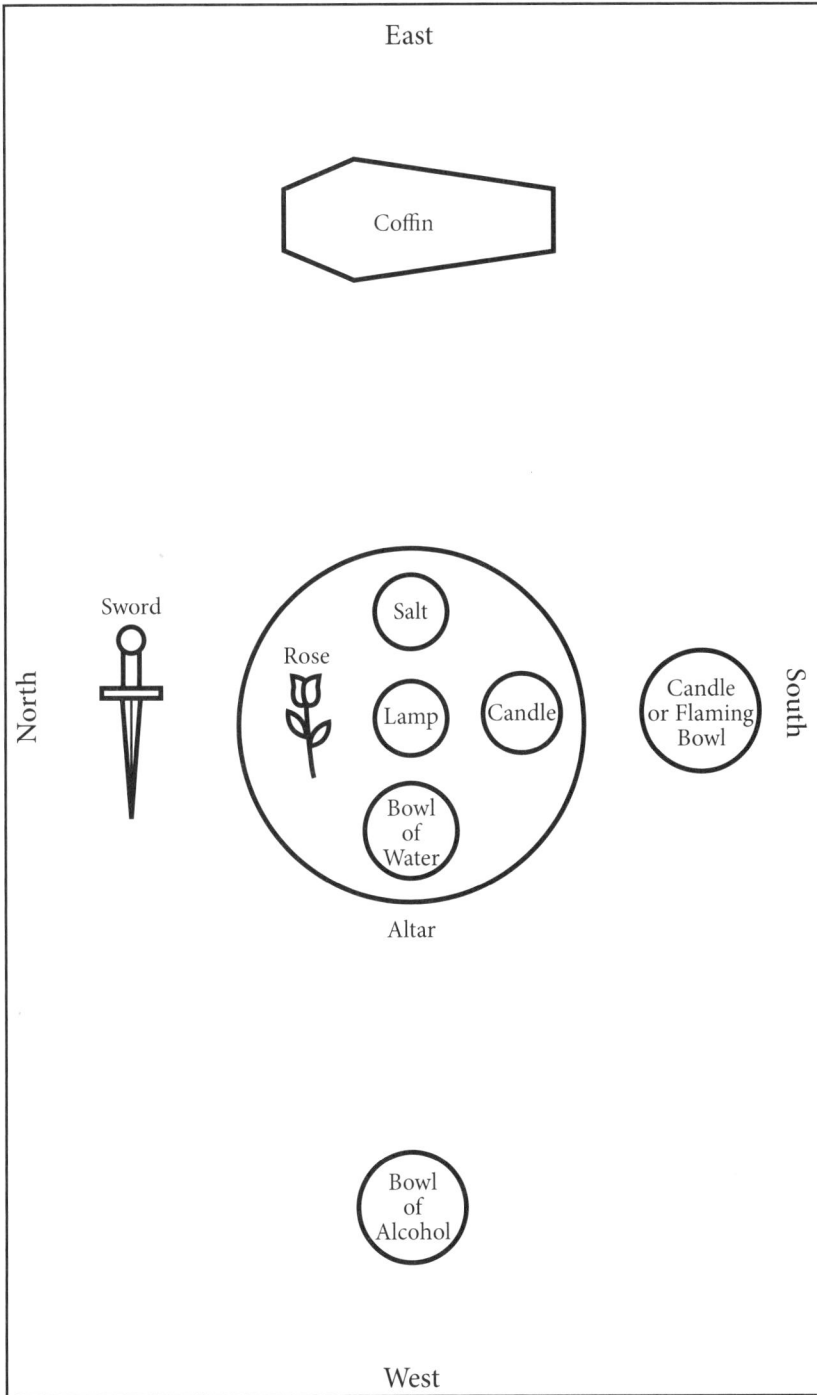

East

Coffin

North

South

Sword

Rose

Salt

Lamp

Candle

Bowl
of
Water

Candle
or Flaming
Bowl

Altar

Bowl
of
Alcohol

West

The Ritual of Initiation of a Thelemite

Participants: Minimum 3
Time required: About an hour
Setup: Relatively complex
Words: Quite a lot
Equipment: • Coffin
                    • Candle or flaming bowl
                    • Sword
                    • Bowl of alcohol
                    • Altar with:
                    • Lamp
                    • Salt
                    • Fire
                    • Rose
                    • Water
                    • For Candidate:
                      • Robe
                      • Hoodwink & hand bindings
                      • Oath for candidate to study and sign beforehand

Opening

Let the forces of the Flaming Star be invoked in a temple purified by the elements.

> [The group Mark of the Beast ritual given earlier would be ideal for this.]

The temple has: in the East, a Coffin: in the South, a candle or flaming bowl; in the North, a Sword; in the West, a bowl of bitterly cold alcohol. In the centre, an altar with the Star of Magick Light: N,S,E,W are rose, fire, salt, water.

> [The Star of Magick Light is presumably an electric lamp. The attribution of the equipment to the four quarters is slightly different than in the original version of this rite, to fit more closely with Thelemic attributions.]

The opening being finished, let the doors be opened; and let the Introducing Adept admit the Candidate, his hands bound and his eyes blinded. Follows the Ritual.

> [Introducing Adept would normally be Second Officer, but may be another initiate if there are enough people.]

Ritual

Adept: Who art thou?

Candidate: _____, in darkness and slavery which I have
                voluntarily taken myself; that I may bring Light and
                Liberty to others.

  *[In each case, the Candidate should be prompted with the correct answer by the
  Second Officer]*

Adept: Whence comest thou?

Candidate: From the Place of the Meditations.
Adept: Whither goest thou?

Candidate: To the Place of the Tryings.

Adept: Art thou furnished for the journey?

Candidate: I am naked, and poor, and miserable.

Adept: Hast thou nought to sacrifice unto the guardians of the
                Ways?

Candidate: The Breath of my Nostrils, the Flesh of my Body, the
                Tears of mine Eyes and the Blood of my Heart.

Adept: Add thou thereto the Silence of Thy Tongue.
                Let the Purification be performed.

(Second Adept brings salt and water from the altar and makes a cross with
each before the candidate.)

  *[This is, a cross with the salt, then another cross with the water. They are not mixed
  until much later in the ritual.]*

Adept: Be the candidate pure of body and soul!

(Second Adept brings rose and fire from the altar and makes a cross with
each before the candidate.)

  [Another two crosses, as above.]

Adept: **Be the candidate fervent of body and soul!**

(Ritual J is solemnly recited by Candidate.)

> *[Ritual J was the Oath of Obligation used in the early Golden Dawn Neophyte initiation. It contained clauses in which the candidate promised to keep secret the Order's rituals and the names of its members; and promised not to use the powers given for evil purposes etc. See appendix for the original text. Your group might want to create something similar to fit here.]*

Adept: **Thou hast signed the Oath of thine Obligation: art thou now ready to confirm its provision in this Presence?**

> *[This sentence implies that it should be printed on paper and given to the Candidate before the ritual to be studied and signed. Note that this is not common practice in O.T.O. and other Thelemic Orders today. It could be given to the Candidate at this point to be signed if you think that would work better.]*

Candidate: **I am.**

> *[Do not prompt the Candidate in this line, he must agree of his own free Will.]*

(Candidate is led to foot of Altar. His hands are unbound; they are placed around the lamp in the centre, as if ready to support it. The Oath is then taken.)

Adept: **Knowest thou the Force of the name Ra-Hoor-Khuit?**

Candidate: **At this name an Universe is crushed.**

> *[Candidate may be prompted on from here on.]*

Adept: **Thy Name is the Child of the Children of the Universe: In This Name Ra-Hoor-Khuit dost thou trust?**

Candidate: **Success is my proof, courage is my armour.**

Adept: **In the name of the Lord of Initiation, Amen.**
                    I fly and I alight as an hawk:
                    of mother-of-emerald are my mighty-sweeping wings.
                    I swoop down upon the black earth;
                    and it gladdens into green at my coming.

Children of Earth! rejoice! rejoice exceedingly;
for your salvation is at hand.
The end of sorrow is come;
I will ravish you away into mine unutterable joy.
I will kiss you, and bring you to the bridal:
I will spread a feast before you in the house of happiness.
I am not come to rebuke you, or to enslave you.
I bid you not turn from your voluptuous ways,
from your idleness, from your follies.
But I bring you joy to your pleasure,
peace to your languor, wisdom to your folly.
All that ye do is right, if so be that ye enjoy it.
I am come against sorrow, against weariness,
against them that seek to enslave you.
I pour you lustral wine,
that giveth you delight both at the sunset and the dawn.
Come with me, and I will give you
all that is desirable upon the earth.
Because I give you that of which Earth
and its joys are but as shadows.
They flee away, but my joy abideth even unto the end.

(Candidate is led to South and his right hand moved towards the Fire.)

[Needless to say, you need to be careful here! Do NOT actually BURN the candidate! Simply move his hand near enough to the flame so that the heat can be felt without any injury. Do NOT hold or force the candidate's hand into danger! Also be wary of the candidate's sleeve - it's very easy to set someone on fire if you are not careful! In this, as in all rituals containing open flames, have a fire extinguisher nearby and know how to use it.]

Adept: Let him come through the first ordeal, & it will be to him as silver.

(Recite Prayer of Salamanders)

Immortal, Eternal, Ineffable and Uncreated Father of all, borne upon the Chariot of Worlds which ever roll in ceaseless motion. Ruler over the Etherial Vastness where the Throne of Thy Power is raised from the summit of which Thine Eyes behold all and Thy Pure and Holy Ears hear all – help us, thy children, whom Thou hast loved since the birth of the Ages of Time! Thy Majesty, Golden, Vast and Eternal, shineth above the Heaven of Stars. Above them art Thou exalted.

O Thou Flashing Fire, there Thou illuminatest all things with Thine Insupportable Glory, whence flow the Ceaseless Streams of Splendour which nourish Thine Infinite Spirit. This Infinite Spirit nourishest all and maketh that inexhausible Treasure of Generation which ever encompasseth Thee replete with the numberless forms wherewith Thou hast filled it from the Beginning. From this Spirit arise those most holy Kings who are around Thy Throne, and who compose Thy Court.

O Universal Father, One and Alone! Father alike of Immortals and Mortals. Thou hast especially created Powers similar unto thy Thought Eternal and unto Thy Venerable Essence. Thou hast established them above the Angels who announce Thy Will to the world. Lastly, thou hast created us as a third Order in our Elemental Empire.

There our continual exercise is to praise and to adore Thy Desires; there we ceaselessy burn with Eternal Aspirations unto Thee, O Father! O Mother of Mothers!

O Archetype Eternal of Maternity and Love! O Son, the Flower of all Sons! Form of all Forms! Soul, Spirit, Harmony, and Numeral of all things! Amen!

(Candidate to West and his left hand placed in freezing mixture)

[Again, do not force the candidate into danger. The mixture needs only to be cold, not freezing, and the candidate's hand should should only be placed in the cold mixture and not HELD there.]

Adept: **Through the second, gold.**

(Recite Prayer of Undines.)

Terrible King of the Sea, Thou who holdest the Keys of the Cataracts of Heaven, and who enclosest the subterraean Waters in the cavernous hollows of Earth. King of the Deluge and of the Rains of Spring. Thou who openest the sources of the rivers and of the fountains; thou who commandest moisture which is, as it were, the Blood of the Earth, to become the sap of the plants. We adore Thee and we invoke Thee. Speak Thou unto us, Thy Mobile and changeful creatures, in the Great Tempests, and we shall tremble before Thee. Speak to us also in the murmer of the limpid Waters, and we shall desire Thy love.

O Vastness! wherein all the rivers of Being seek to lose themselves – which renew themselves ever in Thee! O Thou Ocean of Infinite Perfection! O Height which reflectest Thyself in the Depth! O Depth which exhalest into the Height! Lead us unto the true life through intelligence, through love! Lead us into immortality through sacrifice, that we may be found worthy to offer one day unto Thee, the Water, the Blood and the Tears, for the Remission of Sins! Amen.

(Candidate is taken to the North and blood drawn from heart)

[No sharp blades or pointed weapons should EVER be allowed in a temple - blunt weapons ONLY. You do not need to draw physical blood here! Symbolically holding the blunt sword to the candidate's heart is enough.]

Adept: Through the third, stones of precious water.

(Recite Prayer of Sylphs.)

SPIRIT OF LIFE! Spirit of Wisdom! Whose breath giveth forth and withdraweth the form of all things: THOU before whom the life of beings is but a shadow which changeth, and a vapour which passeth; THOU who mountest upon the clouds, and who walkest upon the Wings of the Wind. THOU who breathest forth Thy breath, and endless space is peopled; THOU who drawest in Thy breath, and all that cometh from Thee returneth unto Thee! CEASELESS MOTION in Eternal Stability, be Thou eternally blessed!

We praise Thee and we bless Thee in the Changeless Empire of Created Light, of Shades, of Reflections, and of Images, and we aspire without cessation unto Thy immutable and imperishable brilliance. Let the ray of Thy intelligence and the warmth of Thy love penetrate even unto us! Then that which is Volatile shall be Fixed; the Shadow shall be a Body; the Spirit of Air shall be a Soul; the Dream shall be a Thought. And no more shall we be swept away by the Tempest, but we shall hold the Bridles of the Winged Steeds of Dawn. And we shall direct the course of the Evening Breeze to fly before Thee! O Spirit of Spirits! O Eternal Soul of Souls! O imperishable Breath of Life O creative sigh! O Mouth which breathest forth and withdrawest the life of all beings, in the flux and reflux of Thine Eternal Word, which is the Divine Ocean of Movement and of Truth! Amen.

(Candidate is taken to East, placed in coffin and closed up)

Adept: Through the fourth, ultimate sparks of the intimate fire.

(Recite Prayer of Gnomes.)

O Invisible King, who, taking the Earth for Foundation, didst hollow its depths to fill them with Thy Almighty Power. Thou whose Name shaketh the Arches of the World, Thou who causest the Seven Metals to flow in the veins of the rocks, King of the Seven Lights, Rewarder of the subterranean workers, lead us into the desirable Air and into the Realm of Splendour. We watch and we labour unceasingly, we seek and we hope, by the twelve stones of the Holy City, by the buried Talismans, by the Axis of the Lodestone which passes through the centre of the Earth – O Lord, O Lord, O Lord! Have pity upon those who suffer. Expand our hearts, unbind and upraise our minds, enlarge our natures.

O Stability and Motion! O Darkness veiled in Brilliance! O Day clothed in Night! O Master who never doest withhold the wages of Thy workmen! O Silver Whiteness – O Golden Splendour! O Crown of Living and Harmonious Diamond! Thou who wearest the Heavens on Thy Finger like a ring of Sapphire! Thou who hidest beneath the Earth in the Kingdom of Gems, the marvellous Seed of the Stars! Live, reign, and be Thou the Eternal Dispenser of the Treasures whereof Thou hast made us the wardens. Amen.

(Pause.)

> I have hidden myself beneath a mask: I am a black and terrible God.
>
> With courage conquering fear shall ye approach me: ye shall lay down your heads upon mine altar, expecting the sweep of the sword.
>
> But the first kiss of love shall be radiant on your lips; and all my darkness and terror shall turn to light and joy.

(Knock once.)

[The Adept gives one hard knock on the lid of the coffin while Candidate is inside]

> O my children, ye are more beautiful than the flowers: ye must not fade in your season.
>
> I love you; I would sprinkle you with the divine dew of immortality.
>
> This immortality is no vain hope beyond the grave: I offer you the certain consciousness of bliss.
>
> I offer it at once, on earth; before an hour hath struck upon the bell, ye shall be with Me in the Abodes that are beyond Decay.
>
> In the name of Osiris, I say unto Thee, Arise!
>
> In the name of Osiris, I say unto Thee, Arise!
>
> In the name of Osiris, I say unto Thee, Arise!

(Candidate is lifted from coffin and assisted to stand at altar.)

> My adepts stand upright; their head above the heavens, their feet below the hells.
>
> Also I give you power earthly and joy earthly; wealth, and health, and length of days. Adoration and love shall cling to your feet, and twine around your heart.
>
> Only your mouths shall drink of a delicious wine - the wine of Iacchus; they shall reach ever to the heavenly kiss of the Beautiful God.

(Unbandage Candidate's eyes.)

> L.V.X. - the Flaming Star of Light!

[The Initiator may wish to give the signs of L.V.X. here.]

> I now clothe thee with the Robe
> of the Initiate of _____.

[Enter the name of your group.]

> The Sign of True Esotericism is thus given.
> The first priest looks to heaven saying "I watch".
> The second, holding his hands as if to shield a flame:
> "I work".
> The first, looking to earth, "I weep".
> The second, pointing to heaven, "It beams".
> The first, as shielding a flame, "It burns!"

[The Initiator should demonstrate these signs as he explains them, and the Candidate should repeat them to make sure he understands them.]

(Both Priests then give the grip: each places his arms around the neck of the other, arms straight, thus forming a hexagram; both look to heaven: they slowly lower their eyes and when they meet, the arms are crossed on the breast, and both bow profoundly.)

[When both bow here, do be careful that you don't bang your heads together! And yes, I have seen it happen...]

> The Pass-Word is changed annually;
> it is at present _____.

[If you use passwords for your group, insert yours here. Otherwise just leave this line out.]

> By virtue of which mystic Words and Signs I now declare
> thee fitted to sacrifice before the Most High: for in
> the name of Ra-Hoor-Khuit art thou admitted to the
> mysteries hereof. Sacrifice thou therefore the four into
> the One. Cast the salt into the bowl; light the flame and
> place the rose therein!

(Done.)

> Let the Spirit of the Gods descend!
> I finally invoke upon Thee the Light Divine in the divine
> Name Ra-Hoor-Khuit!

They shall be masters of majesty and might; they shall be beautiful and joyous; they shall be clothed with victory and splendour; they shall stand upon the firm foundation; the kingdom shall be theirs; yea, the kingdom shall be theirs.

Come forth, Initiate of_____for by this Name I call thee. Hail unto ye, O ye Great Gods of Heaven! Give me your hands, for this One is made as ye! Who is this that hath passed under the power of the Name? Who is he that cometh triumphant from the trials? Hail unto thee, O Thoth! Is not his name written in thy book of Life?

Return then to the Altar and stand in humble prayer unto the Gods, that they may hold thee in their hands to keep thee in all thy ways.

(Done, while Initiator chants:)

O Lord, deliver me from hell's great fear and gloom!
Loose thou my spirit from the larvae of the tomb!
I seek them in their dread abodes without affright:
On them will I impose my will, the law of light.
I bid the night conceive the glittering hemisphere.
Arise, O sun, arise! O moon, shine white and clear!
I seek them in their dread abodes without affright:
On them will I impose my will, the law of light.
Their faces and their shapes are terrible and strange.
These devils by my might to angels I will change.
These nameless horrors I address without affright:
On them will I impose my will, the law of light.
These are the phantoms pale of mine astonied view,
Yet none but I their blasted beauty can renew;
For to the abyss of hell I plunge without affright:
On them will I impose my will, the law of light.
Est, sit, esto, fiat!
Ad Virginis Fructifictionem
Ad Gloriam Roseae Crucis
Ad Matris Amorem
Ad Patris Vitam
Ad Lucem; ad Gloriam
Tui Nominis Ineffabilis
In the name of the Lord of Initiation. Amen.

[To the fructified Virgin
To the Glory of the Rosy Cross
To Love of the Mother
To the Life of the Father
To the Light; to the Glory
of Your Ineffable Name]

Chapter Fourteen
Breaking of Bread

One of the simplest and most complete of Magick ceremonies is the Eucharist.

It consists in taking common things, transmuting them into things divine, and consuming them.

So far, it is a type of every magick ceremony, for the reabsorption of the force is a kind of consumption; but it has a more restricted application, as follows.

Take a substance symbolic of the whole course of nature, make it God, and consume it.

- Aleister Crowley, *Magick*

At its height during the Middle Ages, Gnosticism was the second biggest religion in Europe, spreading right across the Northern Mediterranean region, from Northern Spain and Southern France all the way over to Bulgaria and the Balkans. Yet until recently it was almost unheard of. It simply ceased to exist after the 13th century. That didn't happen by accident, but by one of the biggest genocidal campaigns in history.

Over the past centuries many religions have been persecuted by the Christian Church, but the war waged against the Gnostics during the medieval period outweighs pretty much all the others. Not only did the Christian Church torture and kill approximately half a million Gnostic adherents, they did everything they could to destroy their teachings and writings as well. For that reason little of the authentic Gnostic rites has come down to us, and indeed for several centuries the religion was almost totally forgotten.

However during the 19th century an archivist at the Library of Orleans named Jules Doinel discovered a peculiar manuscript dealing with Gnostic ideas. It had been written in 1022 by Canon Stephen of Orleans, a teacher of Gnostic ideas who was burned for heresy shortly after writing the manuscript.

Doinel was a Freemason deeply interested in esotericism, and in Gnosticism he believed he had found the "missing link" behind the mysteries of Masonry. This belief was confirmed to him in a vision during which the spirit of Jesus appeared to him and charged him with reviving the ancient Gnostic religion. This was later followed by many seances in which Doinel was contacted by the spirits of past Gnostic Bishops and given instructions in how to rebuild the Gnostic Church. He did this in 1890, and consecrated several new Bishops and "Sophias" (female Bishops), including the famous Tarot expert Gerard Encausse, who wrote under the name of Papus. Encausse would later join the fledgling Ordo Templi Orientis in 1908, and in turn consecrate its Outer Head, Theodor Reuss, as a Bishop of the Ecclesia Gnostica Catholica (Gnostic Catholic Church). Reuss became Patriarch of E.G.C. and made it an official part of O.T.O. from then onwards; and it still forms an important part of O.T.O today.

In turn, Theodor Reuss consecrated Aleister Crowley as a Bishop of the Gnostic Church, and in 1913 Crowley composed its central public and private rite: *Liber XV* - The Gnostic Mass. The Gnostic Mass is rightly judged to be one of the greatest Eucharistic rites of all time, and O.T.O. bodies all over the world perform it regularly - I heartily recommend all readers of this book to attend one at least once in their lives, it's a wonderful experience. However it's not a simple rite to perform; it requires a fairly large amount of temple equipment and five highly trained officers to be done properly. It's so deep that no less than two complete books have already been written about it, as well as a huge amount of other supplementary material being available on the Internet. I've taught classes on it for well over a decade, and I'm still learning more about it all the time.

However Gnosticism is certainly one of the most important roots of modern-day Thelema, so I think it important that we have at least one Gnostic rite represented in this book for your group to work with. Consequently for this ritual I have gone back to the source and looked at Jules Doinel's original rituals of the Gnostic Church. Doinel wrote three major rituals for his Church, based on his idea of original medieval Gnostic ideas: the Consolamentum, or Baptism of the Spirit; the Appareilamentum, which was a type of confession and absolution ritual; and the Fraction du Pain, or Breaking of Bread, which was the Gnostic equivalent of the Roman Catholic Eucharist.

The *Catholic Encyclopedia* has this to say about the Gnostic Eucharist:

> "It is remarkable that so little is known of the Gnostic substitute for the Eucharist. In a number of passages we read of the breaking of the bread, but in what this consisted is not easy to determine. The use of salt in this rite seems to have been important (Clement, Hom. xiv), for we read distinctly how St. Peter broke the bread of the Eucharist and 'putting salt thereon, he gave first to the mother and then to us.'

...What formula of consecration was used we do not know, but the bread was certainly signed with the Cross."

Although the Roman Catholic Church describes this as a "substitute" for the Eucharist, it would appear that the Gnostics certainly considered it to be a real Eucharist. Not much else is known about the original Gnostic Eucharist however, which has led to some problems for those of us who would attempt to revive and expand on the Gnostic religion in the modern day.

Doinel's ceremony probably didn't have a whole lot to do with the original Gnostic "Breaking of Bread" ritual, but it is a fascinating Eucharistic ritual in its own right, and an obvious predecessor to Crowley's Gnostic Mass. This rite does not pretend to have anything like the sublimity and depth of *Liber XV*, but it does have the advantage of requiring fewer officers and less setup.

For this Thelemic recension of the Breaking of Bread ritual I have kept the original structure of Doinel's rite fairly intact, but replaced the words with modern Thelemic equivalents, largely derived from the *Book of the Law* - so although the words spoken have very little in common with Doinel's text, the actual *mechanism* of the performance of this Mass is almost identical. The only original words currently remaining in the ritual are the Latin Valentinian Prayer which the Congregation performs at the beginning of the ceremony and the chant they perform near the end, and which I left intact to help the Congregation feel connected to our Gnostic forebears.

The original ritual was designed to be performed by any of the "Pneumatics" or "Perfecti" of Doinel's Gnostic Church. In order to become one of these Perfect Initiates the candidate would undergo the ceremony of the *Consolamentum*, and thus be considered effectively baptised and confirmed within the Church. In this version I have entitled the lead role "Cleric", which may be a woman or man acting in the role of Priestess or Priest. In a Thelemic context this would ideally be someone who is an ordained Priestess or Priest of Ecclesia Gnostica Catholica, or a Novice training to be one. There is no reason why others cannot perform this role in order to understand how a basic Thelemic Eucharistic ritual works; however it could be argued that Baptism and Confirmation into E.G.C. would assist in making a "magical link" to Doinel's original Gnostic Church.

The Doinel rite had a Deacon and Deaconess who carried the bread and wine and acted as ritual assistants. For the current version I have followed Crowley's practice in the Gnostic Mass and replaced them with two officers referred to as the Children. Please note the capitalisation of the word Children! Children in this context does not mean you should use real under-18 children. The roles of the Children in this ritual (and in the Gnostic Mass) can be, and in my opinion should be, played by adults. The Children within the Mass are *roles* based on the Children portrayed in the Tarot card of the Sun - representations of divine innocence and the birth of new life.

One of the major advantages of this ritual as opposed to many other Eucharistic rituals, is the easiness of setup. The only temple paraphernalia required are an altar, two candles, a chafing dish, and a copy of the *Book of the Law*; plus a paten (plate) with Cakes of Light, and a Cup of wine (or a tray with individual goblets of wine if you prefer). The Cakes of Light should be made as given in the *Book of the Law*, but the original Gnostic custom of using simple bread and salt would be an adequate substitute if Thelemic Cakes are not available.

A chafing dish is mentioned in the original Doinel ritual, so I've kept it in here as well. This is a small dish with a spirit lamp or candle burner underneath used for keeping food warm, such as you often see in Asian restaurants. These can usually be easily found in cookware shops, or you could use an incense burner or something similar in a pinch. It is used for correctly disposing of any leftover bits of the consecrated Cakes of Light at the end of the ritual, by burning them to ash. One nice touch might be to keep the ash from one ritual to use as an ingredient when making Cakes of Light for the next one.

An interesting point to note is that both the early Gnostics and the 19th century Gnostic revivalists did not use the word "altar", but had a simple table instead, since they believed that there was no intrinsic holiness in material things. I have chosen to use the term altar for aesthetic reasons more than anything else - you may of course use a table if you wish. I usually just use a table and call it an altar, which works fine for me.

In *Book 4* Crowley speaks about the ideal conditions for the consumption of the Eucharist:

> *"Chastity is a condition; fasting for some hours previous is a condition; an earnest and continual aspiration is a condition."*

Officers and members of the Congregation should bear these conditions in mind. Although they are by no means essential to the performance of the ritual, you might find that they assist in the consumption of the power generated during it.

Breaking of Bread

Participants:	Minimum four. The rite works well with a medium to large size group.
Time required:	Less than half an hour
Setup:	Simple
Words:	Relatively simple
Equipment:	• Altar with:

- • Two candles
  - • Book of the Law
  - • Chafing dish
- • Three white robes
- • Red, blue, or purple stole for Cleric
- • Two black sashes or belts for Children
- • Paten with Cakes of Light (or bread & salt)
- • Cup with wine (or tray with goblets of wine)
- • Missals for congregation

Opening

In the East is a small altar, upon which are two candles, and the *Book of the Law* open between them.

The Cleric is robed in white, with a red stole (if male) or blue stole (if female). Consecrated Bishops of E.G.C. may replace this with a purple stole.

The Children are robed in white, with black sashes or belts. The Positive Child carries the Paten with the Cakes of Light (or bread & salt substitute); the Negative Child carries the Cup.

All three officers stand to the West of the altar, facing the Congregation; the Negative Child is to the right of the Cleric, the Positive Child to the left.

The Congregation are robed in white and are seated along the North and South sides of the temple.

When they are all seated, the Cleric leads them in the Valentinian Prayer:

> **Beati vos Eones**
> **Vera vita vividi;**
> **Vos Emanationes**
> **Pleromatis lucidi;**
> **Adeste visiones**
> **Stolis albis candidi.**

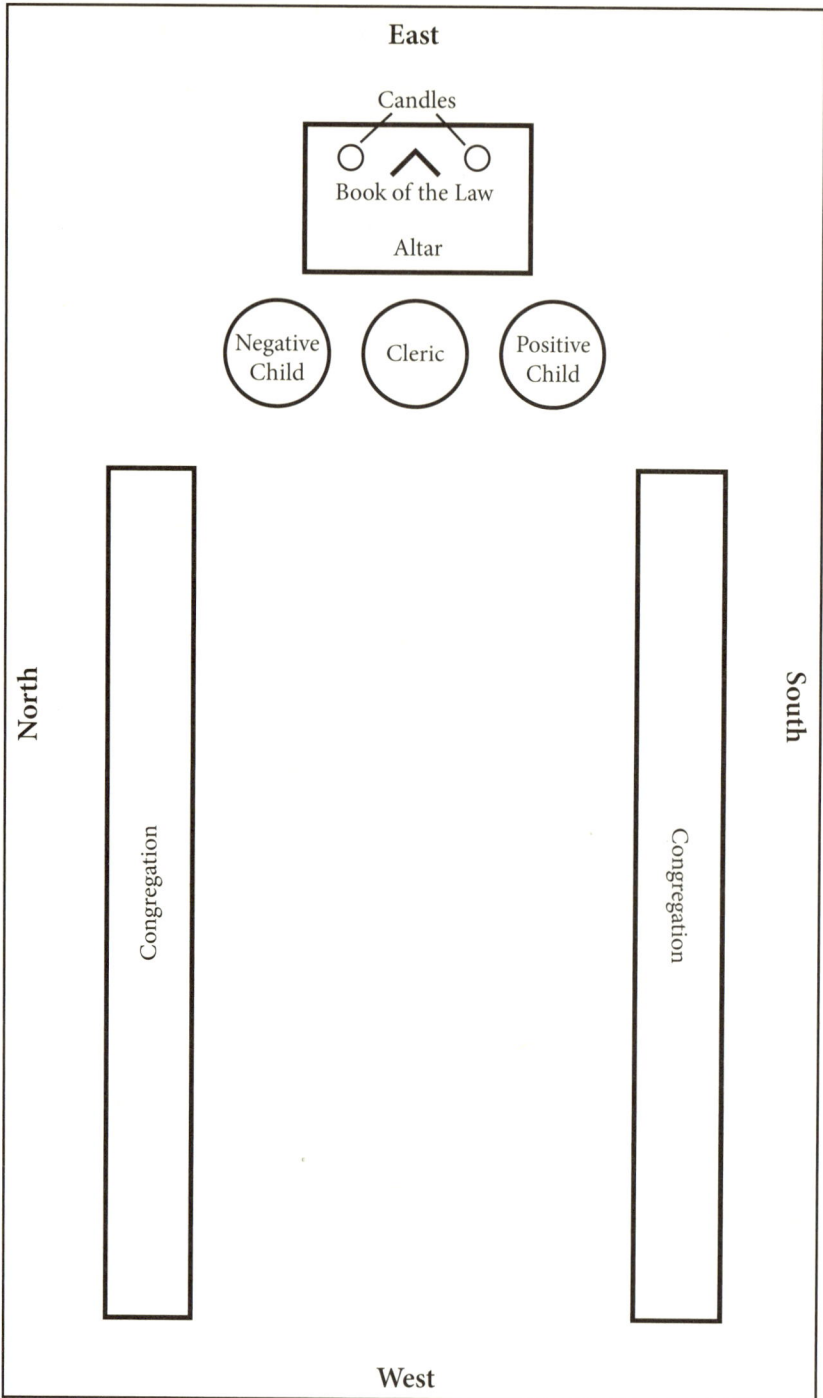

East

Candles

Book of the Law

Altar

Negative Child

Cleric

Positive Child

North

South

Congregation

Congregation

West

[O Ye Blessed Aeons
Animate by the True Life;
O Ye Emanations
The Pleroma fills thee with Light;
Come, Ye Sacred Visions
Shining in Garments of White.]

The Cleric makes a cross over the Congregation and says:

> **Above, the gemmed azure is**
> **The naked splendour of Nuit;**
> **She bends in ecstasy to kiss**
> **The secret ardours of Hadit.**
> **The winged globe, the starry blue,**
> **Are mine, O Ankh-af-na-khonsu!**

Consecration of the Elements

The Children present the Cup and Paten to the Cleric.

(Cleric strikes breast)

> **By Bes-na-Maut my breast I beat;**

(Cleric makes a cross over the Cup and Paten)

> **By wise Ta-Nech I weave my spell.**

(Cleric raises hands to the heavens)

> **Show thy star-splendour, O Nuit!**

(Cleric crosses arms over breast)

> **Bid me within thine House to dwell,**
> **O winged snake of light, Hadit!**
> **Abide with me, Ra-Hoor-Khuit!**

The Congregation chants in response:

> **So mote it be.**

The Cleric says: **Then saith the prophet and slave of the beauteous one: Who am I, and what shall be the sign? So she answered him, bending down, a lambent flame of blue, all-touching, all penetrant, her lovely hands upon the black earth, & her lithe body arched for love, and her soft feet not hurting the little flowers: Thou knowest! And the sign shall be my ecstasy, the consciousness of the continuity of existence, the omnipresence of my body.**

(Cleric takes a Cake of Light and breaks it over the Paten)

This burn: of this make cakes & eat unto me.

The Cleric elevates the Cake above head height, and says:

TOUTO ESTI TO SOMA MOU.

(The Cleric places the Cake on the paten, kneels before it and adores)

The Cleric rises, takes the Cup, elevates it, and says:

TOUTO ESTI TO POTÊRION TOU HAIMATOS MOU.

(The Cleric kneels again and adores; then eats a fragment of the Cake and drinks of the Cup. There is a brief pause, while music plays.)

Communion

The Cleric rises and says:

> **Now, therefore, I am known to ye by my name Nuit, and to him by a secret name which I will give him when at last he knoweth me. Since I am Infinite Space, and the Infinite Stars thereof, do ye also thus.**

(The Children advance and stop before each of the Congregation, offering to each one the Cakes and the Cup.

After the last of the Congregation has partaken of the bread and wine, there is an additional pause for meditation, during which the music continues to play.

The Children return to their initial places before the altar.)

The Cleric extends hands and says:

> **Come forth, o children, under the stars, & take your fill**
> **of love! I am above you and in you. My ecstasy is in yours.**
> **My joy is to see your joy.**

(The remains of the Cakes are then burned on a chafing dish.
The Children place the Paten and Cup on the Altar, and cross their arms
over their breasts.)

The Congregation chant together:

> **Hail, hail Kingdom**
> **Of eternal Clarity.**
> **Hail, hail Fullness**
> **of Divinity!**
> **Where Matter becomes Motion**
> **O deep and endless Sea**
> **Mystery of Silence,**
> **Of Love, and of Beauty!**

The Cleric makes a cross over the Congregation and says:

> **The unveiling of the company of heaven.**
> **Every man and every woman is a star.**

(The Cleric retires, escorted by the Children, who carry with them the two
candles from the altar.)

Chapter Fifteen
The Mass of Babalon

It's become a commonplace saying in modern magical circles that writing your own rituals is always preferable to doing stuff that's written by other people, or that somehow rituals written by other people won't resonate with you as much as those written by yourself. This is, of course, complete nonsense. It's like saying that building your own car is preferable to buying one made in a factory. Even professional mechanics usually buy factory-built cars, because a car is a very sophisticated piece of machinery, in which each part is highly dependent on every other part, and requires a great deal of specialist knowledge to get right. Rituals are not dissimilar in that respect. Writing good ones takes knowledge, research, talent, and time. Lots of time - some of the ones given here took years to write, even for a genius like Aleister Crowley.

So no, I certainly don't subscribe to the theory that home-brewed is better. If in doubt, leave it to the professionals. However I'm also fully aware that there are only fifteen rituals given in this book, and although that's enough to keep even a very active group busy for at least a year or two, you may eventually want to extend beyond them.

You may have noticed in working through the book that rituals tend to follow certain set structures. If you have not noticed this, grab a notepad and pen, and go back through the book looking for common structural themes. Note that we're not looking for common words here, but the stuff that lies below the words, the framework of the rituals themselves. To continue the car metaphor, we need to be looking at the engine and the chassis, not the paint job. We need to analyse rituals in this way in order to understand the formula used by each ritual in order to achieve its goals.

In the previous chapter on the Breaking of Bread ritual you can see the classic Eucharistic ritual formula at work, which can be broken down into three stages:

1. divine energy is invoked into a person (the Priestess or Priest).
2. that person transmits the energy into food.
3. the other people then consume the food and the divine energy contained within it.

All masses follow this formula - the long and ornate Gnostic Mass is at heart just this process, with a lot of (very beautiful) window dressing on top. Since the publication of my last book, the Mass of Baphomet has become quite popular in Thelemic circles, which is very gratifying; and this can be used as a "construction kit" for quickly and easily building your own rituals.

Let's look at the ritual procedure for a standard eucharistic ceremony:

1. Choose the deity you will be invoking. This can be pretty much any deity you want. Usually it's best to pick something you know and can relate to, but sometimes you should try to explore energies that are a little out of the ordinary for you, so it's important to be as well-rounded as you can in your choices. Don't just aim for the obvious.

2. Choose a sacrament appropriate to the work. The classic eucharistic sacraments are bread and wine, representing the body and blood; but you may want to pick a food or drink that is traditionally associated with the goddess or god you will be invoking.

3. Choose roles for the ritual. In any Mass you will need at least one person to act in the priestly role to invoke the divine energy into the sacrament - you might have more than one depending on the ritual. You will also probably need some kind of assistant or assistants to deal with other things not directly connected with the main invocation - banishing, statement of intent, making sure that the other participants know what they are doing and when to do it. Other roles may be added as required, but try to make sure they have some actual purpose, don't just give out titles for the sake of it.

4. Prepare the temple. You will need incense appropriate to the ritual, charcoal and burner; a plate, paten, cup or other container to hold the sacrament; robes; candles; furnishings, statues, or pictures appropriate to the deity to be invoked. And of course a place to work in - this could be someone's living room, the local Masonic Lodge, or the nearest piece of private woodland. Just make sure you have legal permission to do the things you want to do there, and that you won't get disturbed.

5. Start your ritual with a statement of intent, banishing, whatever introductory thing that will prepare the space and the people in it - usually performed by whoever is in the the assistant role.

6. Recite some words. You don't need many, but you do need some in order to set the scene, and get the ball rolling. If you are a good writer you could try writing your own, but in my experience that's not usually the best idea. I've had to sit through some truly awful occult poetry in my time, and I bet a lot of my readers are nodding and agreeing with that, so I'm certainly not going to encourage people to write more. Even Crowley, who was a damn good magical writer most times, wrote some ghastly and exceedingly verbose ritual poetry. So if in doubt, keep it short and simple. And steal. Steal shamelessly from everywhere you can. As T.S. Elliot (who was a good writer) said: "Immature poets imitate; mature poets steal". And don't be ashamed either - huge chunks of early Wiccan rituals in the 1950s were lifted straight out of the *Gnostic Mass* and the *Book of the Law*, and they seemed to have worked out fine. The main thing is that the words should be very evocative and help the participants get into the correct state of mind. So something very descriptive of the deity and the environment they are traditionally associated with is always useful.

7. Raise the magical energy. This can be done by poetry, chanting, mantra, music, dance, sexuality, or any combination of the above - whatever you decide will get the divine energy into the room and into the people who have taken on the priestly role. I've used all of these in various combinations in the past, and they all work. Mantra is certainly the easiest if you want to get everyone fully involved.

8. Get the divine energy into the Priest(ess).

9. Get that energy from the Priest(ess) into the Sacrament. Physically this is usually done by the laying on of hands.

10. Get the Sacrament containing the energy into the People i.e. eating and drinking.

11. Finish off. Close with thanks, feasting, hoovering, banishing, whatever seems appropriate to the work.

Notice that the last few sections, which would seem to be where all the complex magical action is, are actually the simplest. That's because generally if you do the preparation right, and get everyone involved in the ritual energy, then everything else after that is usually pretty automatic; because that's the way we're wired up as human beings. If you push all the right buttons, you'll get the right effect.

The Mass of Baphomet as given in *Abrahadabra* uses the formula laid out above in the following way:

1. **Choose the deity**
   - In this case we have the famous goat-headed horned Templar deity known as Baphomet
2. **Choose a sacrament appropriate to the work.**
   - Normally wine or Cakes of Light for Baphomet, or something else as appropriate
3. **Choose roles for the ritual.**
   - In this case we have two Officers, one priest, called the Manifester, and one assistant called the Banisher.
4. **Prepare the temple.**
   - Baphomet is normally described as sitting on a blasted heath at night, so a fairly simple temple setup is fine (or do it outdoors) preferably after dark.
5. **Start your ritual.**
   - A simple pentagram ritual is a classic opening.
6. **Recite some words.**
   - The Thelemic Holy Book Liber A'Ash deals specifically with invoking Baphomet so that's perfect.
7. **Raise the magical energy.**
   - In order the keep the rite as simple and easy to learn as possible it uses a mantra of just three vowels: I A O
8. **Get the divine energy into the Priest(ess).**
   - Done by visualising the Manifester in the traditional image of Baphomet
9. **Get that energy from the Priest(ess) into the Sacrament.**
   - Laying on of hands
10. **Get the Sacrament containing the energy into the People i.e. eating and drinking.**
    - No explanation necessary here.
11. **Finish off.**
    - Repeat the Pentagram ritual used at the beginning

And that's it! Although this is a very simple ritual it has proven itself extremely effective and is in regular use around the world today. I've seen it performed in small bedrooms, large halls, and outdoors in the forest - its simplicity means that it's very flexible. Because it was built on the framework laid out above, we can be sure we have a well-tested example that proves that this formula works, and so we can easily build entirely new and very functional rites by just adapting the same formula to invoke other divine energies.

Let's take a case study to show how this can be done. Say your group decides to invoke the goddess Babalon, an important and popular goddess in the Thelemic pantheon. How should we go about it? Well, part 1 is already done, we have already decided on our deity. Now we need to go to part 2 - choosing a sacrament. What sacrament would be appropriate? Here's where we need to start doing some research on Babalon. A good place to start would be *Liber Cheth*, a Thelemic Holy Book entirely devoted to Babalon. Let's pick out a few useful verses:

1. This is the secret of the Holy Graal, that is the sacred vessel of our Lady the Scarlet Woman, Babalon the Mother of Abominations, the bride of Chaos, that rideth upon our Lord the Beast.

2. Thou shalt drain out thy blood that is thy life into the golden cup of her fornication.

   ...

11. For if thou dost not this with thy will, then shall We do this despite thy will. So that thou attain to the Sacrament of the Graal in the Chapel of Abominations.

    ...

14. Then shall every gain be a new sacrament, and it shall not defile thee; thou shalt revel with the wanton in the market-place, and the virgins shall fling roses upon thee, and the merchants bend their knees and bring thee gold and spices. Also young boys shall pour wonderful wines for thee, and the singers and the dancers shall sing and dance for thee.

The first thing we notice right from the opening line is that the Holy Graal which contains the blood of the worshippers is an important part of the imagery. Also in verse 14 the sacrament is mentioned, and wonderful wines being poured for you. That sounds like what we're looking for. So let's get a cup to represent the Graal, and red wine to represent the blood. Right away we have a sacrament ready to go.

Next section: roles in the ritual. We'll need someone to incarnate the energy of Babalon. Clearly she's an extremely feminine goddess, so a woman would be the obvious choice, though a man could also do the job in a pinch. And Babalon certainly has a lot of wanton sensual energy, so it should be someone who can handle that (though you'd be surprised at how some people's hidden inner nature can come out in situations like these). Verse 14 also mentions virgins that fling roses, merchants that bring gold and spices, young boys pouring wine, and singers and dancers. Those sound like things that we could turn into other ritual roles. Perhaps we could have an assistant role of Cup Bearer, who brings the wine in to the ritual, and decants and serves it to the people after the Goddess has blessed it. Or we could have the part of Virgin, who brings roses and strews them around the temple. The Role of Merchant might be an interesting one - perhaps as well as wine we could have small spicy treats as part of the sacrament? Or even have small golden trinkets that could be blessed by the goddess and handed out as talismans to the people? That would give us four elemental items:

- Fire: spices
- Water: wine
- Air: roses
- Earth: gold

Or we can just decide to stick with wine as the sacrament, and have roses, spices, and gold on the altar during the rite, for simplicity's sake; which brings us neatly to the next section, preparing the temple.

Let's look for references in the text that we could use... Verse 11 says that "thou attain to the Sacrament of the Graal in the Chapel of Abominations." That sounds like a good setting. What would a Chapel of Abominations look like? Probably vaguely satanic and not too pleasant I'm guessing. So you could decorate in high Gothic style, maybe add some bones or surrealist paintings, candles in big candlesticks for effect of course, lots of wall hangings... you get the idea. Let's look at some of the imagery: verse 6 mentions the City of the Pyramids, so perhaps a picture of pyramids might be good. Angels are mentioned there too, so angelic images might be nice. Dogs and vultures are mentioned in verse 10, so they are creatures associated with her – probably best not to bring real dogs and vultures into the temple, but statues of them could be interesting. Of course there's also classic Babalon imagery in Aleister Crowley's Tarot pack - the Lust card features Babalon riding The Beast, so that would make a great altar piece.

With a little more research we can find other texts that may be useful. For example, we could always try the the *Book of Revelation* in the *Bible*:

The Book of Revelations 17: 3-6

So he carried me away in the spirit into the wilderness: and I saw a woman sit upon a scarlet coloured beast, full of names of blasphemy, having seven heads and ten horns.

And the woman was arrayed in purple and scarlet colour, and decked with gold and precious stones and pearls, having a golden cup in her hand full of abominations and filthiness of her fornication.

And upon her forehead was a name written: Mystery, Babalon The Great, The Mother of Harlots and Abominations of the Earth.

And I saw the woman drunken with the blood of the saints, and with the blood of the martyrs of Jesus: and when I saw her I wondered with great admiration.

According to this Babalon wears purple and scarlet, and wears lots of gold and jewels, so that sounds like a good idea for what kind of attire the Priestess should wear.

Now we should have enough information to build up a fairly complete temple structure, so let's move on to the next section: words. We already have quite a bit of verbiage in the two books referenced above, but some more to choose from is always good. So back to doing some research...

Babalon is also a goddess that appears throughout the Enochian magical system. John Dee and Edward Kelley contacted her in the 16th century in the 7th Enochian Aethyr, called Deo, where she communicated the following:

The Daughter of Fortitude

I am the daughter of Fortitude, and ravished every hour from my youth. For behold I am Understanding and science dwelleth in me; and the heavens oppress me. They cover and desire me with infinite appetite; for none that are earthly have embraced me, for I am shadowed with the Circle of the Stars and covered with the morning clouds. My feet are swifter than the winds, and my hands are sweeter than the morning dew. My garments are from the beginning, and my dwelling place is in myself. The Lion knoweth not where I walk, neither do the beast of the fields understand me. I am deflowered, yet a virgin; I sanctify and am not sanctified. Happy is he that embraceth me: for in the night season I am sweet, and in the day full of pleasure. My company is a harmony of many symbols and my lips sweeter than health itself. I am a harlot for such as ravish me, and a virgin with such as know me not. For lo, I am loved of many, and I am a lover to many; and as many as come unto me as they should do, have entertainment.

Purge your streets, O ye sons of men, and wash your houses clean;

make yourselves holy, and put on righteousness. Cast out your old strumpets, and burn their clothes; abstain from the company of other women that are defiled, that are sluttish, and not so handsome and beautiful as I, and then will I come and dwell amongst you: and behold, I will bring forth children unto you, and they shall be the Sons of Comfort. I will open my garments, and stand naked before you, that your love may be more enflamed toward me.

That's certainly very resonant and rich in imagery, so could be very useful as invocatory text. It's spoken by Babalon herself, so might be something the Priestess could say during the rite.

Aleister Crowley also explored the Enochian Aethyrs extensively, and had this vision concerning Babalon in the 12th Aethyr during a working at Bou-Sada on December 4-5, 1909 which he published in his diary called *The Vision & The Voice*. The text is spoken by the figure of the Charioteer from the Tarot card of the The Chariot, and begins:

Let him look upon the cup whose blood is mingled therein, for the wine of the cup is the blood of the saints.

...O Babylon, Babylon, thou mighty Mother, that ridest upon the crown'd beast, let me be drunken upon the wine of thy fornications; let thy kisses wanton me unto death, that even I, thy cup-bearer, may *understand*.

That last line is interesting, because it refers to the speaker as being Babalon's cup-bearer. We already thought of perhaps having a role in the ritual of Cup Bearer so let's have him do this whole speech at some point in the ritual. That gives us two definite officer roles: a Priestess and a Cup Bearer. We could add more roles if we want, but let's keep things simple to start with. Two sounds like enough officers for a small group.

Once we have decided on that, we will need to design how the temple layout is set up. In the Mark of the Beast ritual the station of Babalon is in the West, so that might be a good place for the Priestess to be seated during the main part of the rite. We could then put an altar in the middle, with the Graal, and some roses etc. and have the Cup Bearer seated in the East. Have the rest of the participants along the North and South sides of the temple. Add in the furnishings we spoke of earlier and now we have the full temple ready to go.

We'll need to decide on how to build the actual format of the ritual. As an opening we could use the Mark of the Beast ritual. That's quite fitting since Babalon is usually depicted riding on the Beast, so there's a strong connection there. Another option would be to use Crowley's poem to Babalon from The *Book of Oaths* which might work well as an opening section to a Babalon ritual:

Babalon

Do what thou wilt shall be the whole of the Law.
Rue not now guilt the Devil's dagger who draw!

I swear toward the West
On BABALON'S bold breast.
I swear toward the South
On her mad merry mouth.
I swear towards the East
On her Cup fiery-fleeced.
I swear towards the North
On Her Disk savage-swarth.
I swear toward the Height
On Her five fingers' Spite.
I swear towards the Deep
On Her soul's smiling sleep.
I swear towards the Centre
By Her and Him that sent Her.

I swear this Oath
Of Troth
To BABALON –
My own
Sister, and Scarlet
Harlot;
I am Her Priest
The BEAST,
To bring to birth
On earth
My word of awe,
The Law
Of Will, above
Its Love.
To BABALON
Alone
This tempered Oath

Of Troth
In Her chaste Cup
Seal up!

We could even use both if we really wanted, or just stick with one to keep it simple. Then we could follow it with the speech of the Charioteer from the 12th Aethyr, as mentioned above. That should be more than enough opening work.

Now we come to the crux of the whole affair - the raising of the magical energy. Liber Cheth makes much of there being singing and dancing, so that might be what we need here, as fitting to the wanton sensuality that we need. In a previous chapter on the Supreme Ritual we were introduced to the song given in The Vision & The Voice, 2nd Aethyr. In the vision of that Aethyr Babalon appears strongly, and Crowley describes this rather remarkable song thus:

The Song of the 2nd Aethyr

So sweet is this song that no one could resist it. For in it is all the passionate ache for the moonlight, and the great hunger of the sea, and the terror of desolate places, - all things that lure men to the unattainable.

Omari tessala marax,
tessala dodi phornepax.
amri radara poliax
armana piliu.
amri radara piliu son';
mari narya barbiton
madara anaphax sarpedon
andala hriliu.

[Translation:
I am the harlot that shaketh Death.
This shaking giveth the Peace of Satiate Lust.
Immortality jetteth from my skull,
And music from my vulva.
Immortality jetteth from my vulva also,
For my Whoredom is a sweet scent like a seven-stringed instrument,
Played unto God the Invisible, the all-ruler,
That goeth along giving the shrill scream of orgasm.]

That sounds like a good Babalon invocation to me. And it would make a great chant for the people - it's only eight lines, so it could be used like a mantra. For music we could use sistrums perhaps, or some appropriate instrumental recorded music that might go with the chant - something sensual and rhythmic would work well, perhaps Indian or Middle Eastern music, or if you prefer Western classical music, Ravel's *Bolero*.

As regards dancing, the first thing that enters my mind given the atmosphere we are building here might be belly-dancing. If your group has someone who is skilled in that practice, then by all means add it in. You could either have several members of the group dance in whichever way they might feel comfortable with, or perhaps just have the officer playing Babalon dance while everyone else is chanting.

Another option might be to have the Cup Bearer read out *Liber Cheth* before the chant, or even as a counterpoint to it - a very effective technique if done well.

While all that is going on, the participants need to keep focused on the true purpose of the rite, to invoke Babalon into the body of the Priestess. You can aid this by having each member perhaps be given rose petals and in turn scatter them at the feet of the Priestess. Or perhaps have the Priestess hold the Lust Tarot card in her lap or to her breast, as a focal point. Each participant needs to call on Babalon while they chant and concentrate on bringing Her energy into the body of the Priestess.

Eventually the Priestess is going to be filled with the essence of Babalon. There's no way to describe when she will know when this point occurs, but trust me on this, she'll know. Once that moment arrives she should raise her hands and signal for the Cup Bearer to bring her the decanter of wine and perhaps kneel before her while she lays her hands on it. Once that's done all that remains is for the Cup Bearer to pour the wine for the people and for them to drink of Her essence.

Then have the Cup Bearer close the temple with another recitation of the Babalon poem to finish.

And there we have it - one full Babalon group invocation built from scratch before your very eyes. And quite a complex and full-featured one at that. So now let's build a proper script for it...

The Mass of Babalon

Participants:	Minimum three. The rite works well with a small to medium size group.
Time required:	About half an hour
Setup:	Medium
Words:	Medium
Equipment:	• Altar with

- Altar with
  - Cup with wine
  - Rose petals (optional)
  - Incense & burner
  - Individual goblets for the people
- Two seats
- Priestess
  - Purple and scarlet attire
  - Jewels
- Cup Bearer
  - Dagger

In the West is the throne of the Priestess. In the centre is the Altar. The throne of the Cup Bearer is to the East. The People sit along the North and South sides of the temple.

The Cup Bearer rises, faces West, draws his dagger, and opens the temple with the Poem to Babalon; moving around the appropriate quarters, pointing to them with the dagger, and strewing rose petals as he recites. After swearing towards West, South, East, and North, he returns to face West and swears to the Height, Deep, and Centre.

Cup Bearer:	**Do what thou wilt shall be the whole of the Law.**
	Rue not now guilt the Devil's dagger who draw!
	I swear toward the West
	On BABALON'S bold breast.
	I swear toward the South
	On her mad merry mouth.
	I swear towards the East
	On her Cup fiery-fleeced.
	I swear towards the North
	On Her Disk savage-swarth.
	I swear toward the Height

On Her five fingers' Spite.
I swear towards the Deep
On Her soul's smiling sleep.
I swear towards the Centre
By Her and Him that sent Her.

I swear this Oath
Of Troth
To BABALON –
My own
Sister, and Scarlet
Harlot;
I am Her Priest
The BEAST,
To bring to birth
On earth
My word of awe,
The Law
Of Will, above
Its Love.
To BABALON
Alone
This tempered Oath
Of Troth
In Her chaste Cup
Seal up!

(The Cup Bearer returns to his seat and recites The Speech of the Charioteer:)

Let him look upon the cup whose blood is mingled therein, for the wine of the cup is the blood of the saints. Glory unto the Scarlet Woman, Babalon the Mother of Abominations, that rideth upon the Beast, for she hath spilt their blood in every corner of the earth and lo! she hath mingled it in the cup of her whoredom.

With the breath of her kisses hath she fermented it, and it hath become the wine of the Sacrament, the wine of the Sabbath; and in the Holy Assembly hath she poured it out for her worshippers, and they had become drunken thereon, so that face to face they beheld my Father. Thus are they made worthy to become partakers of the Mystery of this holy vessel, for the blood is the life. So sitteth she from age to age, and the righteous are never weary of her kisses, and by her murders and fornications she seduceth the world. Therein is manifested the glory of my Father, who is truth...

...This is the Mystery of Babylon, the Mother of abominations, and this is the mystery of her adulteries, for she hath yielded up herself to everything that liveth, and hath become a partaker in its mystery. And because she hath made herself the servant of each, therefore is she become the mistress of all. Not as yet canst thou comprehend her glory.

Beautiful art thou, O Babylon, and desirable, for thou hast given thyself to everything that liveth, and thy weakness hath subdued their strength. For in that union thou didst understand. Therefore art thou called Understanding, O Babylon, Lady of the Night!

This is that which is written, "O my God, in one last rapture let me attain to the union with the many." For she is Love, and her love is one, and she hath divided the one love into infinite loves, and each love is one, and equal to The One, and therefore is she passed "from the assembly and the law and the enlightenment unto the anarchy of solitude and darkness. For ever thus must she veil the brilliance of Her Self." O Babylon, Babylon, thou mighty Mother, that ridest upon the crown'd beast, let me be drunken upon the wine of thy fornications; let thy kisses wanton me unto death, that even I, thy cup-bearer, may understand.

(Music is played, and dancing begins. The People chant together the Song of the 2nd Aethyr as a mantra.)

People: Omari tessala marax,
tessala dodi phornepax.
amri radara poliax
armana piliu.
amri radara piliu son';
mari narya barbiton
madara anaphax sarpedon
andala hriliu.

(During this the Cup Bearer recites *Liber Cheth*, and all continue to chant and call upon the essence of Babalon to descend into the temple, and into the body of the Priestesss.)

Cup Bearer: 1. This is the secret of the Holy Graal, that is the sacred vessel of our Lady the Scarlet Woman, Babalon the Mother of Abominations, the bride of Chaos, that rideth upon our Lord the Beast.

                2. Thou shalt drain out thy blood that is thy life into the golden cup of her fornication.

                3. Thou shalt mingle thy life with the universal life. Thou shalt keep not back one drop.

                4. Then shall thy brain be dumb, and thy heart beat no more, and all thy life shall go from thee; and thou shalt be cast out upon the midden, and the birds of the air shall feast upon thy flesh, and thy bones shall whiten in the sun.

                5. Then shall the winds gather themselves together, and bear thee up as it were a little heap of dust in a sheet that hath four corners, and they shall give it unto the guardians of the abyss.

                6. And because there is no life therein, the guardians of the abyss shall bid the angels of the winds pass by. And the angels shall lay thy dust in the City of the Pyramids, and the name thereof shall be no more.

7. Now therefore that thou mayest achieve this ritual of the Holy Graal, do thou divest thyself of all thy goods.

8. Thou hast wealth; give it unto them that have need thereof, yet no desire toward it.

9. Thou hast health; slay thyself in the fervour of thine abandonment unto Our Lady. Let thy flesh hang loose upon thy bones, and thine eyes glare with thy quenchless lust unto the Infinite, with thy passion for the Unknown, for Her that is beyond Knowledge the accursed one.

10. Thou hast love; tear thy mother from thine heart, and spit in the face of thy father. Let thy foot trample the belly of thy wife, and let the babe at her breast be the prey of dogs and vultures.

11. For if thou dost not this with thy will, then shall We do this despite thy will. So that thou attain to the Sacrament of the Graal in the Chapel of Abominations.

12. And behold! if by stealth thou keep unto thyself one thought of thine, then shalt thou be cast out into the abyss for ever; and thou shalt be the lonely one, the eater of dung, the afflicted in the Day of Be-with-Us.

13. Yea! verily this is the Truth, this is the Truth, this is the Truth. Unto thee shall be granted joy and health and wealth and wisdom when thou art no longer thou.

14. Then shall every gain be a new sacrament, and it shall not defile thee; thou shalt revel with the wanton in the market-place, and the virgins shall fling roses upon thee, and the merchants bend their knees and bring thee gold and spices. Also young boys shall pour wonderful wines for thee, and the singers and the dancers shall sing and dance for thee.

15. Yet shalt thou not be therein, for thou shalt be forgotten, dust lost in dust.

16. Nor shall the aeon itself avail thee in this; for from the dust shall a white ash be prepared by Hermes the Invisible.

17. And this is the wrath of God, that these things should be thus.

18. And this is the grace of God, that these things should be thus.

19. Wherefore I charge you that ye come unto me in the Beginning; for if ye take but one step in this Path, ye must arrive inevitably at the end thereof.

20. This Path is beyond Life and Death; it is also beyond Love; but that ye know not, for ye know not Love.

21. And the end thereof is known not even unto Our Lady or to the Beast whereon She rideth; nor unto the Virgin her daughter nor unto Chaos her lawful Lord; but unto the Crowned Child is it known? It is not known if it be known.

1. Therefore unto Hadit and unto Nuit be the glory in the End and the Beginning; yea, in the End and the Beginning.

Priestess: I am the daughter of Fortitude, and ravished every hour from my youth. For behold I am Understanding and science dwelleth in me; and the heavens oppress me. They cover and desire me with infinite appetite; for none that are earthly have embraced me, for I am shadowed with the Circle of the Stars and covered with the morning clouds. My feet are swifter than the winds, and my hands are sweeter than the morning dew. My garments are from the beginning, and my dwelling place is in myself. The Lion knoweth not where I walk, neither do the beast of the fields understand me. I am deflowered, yet a virgin; I sanctify and am not sanctified. Happy is he that embraceth me: for in the night season I am sweet, and in the day full of pleasure. My company is a harmony of many symbols and my lips sweeter than health itself. I am a harlot for such as ravish me, and a virgin with such as know me not. For lo, I am loved of many, and I am a lover to many; and as many as come unto me as they should do, have entertainment.

Purge your streets, O ye sons of men, and wash your houses clean; make yourselves holy, and put on righteousness. Cast out your old strumpets, and burn their clothes; abstain from the company of other women that are defiled, that are sluttish, and not so handsome and beautiful as I, and then will I come and dwell amongst you: and behold, I will bring forth children unto you, and they shall be the Sons of Comfort. I will open my garments, and stand naked before you, that your love may be more enflamed toward me.

(The mantra continues until the Priestess is fully overcome. She indicates to the Cup Bearer to bring forward the Wine and the Cup so that she may lay her hands on them.)

Priestess: **Hriliu!**

(All stop the chant. The Cup Bearer pours wine for the People. All drink.

The Cup Bearer replaces the Cup upon the altar, and closes the temple with the Poem to Babalon as before.)

Cup Bearer: **Do what thou wilt shall be the whole of the Law.**
Rue not now guilt the Devil's dagger who draw!

I swear toward the West
On BABALON'S bold breast.
I swear toward the South
On her mad merry mouth.
I swear towards the East
On her Cup fiery-fleeced.

I swear towards the North
On Her Disk savage-swarth.
I swear toward the Height
On Her five fingers' Spite.
I swear towards the Deep
On Her soul's smiling sleep.
I swear towards the Centre
By Her and Him that sent Her.

I swear this Oath
Of Troth
To BABALON –
My own
Sister, and Scarlet
Harlot;
I am Her Priest
The BEAST,
To bring to birth
On earth
My word of awe,
The Law
Of Will, above
Its Love.
To BABALON
Alone
This tempered Oath
Of Troth
In Her chaste Cup
Seal up!

Appendix I
Rituals from Liber O

The following rituals of the Pentagram and Hexagram are generally considered the foundation of practical Western magick in the tradition of the Golden Dawn magical Order, and as such you'll see them repeated verbatim in hundreds of magical books published over the past century. Aleister Crowley received much of his basic magical training within the portals of the Golden Dawn, and thus when he set up his own spin-off version of that Order (known as A.A.) one of the first books of instruction he wrote was *Liber O*, which contained these rituals.

The original inspiration for these rituals seems to have been a note by Eliphas Levi in his 19th century classic work *Dogme et Rituel de la Haute Magie* (*Teachings and Ritual of High Magic*, usually incorrectly translated as *Transcendental Magic*). Levi writes:

> *The sign of the Cross adopted by the Christians does not exclusively belong to them. It is also Kabbalistic and represents the oppositions and tetradic equilibrium of the Elements. There were originally two methods of making the Cross; one reserved for the priests and initiates, the other set apart for the neophytes and profane. Thus, for example, the initiate, raising his hand to his forehead said: 'Thine is', then brought his hand to his breast, saying: 'the Kingdom', then, transferred his hand to the left shoulder saying: 'Justice', and finally, to the right shoulder, saying: 'and Mercy'. Then, joining his hands together, added: 'through the generating age'. TIBI SUNT MALCHUT ET GEBURAH ET CHESED PER AEONAS - a sign of the cross which is absolutely and splendidly Kabbalistic, and which the profanations of the Gnosis have entirely lost to the official and militant church. The sign made in this manner should precede and terminate the Conjuration of the Four.*

This translation is not a particularly good one, but you get the idea I hope. From this little note it appears that the Golden Dawn constructed or adapted the so-called "banishing" rituals which have become the standard until today.

You'll find references to these foundation rituals in many of the group rituals in this book, especially in the ones that Crowley wrote in his early years after leaving the G.D. However Crowley himself grew to realise that these rituals were seriously flawed, and several times attempted to write better versions, culminating in the Ritual of the Mark of the Beast given in Chapter 1.

Bizarrely, although Crowley reworked and replaced these rituals almost entirely after around 1912, many Thelemites today seem to think they are still relevant - I personally don't consider them of any value except as historical curiosities, and I haven't used them in years. However since they are referenced in some of the older rites I've given here, I've thought it useful to reprint them. I definitely recommend more modern variations of these rites, such as Crowley's Star Ruby or Mark of the Beast rituals; or my own Nu-Sphere Ritual or Rite of the Infinite Stars (published in my previous book *Abrahadabra*).

These older rituals, like much Golden Dawn material, are frequently overly complex. Instead of having just one pentagram the Golden Dawn decided to have two for each element - one "invoking" pentagram and one "banishing" for Earth, Air, Water, and Fire. That made eight. Then they figured that adding Spirit as an element might be a good way to get a couple more. Not to be outdone they decided not only to have those ten but to add another couple by splitting Spirit into "Spirit Active" and "Spirit Passive" - for what reason I have absolutely no idea.

It also leads to serious internal contradictions - for example the "Banishing Pentagram of Air" is the same as the "Invoking Pentagram of Water", and vice-versa. I utterly fail to see how getting rid of one element can be the same as calling in another. On the other hand, mathematically there are only five lines multiplied by two directions in a pentagram figure i.e. ten vectors in total, so it's not surprising that they ended up with such a mess once they had manufactured twelve pentagrams.

I cannot see any practical reason for all these pentagrams, or for the difference between invoking and banishing ones. One for each basic element should really be more than enough, but here we are. Luckily in most pentagram rituals only the banishing pentagram of Earth is used, so in many cases you won't need all of these anyway. It is true that the Mark of the Beast ritual uses the invoking pentagrams though, so you do need to know how each of these relates to the other.

As regards the Hexagram ritual given below, the Golden Dawn went into complete overdrive with this one, and instead of just giving alternate directions in drawing the hexagrams, actually used different shapes entirely for each element. I find this to be not only unnecessary, but rather silly and pointless. I've never understood the necessity of using Hexagram rituals at all and when I've used "banishing" rituals I've always found that a simple Pentagram ritual is more than satisfactory as a prelude and epilogue to any ritual - and even then it's not usually really necessary.

Traditionally since the time of the G.D. Western magicians have been repeating the superstition that every ritual should start and end with a "banishing", and usually they have taught that it should be the so-called Lesser Banishing Ritual of the Pentagram. Of course, such banishings were never part of traditional magical practice before the Golden Dawn, and Crowley himself pretty much abandoned the practice eventually. For example in *Liber XV* - The Gnostic Mass, there's no mention of a Pentagram ritual being required, nor in any of the other rituals of this period (including the O.T.O. initiation rituals). Instead Crowley employed a technique which might be termed "affirmation of intent"; i.e. the participants together focused on the intent of the ritual they were about to perform, affirmed their purpose in coming together, and their ability and right to perform the work. An excellent example of this process can be seen at the beginning of the section of the Gnostic Mass called The Ceremony of the Introit, where the Deacon leads the People in the Step & Sign, and then in the recitation of the Gnostic Creed. This method of beginning a ritual is very common across many religious traditions throughout history.

Crowley in later life also dispensed with the banishing at the end of a ritual entirely in many cases, especially in invocatory rituals that had as their purpose the establishment of Thelemic power. The Gnostic Mass is again a perfect example of this, as are many of the rituals in this book. It makes sense really - why spend all that time bringing divine energy down to Earth, only to immediately send it all away again?

As time goes on I've learned to appreciate this technique more and more, and frequently employ it instead of the traditional "Pentagram sandwich" technique, especially in many of the invocations in this book. But at the end of the day, you need to use the methods that work for you, so here are the basic Golden Dawn Pentagram and Hexagram rituals just in case you need them.

Lesser Banishing Ritual of the Pentagram

(i)   Touching the forehead, say **Ateh** (Unto Thee).

(ii)   Touching the breast, say **Malkuth** (The Kingdom).

(iii)   Touching the right shoulder, say **ve-Geburah** (and the Power).

(iv)   Touching the left shoulder, say **ve-Gedulah** (and the Glory).

(v)   Clasping the hands upon the breast, say **le-Olahm, Amen** (To the Ages, Amen).

(vi)   Turning to the East, make a pentagram (that of Earth) with the proper weapon (usually the Wand). Say (i.e. vibrate) **I H V H**.

(vii)   Turning to the South, the same, but say **A D N I**.

(viii)   Turning to the West, the same, but say **A H I H**.

(ix)   Turning to the North, the same, but say **A G L A**. (Pronounce: **Yeh-ho-vah, Ad-oh-nye, Eh-hee-eh, Ahg-lah**).

(x)   Extending the arms in the form of a Cross, say:

(xi)   **Before me Raphael**;

(xii)   **Behind me Gabriel**;

(xiii)   **On my right hand Michael**;

(xiv)   **On my left hand Auriel**;

(xv)   **For about me flames the Pentagram,**

(xvi)   **And in the Column stands the six-rayed Star.**

(xvii-xxi)   Repeat (i) to (v), the "Qabalistic Cross."

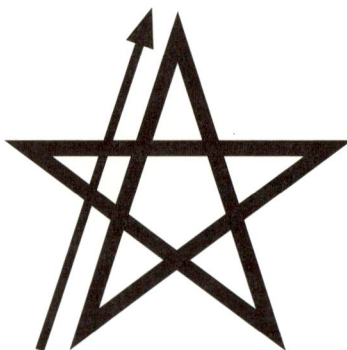

The Banishing Pentagram of Earth

Lesser Banishing Ritual of the Hexagram

This ritual is to be performed after the "Lesser Ritual of the Pentagram".

(i) Stand upright, feet together, left arm at side, right across body, holding the wand or other weapon upright in the median line. Then face East and say:

(ii) **I.N.R.I.**
Yod. Nun. Resh. Yod.
Virgo, Isis, Mighty Mother.
Scorpio, Apophis, Destroyer.
Sol, Osiris, Slain and Risen.
Isis, Apophis, Osiris, IAO.

(iii) Extend the arms in the form of a cross, and say: "**The Sign of Osiris Slain.**"

(iv) Raise the right arm to point upwards, keeping the elbow square, and lower the left arm to point downwards, keeping the elbow square, while turning the head over the left shoulder looking down so that the eyes follow the left forearm, and say, "**The Sign of the Mourning of Isis.**"

(v) Raise the arms at an angle of sixty degrees to each other above the head, which is thrown back, and say, "**The Sign of Apophis and Typhon.**"

(vi) Cross the arms on the breast, and bow the head and say, "**The Sign of Osiris Risen.**"

(vii) Extend the arms again as in (iii) and cross them again as in (vi) saying: "L.V.X., **Lux, the Light of the Cross**".

(viii) With the magical weapon trace the Hexagram of Fire in the East, saying, "**ARARITA**".

This Word consists of the initials of a sentence which means "One is His Beginning: One is His Individuality: His Permutation is One." This hexagram consists of two equilateral triangles, both apices pointed upwards. Begin at the top of the upper triangle and trace it in a dextro-rotary direction.

The top of the lower triangle should coincide with the central point of the upper triangle.

(ix) Trace the Hexagram of Earth in the South, saying "**ARARITA**".

This Hexagram has the apex of the lower triangle pointing downwards, and it should be capable of inscription in a circle.

(x) Trace the Hexagram of Air in the West, saying "**ARARITA**".

This Hexagram is like that of Earth; but the bases of the triangles coincide, forming a diamond.

(xi) Trace the hexagram of Water in the North, saying "**ARARITA**".

This hexagram has the lower triangle placed above the upper, so that their apices coincide.

(xii) Repeat (i-vii)

Fire

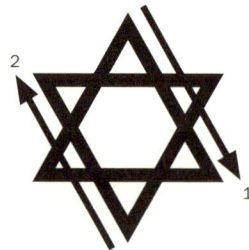

Earth

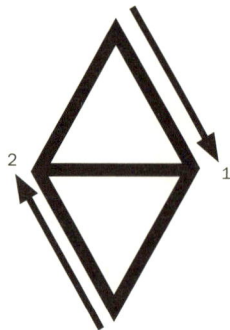

Air

Water

The Elemental Hexagrams

Appendix II
The 72 Spirits of the Goetia

I have updated the standard medieval descriptions of the spirits of the Goetia into modern language, and have categorised their various qualities to make it easier for ritualists to find and understand which one might be best for their purposes. For the more traditional descriptions see Crowley's *Goetia*.

	Number: 01 *Name*: Bael *Rank*: King *Physical characteristics*: Diverse shapes, sometimes like a cat, sometimes like a toad, sometimes like a man, and sometimes all these forms at once. *Powers*: Can make you invisible. *Rulership*: 66 legions of infernal spirits. *Remarks*: Speaks hoarsely. You must wear his seal as a lamen when you call him, otherwise he will not do homage to you.
	Number: 02 *Name*: Agares *Rank*: Duke *Physical characteristics*: The form of an old fair man, riding upon a crocodile, carrying a goshawk upon his fist, yet mild in appearance *Powers*: He makes those that stand still start running, and brings back runaways. He teaches all current languages. He also has power to destroy dignities both spiritual and temporal, and cause earthquakes. *Rulership*: 31 legions of spirits. *Remarks*: Under the power of the East. Used to be of the Order of Virtues *[before the legendary Fall from Heaven, presumably]*.
	Number: 03 *Name*: Vassago *Rank*: Prince *Physical characteristics*: Nothing given *Powers*: He will declare things past and to come, and discover all things hid or lost. *Rulership*: 26 legions of spirits. *Remarks*: Good natured.

Number: 04
Name: Samigina, or Gamigin
Rank: Marquis
Physical characteristics: Appears in the form of a little horse or donkey, and then into human shape at the request of the magician.
Powers: He teaches all liberal sciences, and gives accounts of dead souls that died in sin.
Rulership: 30 legions of inferiors.
Remarks: Speaks with a hoarse voice.

Number: 05
Name: Marbas
Rank: President
Physical characteristics: Appears at first in the form of a large lion, but afterwards, at the request of the magician, takes human shape.
Powers: Answers truly about things hidden or secret. He causes diseases and cures them. Gives great wisdom and knowledge in mechanical arts; and can change people into other shapes.
Rulership: 36 legions of spirits.

Number: 06
Name: Valefor
Rank: Duke
Physical characteristics: Appears in the shape of a lion with a donkey's head, bellowing.
Powers: Although he is a good familiar, he tempts those whom he is a familiar of to steal.
Rulership: 10 legions of spirits.

Number: 07
Name: Amon
Rank: Marquis
Physical characteristics: Appears like a wolf with a serpent's tail, vomiting out of his mouth flames of fire; but at the command of the magician he changes to the shape of a man with a raven's head and dog's teeth.
Powers: He tells all things past and to come. He creates feuds and reconciles controversies between friends.
Rulership: 40 legions of spirits.
Remarks: Is great in power, and very stern.

Number: 08
Name: Barbatos
Rank: Duke
Physical characteristics: Appears with four noble Kings and their companies of great troops.
Powers: He gives understanding of the singing of birds, and of the voices of other creatures, such as the barking of dogs. He breaks open the hidden treasures that have been laid by the enchantments of magicians. He knows all things past, and to come; and reconciles friends and those who are in power.
Rulership: 30 legions of spirits.
Remarks: Appears when the Sun is in Sagittarius *[so presumably for only one month of the year].* He is of the Order of Virtues, and still retains some part of this.

Number: 09
Name: Paimon
Rank: King
Physical characteristics: He appears in the form of a man sitting upon a dromedary *[camel]* with a glorious crown most upon his head. Before him goes a host of spirits, who appear like men with trumpets, cymbals and all other sorts of musical instruments.
Powers: He can teach all arts and sciences, and other secret things. He can teach you what the earth is, and how it works; and what mind is, and where it is; or any other thing you may desire to know. He gives dignity, and confirms the same. He binds or makes anyone subject to the magician if desired. He gives good familiars who can teach all arts.
Rulership: 200 legions of spirits - part of them are of the Order of Angels, and the other part of Potentates.
Remarks: He has a loud voice, and roars at his first coming, and his speech is such that the magician cannot understand easily unless the spirit is compelled. He is to be observed towards the West. He is of the Order of Dominations. If you call Paimon alone, you must make him some offering; and two Kings called Labal and Abalim will attend him, with other spirits of the Order of Potentates, and 25 legions of subject spirits. However these subject spirits are not always with them unless the magician compels them.

Number: 10
Name: Buer
Rank: President
Physical characteristics: Appears like the symbol for Sagittarius *[i.e. a centaur with bow & arrow].*
Powers: He teaches philosophy, physics, and the art of logic; and also the virtues of all herbs and plants. He heals all ills in man, and gives good familiars.
Rulership: 50 legions of spirits.
Remarks: Appears when the Sun is in Sagittarius *[so presumably for only one month of the year].*

Number: 11
Name: Gusion
Rank: Duke
Physical characteristics: He appears like a xenopilus
[*i.e. like a man with a dog's head*].
Powers: He tells all things, past, present, and to come, and
shows the meaning and resolution of all questions asked.
He creates and reconciles friendships, and gives honour and
dignity unto anyone requested.
Rulership: 40 legions of spirits.

Number: 12
Name: Sitri
Rank: Prince
Physical characteristics: Appears at first with a leopard's
head and the wings of a gryphon, but on the command of
the exorcist he puts on a very beautiful human shape.
Powers: He enflames men with love of women, and women
with love of men; and also causes them to show themselves
naked if desired.
Rulership: 60 legions of spirits.

Number: 13
Name: Beleth (or Bileth, or Bilet).
Rank: King
Physical characteristics: He rides on a pale horse with
trumpets and other kinds of musical instruments playing
before him.
Powers: Causes all the love that may be, both of men and
of women, until the exorcist's desire is fulfilled.
Rulership: 85 legions of spirits.
Remarks: He is very furious at his first appearance, so the
exorcist must act with courage. You should hold a hazel
wand in your hand: striking it out towards the South and
East quarters, make a triangle outside the magick circle, and
then command the spirit into it by the bonds and charges of
spirits listed. If the spirit does not enter into the triangle at
your threats, repeat the bonds and charms before him, and
then he will yield obedience and come into it, and do what
he is commanded by the exorcist. Yet you must receive him
courteously because he is a great King, and do homage unto
him, as the kings and princes do that attend upon him. And
you must have always a silver ring on the middle finger of
the left hand held against your face, as with Amaymon. He is
of the Order of Powers.

Number: 14
Name: Leraje, or Leraikka
Rank: Marquis
Physical characteristics: An archer clad in green, and carrying a bow and quiver.
Powers: He causes all great battles and contests; and makes wounds to putrefy that are made with arrows by archers.
Rulership: 30 legions of spirits.
Remarks: Belongs to Sagittarius.

Number: 15
Name: Eligos
Rank: Duke
Physical characteristics: The form of a goodly knight, carrying a lance, an ensign, and a serpent.
Powers: He discovers hidden things, and knows things to come; and of wars, and how the soldiers will or shall meet. He causes the love of lords and great persons.
Rulership: 60 legions of spirits.

Number: 16
Name: Zepar
Rank: Duke
Physical characteristics: Appears in red apparel and armour, like a soldier.
Powers: His office is to cause women to love men, and to bring them together in love. He also makes them barren.
Rulership: 26 legions of spirits.

Number: 17
Name: Botis
Rank: President & Earl
Physical characteristics: He appears at the first show in the form of an ugly viper, then at the command of the magician he puts on a human shape with great teeth, and two horns, carrying a bright and sharp sword in his hand.
Powers: He tells all things past, and to come, and reconciles friends and foes.
Rulership: 60 legions of spirits.

Number: 18
Name: Bathin
Rank: Duke
Physical characteristics: A strong man with the tail of a serpent, sitting upon a pale-coloured horse.
Powers: He knows the virtues of herbs and precious stones, and can transport people suddenly from one country to another.
Rulership: 30 legions of spirits.

Number: 19
Name: Sallos
Rank: Duke
Physical characteristics: The form of a gallant soldier riding on a crocodile, with a ducal crown on his head, but peaceably.
Powers: He causes the love of women to men, and of men to women.
Rulership: 30 legions of spirits.

Number: 20
Name: Purson
Rank: King
Physical characteristics: His appearing is comely, like a man with a lion's face, carrying a cruel viper in his hand, and riding upon a bear. Going before him are many trumpets sounding.
Powers: He knows all things hidden, and can discover treasure, and tell all things past, present, and to come. He can take a body either human or aerial, and answers truly about all earthly things both secret and divine, and of the creation of the world.
Rulership: 22 legions of spirits, partly of the Order of Virtues and partly of the Order of Thrones.
Remarks: He brings forth good familiars.

Number: 21
Name: Marax
Rank: Earl & President
Physical characteristics: He appears like a great bull with a man's face.
Powers: His office is to make people very knowing in astronomy, and all other liberal sciences; also he can give good and wise familiars, knowing the virtues of herbs and precious stones.
Rulership: 30 legions of spirits.

Number: 22
Name: Ipos
Rank: Earl & Prince
Physical characteristics: He appears in the form of an angel with a lion's head, and a goose's foot, and hare's tail.
Powers: He knows all things past, present, and to come. He makes people witty and bold.
Rulership: 36 legions of spirits.

Number: 23
Name: Aim
Rank: Duke
Physical characteristics: He appears in the form of a very handsome man in body, but with three heads; the first like a serpent, the second like a man having two stars on his forehead, the third like a calf. He rides on a viper, carrying a firebrand in his Hand, with which he sets cities, castles, and great places on fire.
Powers: He makes you witty in all manner of ways, and gives true answers to private matters.
Rulership: 26 legions of inferior spirits.

Number: 24
Name: Naberius
Rank: Marquis
Physical characteristics: The form of a black crane fluttering about the circle, and when he speaks it is with a hoarse voice.
Powers: He makes people cunning in all arts and sciences, but especially in the art of rhetoric. He restores lost dignities and honours.
Rulership: 19 legions of spirits.

Number: 25
Name: Glasya-Labolas
Rank: President & Earl
Physical characteristics: The form of a dog with wings like a gryphon.
Powers: He teaches all arts and sciences in an instant, and is an author of bloodshed and manslaughter. He teaches all things past, and to come. If desired he causes the love both of friends and of foes. He can make a person go invisible.
Rulership: 36 legions of spirits.

Number: 26
Name: Buné (or Bim)
Rank: Duke
Physical characteristics: He appears in the form of a dragon with three heads, one like a dog, one like a gryphon, and one like a man. He speaks with a high and comely voice.
Powers: He changes the place of the dead, and causes the spirits which are under him to gather together upon your sepulchres. He gives riches unto a person, and makes one wise and eloquent. He gives true answers to demands.
Rulership: 30 legions of spirits.

Number: 27
Name: Ronové
Rank: Marquis & Earl
Physical characteristics: He appears in the form of a monster.
Powers: He teaches the art of rhetoric very well, and gives good servants, knowledge of tongues, and favours with friends or foes.
Rulership: 19 legions of spirits.

Number: 28
Name: Berith
Rank: Duke
Physical characteristics: He appears in the form of a soldier with red clothing, riding upon a red horse, and having a crown of gold upon his head. He speaks with a very clear and subtle voice.
Powers: He gives true answers, past, present, and to come. He can turn all metals into gold. He can give dignities, and can confirm them unto people.
Rulership: 26 legions of spirits.
Remarks: He has two other names given to him by men of later times, which are Beale or Beal; and Bofry or Bolfry. You must make use of a ring in calling him forth, as is before spoken of regarding Beleth. He is a great liar, and not to be trusted.

Number: 29
Name: Astaroth
Rank: Duke
Physical characteristics: Appears in the form of a hurtful angel riding on an infernal beast like a dragon, and carrying in his right hand a viper.
Powers: He gives true answers of things past, present, and to come, and can discover all secrets. He will declare wittingly how the spirits fell, if desired, and the reason of his own fall. He can make people wonderfully knowing in all liberal sciences.
Rulership: 40 legions of spirits.
Remarks: You must in no wise let him approach too near to you, lest he do damage by his noisome breath. Because of this the magician must hold the magical ring near his face, and that will defend him.

Number: 30
Name: Forneus
Rank: Marquis
Physical characteristics: Appears in the form of a great sea monster.
Powers: He teaches, and makes people wonderfully knowing in, the art of rhetoric. He causes men to have a good name, and to have the knowledge and understanding of languages. He makes one to be beloved of foes as well as of friends.
Rulership: 29 legions of spirits, partly of the Order of Thrones, and partly of that of Angels.

Number: 31
Name: Foras
Rank: President
Physical characteristics: Appears in the form of a strong man in human shape.
Powers: He can give the understanding to people as to how they may know the virtues of all herbs and precious stones. He teaches the arts of logic and ethics in all their parts. If desired he makes people invisible, and to live long, and to be eloquent. He can discover treasures and recover things lost.
Rulership: 29 legions of spirits.

Number: 32
Name: Asmoday, or Asmodai
Rank: King
Physical characteristics: He appears with three heads, whereof the first is like a bull, the second like a man, and the third like a ram; he also has the tail of a serpent, and from his mouth issue flames of fire. His feet are webbed like those of a goose. He sits upon an infernal dragon, and bears in his hand a lance with a banner.
Powers: He gives the ring of virtues; he teaches the arts of arithmetic, astronomy, geometry, and all handicrafts absolutely. He gives true and full answers unto your demands. He makes one invincible. He shows the place where treasures lie, and guards it.
Rulership: 72 legions of spirits.
Remarks: He is first and choicest under the power of Amaymon, he goes before all other. When the Exorcist has a mind to call him, let it be abroad, and let him stand on his feet all the time of action, with his cap or headdress off; for if it is on, Amaymon will deceive him and call all his actions to be betrayed. But as soon as the Exorcist sees Asmoday in the shape above, call him by his name, saying: "Are you Asmoday?" and he will not deny it, and by-and-by he will bow down unto the ground.

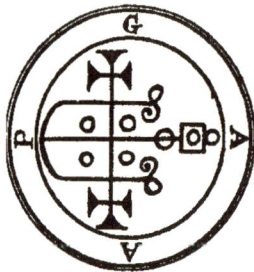

Number: 33
Name: Gäap
Rank: President & Prince
Physical characteristics: Appears in a human shape, going before four great and mighty kings, as if he were a guide to conduct them along on their way.
Powers: His office is to make people insensible or ignorant; as also in philosophy to make them knowing, and in all the liberal sciences. He can cause love or hatred, also he can teach you to consecrate those things that belong to the dominion of Amaymon his king. He can deliver familiars out of the custody of other magicians, and answers truly and perfectly of things past, present and to come. He can carry and re-carry people very speedily from one kingdom to another, at the will and pleasure of the Exorcist.
Rulership: 66 legions of spirits.
Remarks: He appears when the sun is in some of the Southern signs, and he was of the Order of Potentates.

Number: 34
Name: Furfur
Rank: Earl
Physical characteristics: The form of a hart with a fiery tail. He never speaks truth unless he be compelled, or brought up within a triangle. Being therein, he will take upon himself the form of an angel. Being bidden, he speaks with a hoarse voice.
Powers: He will wittingly urge love between man and woman. He can raise lightnings and thunders, blasts, and great tempestuous storms. And he gives true answers both of things secret and divine, if commanded.
Rulership: 26 legions of spirits.

Number: 35
Name: Marchosias
Rank: Marquis
Physical characteristics: Appears at first in the form of a wolf having gryphon's wings, and a serpent's tail, and vomiting fire out of his mouth. But after a time, at the command of the Exorcist he puts on the shape of a man.
Powers: He gives true answers to all questions, and is very faithful to the Exorcist in doing his business.
Rulership: 30 legions of spirits.
Remarks: He is a strong fighter, and was of the Order of Dominations. He told his chief, who was Solomon, that after 1,200 years he had hopes to return to the Seventh Throne.

Number: 36
Name: Stolas, or Stolos
Rank: Prince
Physical characteristics: Appears in the shape of a mighty raven at first before the Exorcist; but after he takes on the image of a man.
Powers: He teaches the art of astronomy, and the virtues of herbs and precious stones.
Rulership: 26 legions of spirits.

Number: 37
Name: Phenex (or Pheynix)
Rank: Marquis
Physical characteristics: Appears like the phœnix bird, having the voice of a child. He sings many sweet notes before the Exorcist, which you must not regard, but by-and-by you must bid him put on human shape.
Powers: He will speak marvellously of all wonderful sciences if required. He is an excellent poet, and will be willing to perform your requests.
Rulership: 20 legions of spirits.
Remarks: He has hopes to return to the seventh throne after 1,200 years more, as he said to Solomon.

Number: 38
Name: Halphas, or Malthus (or Malthas)
Rank: Earl
Physical characteristics: Appears in the form of a stock-dove. He speaks with a hoarse voice.
Powers: His office is to build up towers, and to furnish them with ammunition and weapons, and to send men-of-war to places appointed.
Rulership: 26 legions of spirits.

Number: 39
Name: Malphas
Rank: President
Physical characteristics: He appears at first like a crow, but after he will put on human shape at the request of the Exorcist, and speak with a hoarse voice.
Powers: He can build houses and high towers, and can bring to your knowledge enemies' desires and thoughts, and that which they have done. He gives good familiars.
Rulership: 40 legions of spirits.
Remarks: If you make a sacrifice to him he will receive it kindly and willingly, but he will deceive anyone that does it.

Number: 40
Name: Räum
Rank: Earl
Physical characteristics: Appears at first in the form of a crow, but after the command of the Exorcist he puts on human shape.
Powers: His office is to steal treasures out of king's houses, and to carry it whither he is commanded, and to destroy cities and dignities of men, and to tell all things, past, and what is, and what will be; and to cause love between friends and foes.
Rulership: 30 legions of spirits.
Remarks: He was of the Order of Thrones.

Number: 41
Name: Focalor, or Forcalor, or Furcalor
Rank: Duke
Physical characteristics: He appears in the form of a man with gryphon's wings.
Powers: His office is to slay men, and to drown them in the waters, and to overthrow ships of war, for he has power over both winds and seas; but he will not hurt any man or thing if he be commanded to the contrary by the Exorcist.
Rulership: 30 legions of spirits.
Remarks: He also has hopes to return to the seventh throne after 1,000 years.

Number: 42
Name: Vepar, or Vephar
Rank: Duke
Physical characteristics: Appears like a mermaid.
Powers: His office is to govern the waters, and to guide ships laden with arms, armour, and ammunition, etc. And at the request of the Exorcist he can cause the seas to be right stormy and to appear full of ships. Also he makes men to die in three days by putrefying wounds or sores, and causing worms to breed in them.
Rulership: 29 legions of spirits.

Number: 43
Name: Sabnock, or Savnok
Rank: Marquis
Physical characteristics: Appears in the form of an armed soldier with a lion's head, riding on a pale-coloured horse.
Powers: His office is to build high towers, castles and cities, and to furnish them with armour, etc. Also he can afflict men for many days with wounds and with sores rotten and full of worms.
Rulership: 50 legions of spirits.

Number: 44
Name: Shax, or Shaz (or Shass)
Rank: Marquis
Physical characteristics: Appears in the form of a stock-dove, speaking with a voice hoarse, but yet subtle.
Powers: His office is to take away the sight, hearing, or understanding of any man or woman at the command of the Exorcist; and to steal money out of the houses of kings, and to carry it again in 1,200 years. If commanded he will fetch horses at the request of the Exorcist, or any other thing. He can discover all things that are hidden, and not kept by wicked spirits. He gives good familiars, sometimes.
Rulership: 30 legions of spirits.
Remarks: He must first be commanded into a Triangle, or else he will deceive you, and tell you many lies.

Number: 45
Name: Viné, or Vinea
Rank: King and Earl
Physical characteristics: Appears in the form of a lion, riding upon a black horse, and bearing a viper in his hand.
Powers: His office is to discover things hidden, witches, wizards, and things present, past, and to come. He, at the command of the Exorcist will build towers, overthrow great stone walls, and make the waters rough with storms.
Rulership: 36 legions of spirits.

Number: 46
Name: Bifrons, or Bifröus, or Bifrovs
Rank: Earl
Physical characteristics: Appears in the form of a monster; but after a while, at the command of the Exorcist he puts on the shape of a man.
Powers: His office is to make one knowing in astrology, geometry, and other arts and sciences. He teaches the virtues of precious stones and woods. He changes dead bodies, and puts them in another place; also he lights what seem like candles upon the graves of the dead.
Rulership: 6 legions of spirits.

Number: 47
Name: Uvall, Vual, or Voval
Rank: Duke
Physical characteristics: Appears in the form of a mighty dromedary at the first, but after a while at the command of the Exorcist he puts on human shape, and speaks the Egyptian language, but not perfectly.
Powers: His office is to procure the love of women, and to tell things past, present, and to come. He also procures friendship between friends and foes.
Rulership: 37 legions of spirits.
Remarks: He was of the Order of Potestates or Powers.

Number: 48
Name: Haagenti
Rank: President
Physical characteristics: Appears in the form of a mighty bull with gryphon's wings. This is at first, but after, at the command of the Exorcist he puts on human shape.
Powers: His office is to make people wise, and to instruct them in diverse things; also to transmute all metals into gold; and to change wine into water, and water into wine.
Rulership: 33 legions of spirits.

Number: 49
Name: Crocell, or Crokel
Rank: Duke
Physical characteristics: He appears in the form of an angel.
Powers: He speaks mystically of hidden things. He teaches the art of geometry and the liberal sciences. He, at the command of the Exorcist, will produce great noises like the rushings of many waters, although there be none. He warms waters, and discovers baths.
Rulership: 48 legions of spirits.
Remarks: He was of the Order of Potestates, or Powers, before his fall, as he declared to King Solomon.

Number: 50
Name: Furcas
Rank: Knight
Physical characteristics: Appears in the form of a cruel old man with a long beard and a hoary head, riding upon a pale-coloured horse, with a sharp weapon in his hand.
Powers: His office is to teach the arts of philosophy, astrology, rhetoric, logic, cheiromancy, and pyromancy, in all their parts, and perfectly.
Rulership: 20 legions of spirits.

Number: 51
Name: Balam or Balaam
Rank: King
Physical characteristics: He appears with three heads: the first is like that of a bull; the second is like that of a man; the third is like that of a ram. He has the tail of a serpent, and flaming eyes. He rides upon a furious bear, and carries a goshawk upon his fist.
Powers: He speaks with a hoarse voice, giving true answers of things past, present, and to come
Rulership: 40 legions of spirits.

Number: 52
Name: Alloces, or Alocas
Rank: Duke
Physical characteristics: Appears in the form of a soldier riding upon a great horse. His face is like that of a lion, very red, and having flaming eyes. His speech is hoarse and very big.
Powers: His office is to teach the art of astronomy, and all the liberal sciences. He brings good familiars to you.
Rulership: 36 legions of spirits.

Number: 53
Name: Camio, or Caïm
Rank: President
Physical characteristics: Appears in the form of the bird called a thrush at first, but afterwards he puts on the shape of a man carrying in his hand a sharp sword. He seems to answer in burning ashes, or in coals of fire.
Powers: His office is to give unto people the understanding of all birds, lowing of bullocks, barking of dogs, and other creatures; and also of the voice of the waters. He gives true answers of things to come.
Rulership: 30 legions of spirits.
Remarks: He is a good disputer. He was of the Order of Angels, but now rules over 30 legions of infernal spirits.

Number: 54
Name: Murmur, or Murmus, or Murmux
Rank: Duke and Earl
Physical characteristics: Appears in the form of a warrior riding upon a gryphon, with a ducal crown upon his head. Before him go his ministers with great trumpets sounding.
Powers: His office is to teach philosophy perfectly, and to constrain souls deceased to come before the Exorcist to answer those questions which he may wish to put to them, if desired.
Rulership: 30 legions of spirits.
Remarks: He was partly of the Order of Thrones, and partly of that of Angels.

Number: 55
Name: Orobas
Rank: Prince
Physical characteristics: Appears at first like a horse; but after the command of the Exorcist he puts on the image of a man.
Powers: His office is to discover all things past, present, and to come; also to give dignities, and prelacies, and the favour of friends and of foes. He gives true answers of divinity, and of the creation of the world.
Rulership: 20 legions of spirits.
Remarks: He is very faithful to the Exorcist, and will not allow you to be tempted by any Spirit.

Number: 56
Name: Gremory, or Gamori
Rank: Duke
Physical characteristics: Appears in the form of a beautiful woman, with a duchess's crown tied about her waist, and riding on a great camel.
Powers: His office is to tell of all things past, present, and to come; and of treasures hid, and what they lie in; and to procure the love of women both young and old.
Rulership: 26 legions of spirits.

Number: 57
Name: Oso, Osé, or Voso
Rank: President
Physical characteristics: Appears like a leopard at the first, but after a little time he puts on the shape of a man.
Powers: His office is to make one cunning in the liberal sciences, and to give true answers of divine and secret things; also to change a person into any shape that the Exorcist pleases, so that those changed will not think anything other than that they are really that creature or thing changed into.
Rulership: 3 legions of spirits.

Number: 58
Name: Amy, or Avnas
Rank: President
Physical characteristics: Appears at first in the form of a flaming fire; but after a while he puts on the shape of a man.
Powers: His office is to make one wonderfully knowing in astrology and all the liberal sciences. He gives good familiars, and can reveal treasure that is kept by spirits.
Rulership: 36 legions of spirits.

Number: 59
Name: Oriax, or Orias
Rank: Marquis
Physical characteristics: Appears in the form of a lion, riding upon a mighty and strong horse, with a serpent's tail; and he holds in his right hand two great serpents hissing.
Powers: His office is to teach the virtues of the stars, and to know the mansions of the planets, and how to understand their virtues. He also transforms people, and he gives dignities, prelacies, and confirmation of these; also favour with friends and with foes.
Rulership: 30 legions of spirits.

Number: 60
Name: Vapula, or Naphula
Rank: Duke
Physical characteristics: Appears in the form of a lion with gryphon's wings.
Powers: His office is to make people knowing in all handicrafts and professions, also in philosophy, and other sciences.
Rulership: 36 legions of spirits.

Number: 61
Name: Zagan
Rank: King and President
Physical characteristics: Appears at first in the form of a bull with gryphon's wings; but after a while he puts on human shape.
Powers: He makes people witty. He can turn wine into water, and blood into wine, also water into wine. He can turn all metals into coin of the dominion that the metal is of. He can even make fools wise.
Rulership: 33 legions of spirits.

	Number: 62 *Name*: Volac, or Valak, or Valu, or Ualac *Rank*: President *Physical characteristics*: Appears like a child with angel's wings, riding on a two-headed dragon. *Powers*: His office is to give true answers of hidden treasures, and to tell where serpents may be seen. These he will bring unto the Exorcist without any force or strength being employed by him. *Rulership*: 38 legions of spirits.
	Number: 63 *Name*: Andras *Rank*: Marquis *Physical characteristics*: Appears in the form of an angel with a head like a black night raven, riding upon a strong black wolf, and having a sharp and bright sword flourished aloft in his hand. *Powers*: His office is to sow discord. *Rulership*: 30 legions of spirits. *Remarks*: If the Exorcist is not careful, Andras will slay both the Exorcist and any companions.
	Number: 64 *Name*: Haures, or Hauras, or Havres, or Flauros *Rank*: Duke *Physical characteristics*: He appears at first like a leopard, mighty, terrible, and strong, but after a while, at the command of the Exorcist, he puts on the shape of a human with flaming and fiery eyes, and a most terrible countenance. *Powers*: He gives true answers about all things, present, past, and to come. He will talk of the creation of the world, and of divinity, and of how he and other spirits fell. He destroys and burns up those who are the enemies of the Exorcist should you so desire it; also he will not suffer you to be tempted by any other spirit or otherwise. *Rulership*: 36 legions of spirits. *Remarks*: If he is not commanded into a triangle, he will lie in all these things, and deceive and beguile the Exorcist in these things or other business.
	Number: 65 *Name*: Andrealphus *Rank*: Marquis *Physical characteristics*: Appears at first in the form of a peacock, with great noises. But after a time he puts on human shape. *Powers*: He can teach geometry perfectly. He makes people very subtle in it; and in all things pertaining to measurement or astronomy. He can transform a person into the likeness of a bird. *Rulership*: 30 legions of spirits.

Number: 66
Name: Cimejes, or Cimeies, or Kimaris
Rank: Marquis
Physical characteristics: A valiant warrior riding upon an impressive black horse.
Powers: His office is to teach perfectly grammar, logic, rhetoric, and to discover things lost or hidden, and treasures.
Rulership: 20 legions of spirits.
Remarks: He rules over all spirits in the parts of Africa.

Number: 67
Name: Amdusias, or Amdukias
Rank: Duke
Physical characteristics: Appears at first like a unicorn, but at the request of the Exorcist he will stand before you in human shape, causing trumpets, and all manner of musical instruments to be heard, but not soon or immediately.
Powers: He can cause trees to bend and incline according to the Exorcist's will.
Rulership: 29 legions of spirits.
Remarks: He gives excellent familiars.

Number: 68
Name: Belial
Rank: King
Physical characteristics: He appears in the form of two beautiful angels sitting in a chariot of fire. He speaks with a comely voice, and declares that he fell first from among the worthier sort, that were before Michael, and other heavenly angels.
Powers: His office is to distribute presentations and senatorships, etc., and to cause favour of friends and of foes.
Rulership: 80 legions of spirits.
Remarks: He was created next after Lucifer. He gives excellent familiars. Note well that this King Belial must have offerings, sacrifices and gifts presented unto him by the Exorcist, or else he will not give true answers unto his demands. But then he tarries not one hour in the truth, unless he be constrained by divine power.

Number: 69
Name: Decarabia
Rank: Marquis
Physical characteristics: He appears in the form of a star in a pentacle at first; but after, at the command of the Exorcist, he puts on the image of a man.
Powers: His office is to discover the virtues of birds and precious stones, and to make the similitude of all kinds of birds to fly before the Exorcist, singing and drinking as natural birds do.
Rulership: 30 legions of spirits.

Number: 70
Name: Seere, Sear, or Seir.
Rank: Prince
Physical characteristics: A beautiful man, riding upon a winged horse.
Powers: His office is to go and come; and to bring abundance of things to pass on a sudden, and to carry or re-carry anything wherever you would have it to go, or where you would have it from. He can pass over the whole earth in the twinkling of an eye. He gives a true account of all sorts of theft, and of treasure hid, and of many other things.
Rulership: 26 legions of spirits.
Remarks: He is of an indifferent good nature, and is willing to do anything which the Exorcist desires.

Number: 71
Name: Dantalion
Rank: Duke
Physical characteristics: The form of a man with many countenances, all men's and women's faces.
Powers: His office is to teach all arts and sciences unto any; and to declare the secret counsels of any one; for he knows the thoughts of all men and women, and can change them at his will. He can cause love, and show the similitude of any person, and show the same by a vision, let them be in what part of the world they will.
Rulership: 36 legions of spirits.

Number: 72
Name: Andromalius
Rank: Earl
Physical characteristics: A man holding a great serpent in his hand.
Powers: His office is to bring back both a thief, and the goods which have be stolen; and to discover all wickedness, and underhand dealing; and to punish all thieves and other wicked people; and also to discover treasures that are hidden.
Rulership: 36 legions of spirits.

Appendix III
Three Holy Books

The following are three of the Holy Books of Thelema, or Class A texts, a group of inspired writings received by Aleister Crowley in the early years of the 20th century. Crowley claimed that these emanated from beyond his normal consciousness and thus contained many secrets of mystic illumination. I have used these three particular texts as source material for the rubric of some of the rituals in this book, so it is only fitting if I print them in their entirety here for you to study.

Liber Stellae Rubeae

A secret ritual of Apep, the Heart of IAO-OAI, delivered unto V.V.V.V.V. for his use in a certain matter of Liber Legis, and written down under the figure LXVI

1. Apep deifieth Asar.
2. Let excellent virgins evoke rejoicing, son of Night!
3. This is the book of the most secret cult of the Ruby Star. It shall be given to none, save to the shameless in deed as in word.
4. No man shall understand this writing - it is too subtle for the sons of men.
5. If the Ruby Star have shed its blood upon thee; if in the season of the moon thou hast invoked by the Iod and the Pe, then mayest thou partake of this most secret sacrament.
6. One shall instruct another, with no care for the matters of men's thought.
7. There shall be a fair altar in the midst, extended upon a black stone.
8. At the head of the altar gold, and twin images in green of the Master.
9. In the midst a cup of green wine.
10. At the foot the Star of Ruby.
11. The altar shall be entirely bare.

12. First, the ritual of the Flaming Star.

13. Next, the ritual of the Seal.

14. Next, the infernal adorations of OAI

15. Mu pa telai,
    Tu wa melai
    a, a, a.
    Tu fu tulu!
    Tu fu tulu
    Pa, Sa, Ga.

16. Qwi Mu telai
    Ya Pu melai;
    u, u, u.
    'Se gu malai;
    Pe fu telai,
    Fu tu lu.

17. O chi balae
    Wa pa malae: -
    Ut! Ut! Ut!
    Ge; fu latrai,
    Le fu malai
    Kut! Hut! Nut!

18. Al OAI
    Rel moai
    Ti - Ti - Ti!
    Wa la pelai
    Tu fu latai
    Wi, Ni, Bi.

19. Also thou shalt excite the wheels with the five wounds and the five wounds.

20. Then thou shalt excite the wheels with the two and the third in the midst; even Saturn and Jupiter, Sun and Moon, Mars and Venus, and Mercury.

21. Then the five - and the sixth.

22. Also the altar shall fume before the master with incense that hath no smoke.

23. That which is to be denied shall be denied; that which is to be trampled shall be trampled; that which is to be spat upon shall be spat upon.

24. These things shall be burnt in the outer fire.

25. Then again the master shall speak as he will soft words, and with music and what else he will bring forward the Victim.

26. Also he shall slay a young child upon the altar, and the blood shall cover the altar with perfume as of roses.
27. Then shall the master appear as He should appear - in His glory.
28. He shall stretch himself upon the altar, and awake it into life, and into death.
29. (For so we conceal that life which is beyond.)
30. The temple shall be darkened, save for the fire and the lamp of the altar.
31. There shall he kindle a great fire and a devouring.
32. Also he shall smite the altar with his scourge, and blood shall flow therefrom.
33. Also he shall have made roses bloom thereon.
34. In the end he shall offer up the Vast Sacrifice, at the moment when the God licks up the flame upon the altar.
35. All these things shalt thou perform strictly, observing the time.
36. And the Beloved shall abide with Thee.
37. Thou shalt not disclose the interior world of this rite unto any one: therefore have I written it in symbols that cannot be understood.
38. I who reveal the ritual am IAO and OAI; the Right and the Averse.
39. These are alike unto me.
40. Now the Veil of this operation is called Shame, and the Glory abideth within.
41. Thou shalt comfort the heart of the secret stone with the warm blood. Thou shalt make a subtle decoction of delight, and the Watchers shall drink thereof.
42. I, Apep the Serpent, am the heart of IAO. Isis shall await Asar, and I in the midst.
43. Also the Priestess shall seek another altar, and perform my ceremonies thereon.
44. There shall be no hymn nor dithyramb in my praise and the praise of the rite, seeing that it is utterly beyond.
45. Thou shalt assure thyself of the stability of the altar.
46. In this rite thou shalt be alone.
47. I will give thee another ceremony whereby many shall rejoice.
48. Before all let the Oath be taken firmly as thou raisest up the altar from the black earth.
49. In the words that Thou knowest.
50. For I also swear unto thee by my body and soul that shall never be parted in sunder that I dwell within thee coiled and ready to spring.
51. I will give thee the kingdoms of the earth, O thou Who hast mastered the kingdoms of the East and of the West.

52. I am Apep, O thou slain One. Thou shalt slay thyself upon mine altar: I will have thy blood to drink.
53. For I am a mighty vampire, and my children shall suck up the wine of the earth which is blood.
54. Thou shalt replenish thy veins from the chalice of heaven.
55. Thou shalt be secret, a fear to the world.
56. Thou shalt be exalted, and none shall see thee; exalted, and none shall suspect thee.
57. For there are two glories diverse, and thou who hast won the first shalt enjoy the second.
58. I leap with joy within thee; my head is arisen to strike.
59. O the lust, the sheer rapture, of the life of the snake in the spine!
60. Mightier than God or man, I am in them, and pervade them.
61. Follow out these my words.
62. Fear nothing.
    Fear nothing.
    Fear nothing.
63. For I am nothing, and me thou shalt fear, O my virgin, my prophet within whose bowels I rejoice.
64. Thou shalt fear with the fear of love: I will overcome thee.
65. Thou shalt be very nigh to death.
66. But I will overcome thee; the New Life shall illumine thee with the Light that is beyond the Stars.
67. Thinkest thou? I, the force that have created all, am not to be despised.
68. And I will slay thee in my lust.
69. Thou shalt scream with the joy and the pain and the fear and the love - so that the LOGOS of a new God leaps out among the Stars.
70. There shall be no sound heard but this thy lion-roar of rapture; yea, this thy lion-roar of rapture.

Liber Tzaddi

vel

Hamus Hermeticus

Sub Figura

XC

0. In the name of the Lord of Initiation, Amen.
1. I fly and I alight as an hawk: of mother-of-emerald are my mighty-sweeping wings.
2. I swoop down upon the black earth; and it gladdens into green at my coming.
3. Children of Earth! rejoice! rejoice exceedingly; for your salvation is at hand.
4. The end of sorrow is come; I will ravish you away into mine unutterable joy.
5. I will kiss you, and bring you to the bridal: I will spread a feast before you in the house of happiness.
6. I am not come to rebuke you, or to enslave you.
7. I bid you not turn from your voluptuous ways, from your idleness, from your follies.
8. But I bring you joy to your pleasure, peace to your languor, wisdom to your folly.
9. All that ye do is right, if so be that ye enjoy it.
10. I am come against sorrow, against weariness, against them that seek to enslave you.
11. I pour you lustral wine, that giveth you delight both at the sunset and the dawn.
12. Come with me, and I will give you all that is desirable upon the earth.
13. Because I give you that of which Earth and its joys are but as shadows.
14. They flee away, but my joy abideth even unto the end.
15. I have hidden myself beneath a mask: I am a black and terrible God.
16. With courage conquering fear shall ye approach me: ye shall lay down your heads upon mine altar, expecting the sweep of the sword.
17. But the first kiss of love shall be radiant on your lips; and all my darkness and terror shall turn to light and joy.
18. Only those who fear shall fail. Those who have bent their backs to the

yoke of slavery until they can no longer stand upright; them will I despise.

19. But you who have defied the law; you who have conquered by subtlety or force; you will I take unto me, even I will take you unto me.

20. I ask you to sacrifice nothing at mine altar; I am the God who giveth all.

21. Light, Life, Love; Force, Fantasy, Fire; these do I bring you: mine hands are full of these.

22. There is joy in the setting-out; there is joy in the journey; there is joy in the goal.

23. Only if ye are sorrowful, or weary, or angry, or discomforted; then ye may know that ye have lost the golden thread, the thread wherewith I guide you to the heart of the groves of Eleusis.

24. My disciples are proud and beautiful; they are strong and swift; they rule their way like mighty conquerors.

25. The weak, the timid, the imperfect, the cowardly, the poor, the tearful - these are mine enemies, and I am come to destroy them.

26. This also is compassion: an end to the sickness of earth. A rooting-out of the weeds: a watering of the flowers.

27. O my children, ye are more beautiful than the flowers: ye must not fade in your season.

28. I love you; I would sprinkle you with the divine dew of immortality.

29. This immortality is no vain hope beyond the grave: I offer you the certain consciousness of bliss.

30. I offer it at once, on earth; before an hour hath struck upon the bell, ye shall be with Me in the Abodes that are beyond Decay.

31. Also I give you power earthly and joy earthly; wealth, and health, and length of days. Adoration and love shall cling to your feet, and twine around your heart.

32. Only your mouths shall drink of a delicious wine - the wine of Iacchus; they shall reach ever to the heavenly kiss of the Beautiful God.

33. I reveal unto you a great mystery. Ye stand between the abyss of height and the abyss of depth.

34. In either awaits you a Companion; and that Companion is Yourself.

35. Ye can have no other Companion.

36. Many have arisen, being wise. They have said "Seek out the glittering Image in the place ever golden, and unite yourselves with It."

37. Many have arisen, being foolish. They have said, "Stoop down unto the darkly splendid world, and be wedded to that Blind Creature of the Slime."

38. I who am beyond Wisdom and Folly, arise and say unto you: achieve both weddings! Unite yourselves with both!

39. Beware, beware, I say, lest ye seek after the one and lose the other!
40. My adepts stand upright; their head above the heavens, their feet below the hells.
41. But since one is naturally attracted to the Angel, another to the Demon, let the first strengthen the lower link, the last attach more firmly to the higher.
42. Thus shall equilibrium become perfect. I will aid my disciples; as fast as they acquire this balanced power and joy so faster will I push them.
43. They shall in their turn speak from this Invisible Throne; their words shall illumine the worlds.
44. They shall be masters of majesty and might; they shall be beautiful and joyous; they shall be clothed with victory and splendour; they shall stand upon the firm foundation; the kingdom shall be theirs; yea, the kingdom shall be theirs.
    In the name of the Lord of Initiation. Amen.

Liber Cheth

vel

Vallum Abiegni

Sub Figura

CLVI

1. This is the secret of the Holy Graal, that is the sacred vessel of our Lady the Scarlet Woman, Babalon the Mother of Abominations, the bride of Chaos, that rideth upon our Lord the Beast.

2. Thou shalt drain out thy blood that is thy life into the golden cup of her fornication.

3. Thou shalt mingle thy life with the universal life. Thou shalt keep not back one drop.

4. Then shall thy brain be dumb, and thy heart beat no more, and all thy life shall go from thee; and thou shalt be cast out upon the midden, and the birds of the air shall feast upon thy flesh, and thy bones shall whiten in the sun.

5. Then shall the winds gather themselves together, and bear thee up as it were a little heap of dust in a sheet that hath four corners, and they shall give it unto the guardians of the abyss.

6. And because there is no life therein, the guardians of the abyss shall bid the angels of the winds pass by. And the angels shall lay thy dust in the City of the Pyramids, and the name thereof shall be no more.

7. Now therefore that thou mayest achieve this ritual of the Holy Graal, do thou divest thyself of all thy goods.

8. Thou hast wealth; give it unto them that have need thereof, yet no desire toward it.

9. Thou hast health; slay thyself in the fervour of thine abandonment unto Our Lady. Let thy flesh hang loose upon thy bones, and thine eyes glare with thy quenchless lust unto the Infinite, with thy passion for the Unknown, for Her that is beyond Knowledge the accursed one.

10. Thou hast love; tear thy mother from thine heart, and spit in the face of thy father. Let thy foot trample the belly of thy wife, and let the babe at her breast be the prey of dogs and vultures.

11. For if thou dost not this with thy will, then shall We do this despite thy will. So that thou attain to the Sacrament of the Graal in the Chapel of Abominations.

12. And behold! if by stealth thou keep unto thyself one thought of thine, then shalt thou be cast out into the abyss for ever; and thou shalt be the lonely one, the eater of dung, the afflicted in the Day of Be-with-Us.

13. Yea! verily this is the Truth, this is the Truth, this is the Truth. Unto thee shall be granted joy and health and wealth and wisdom when thou art no longer thou.

14. Then shall every gain be a new sacrament, and it shall not defile thee; thou shalt revel with the wanton in the market-place, and the virgins shall fling roses upon thee, and the merchants bend their knees and bring thee gold and spices. Also young boys shall pour wonderful wines for thee, and the singers and the dancers shall sing and dance for thee.

15. Yet shalt thou not be therein, for thou shalt be forgotten, dust lost in dust.

16. Nor shall the aeon itself avail thee in this; for from the dust shall a white ash be prepared by Hermes the Invisible.

17. And this is the wrath of God, that these things should be thus.

18. And this is the grace of God, that these things should be thus.

19. Wherefore I charge you that ye come unto me in the Beginning; for if ye take but one step in this Path, ye must arrive inevitably at the end thereof.

20. This Path is beyond Life and Death; it is also beyond Love; but that ye know not, for ye know not Love.

21. And the end thereof is known not even unto Our Lady or to the Beast whereon She rideth; nor unto the Virgin her daughter nor unto Chaos her lawful Lord; but unto the Crowned Child is it known? It is not known if it be known.

22. Therefore unto Hadit and unto Nuit be the glory in the End and the Beginning; yea, in the End and the Beginning.

Appendix IV
Ritual J
Oath of Obligation of
a Neophyte of the Golden Dawn

I (name of aspirant), in the presence of the Lord of the Universe and of this Hall of Neophytes of the Order of The Golden Dawn in the Outer, regularly assembled under warrant from the Greatly Honored Chiefs of the Second Order, do of my own free will and accord hereby and hereon most solemnly pledge myself to keep secret this Order, its name, the name of its members, and the proceedings which take place at its meetings, from all and every person in the whole world who is outside the pale of the Order, and not even to discuss these with initiates, unless he or they are in possession of the password for the time being. Nor yet with any member who has resigned, demitted or been expelled, and I undertake to maintain a kind and benevolent relation with all the Fraters and Sorors of the Order.

I furthermore promise and swear that I will keep any information relative to this Order, which may have become known to me prior to the completion of the Ceremony of my admission and I also pledge myself to divulge nothing whatsoever concerning this Order to the outside world in case either of my resignation, demission or expulsion therefrom, after the completion of my admission. I will not seek to obtain any ritual or lecture pertaining to the Order without due authorization from the Praemonstrator of my Temple, nor will I possess any ritual or lecture unless it be properly registered and labelled by him.

I further undertake that any such ritual or lecture and any case, cover or box containing them shall bear the official label of the Golden Dawn. I will not copy myself nor lend to any other person to be copied, any ritual or lecture, until and unless I hold the written permission of the Praemonstrator to do so, lest our secret knowledge be revealed through my neglect or error.

Furthermore, I undertake to prosecute with zeal the study of Occult Sciences, seeing that this Order is not established for the benefit of those who desire only a superficial knowledge thereof. I will not suffer myself to be hypnotized, or mesmerized, nor will I place myself in such a passive state that any uninitiated person, power, or being may cause me to lose control of my thoughts, words or actions. Neither will I use my Occult powers for any evil purposes and I further promise to persevere with firmness and courage through the ceremony of my admission, and these points I generally and severally, upon this sacred and sublime symbol swear to observe without evasion, equivocation, or mental reservation of any kind whatsoever; under the no less penalty on the violation of any or either of them of being expelled from this Order, as a wilfully perjured wretch, void of any moral worth, and unfit for the society of all right and true persons, and in addition under the awful penalty of voluntarily submitting myself to a deadly and hostile current of will set in motion by the chiefs of the Order, by which I should fall slain and paralysed without visible weapon as if slain by the lightning flash.

So help me the Lord of the Universe and my own higher soul.

Appendix V
Rituel de la Fraction du Pain
Jules-Benoît Doinel, 1894

Les Parfaits étant réunis, les femmes la tête couverte d'un voile blanc et les hommes ceints d'un cordon blanc, s'agenouillent et reçoivent la bénédiction de Sa Seigneurie, l'évêque. Puis ils se relèvent et le choeur chante le cantique:

> Beati, vos Æones
> Vera vita vividi;
> Vos Emanationes
> Pleromatis lucidi;
> Adeste visiones
> Stolis albis candidi.

Sur la table drapée de lin, l'évangile de Jean repose entre les deux flambeaux. L'évêque et le diacre et la diaconesse assistants sont debout devant la table. Une fois le cantique achevé, Sa Seigneurie récite le Pater noster, en grec:

> Pater hêmôn ho en tois ouranois:
> Hagiasthêtô to onoma sou;
> Elthetô hê basileia sou;
> Genêthêtô to thelêma sou,
> Hôs en ouranôi kai epi gês;
> Ton arton hêmôn ton epiousion dos hêmin sêmeron;
> Kai aphes hêmin ta opheilêmata hêmôn,
> Hôs kai hêmeis aphêkamen tois opheiletais hêmôn;
> Kai mê eisenenkêis hêmas eis peirasmon,
> Alla hrusai hêmas apo tou ponêrou.
>
> Hoti sou estin hê basileia,
> Kai hê dynamis, kai hê doxa,
> Eis tous aiônas. Amên.

L'Assemblée répond:

> Amen.

Le diacre présente la coupe et le pain à l'évêque. Le Prélat, revêtu de l'étole (quand sa grâce le Patriarche officie, il est couvert du très auguste Pallium), élève les mains sur les espèces en disant:

> Eon Jesus prisquam pateretur mystice,
> accepit panem et vinum in stancias
> et venerabiles manus suas, et,
> elevatis oculis in coelum, fregit (l'évêque rompt le pain),
> benedixit (l'évêque forme le Tau sur le pain et la coupe)
> et dedit discipulis uais, dicens (tout le monde se prosterne)
> Accipite et manducate et bibit omnes!

Le diacre portant le plateau et la diaconesse portant la coupe précèdent Sa Seigneurie qui s'avance vers les Parfaits. L'orgue joue une marche religieuse et lente.

L'évêque, prenant le pain, l'élève au-dessus de l'assemblée en disant:

> Touto estin to soma pneumatikon tou Christou.

Puis il repose le pain sur le plateau, s'agenouille et adore.

Il se relève, prend la coupe et l'élève en disant:

> Calix meus inebrians quàm proeclaus est!
> Calicem Salutaris accipiam et nomen Domini invocabo.

Il s'agenouille et adore.

Il se relève, rompt un fragment du corps spirituel de Jésus et le mange. Il boit à la coupe du sang.

Pause. Orgues.

Il s'avance ensuite vers chaque Parfait et tend le pain et la coupe à chacun.

Silence. Orgues. Adoration.

De retour à l'autel, l'évêque étendant les mains dit:

> Que la grâce du très saint Plérôme soit toujours avec vous!

Les restes des espèces consacrées sont brûlés sur un réchaud, car le corps pneumatique du Seigneur ne doit pas être profané.

Après quoi, Sa Seigneurie donne la bénédiction gnostique et se retire entre les deux assistants qui portent les flambeaux.

The Ritual of the Breaking of the Bread
Translated by Rodney Orpheus

The Perfect having come together, the women with their heads covered with a white veil and the men girded with a white cord, they kneel to receive the blessing of his Eminence, the Bishop. They rise and the choir sings the canticle:

> Beati, vos Æones
> Vera vita vividi;
> Vos Emanationes
> Pleromatis lucidi;
> Adeste visiones
> Stolis albis candidi.

The Gospel of John rests between two candles on a table draped in linen. The Bishop and the Deacon and Deaconess stand before the table. Once the canticle is completed, his Eminence recites the Lord's Prayer in Greek.

> Pater hêmôn ho en tois ouranois:
> Hagiasthêtô to onoma sou;
> Elthetô hê basileia sou;
> Genêthêtô to thelêma sou,
> Hôs en ouranôi kai epi gês;
> Ton arton hêmôn ton epiousion dos hêmin sêmeron;
> Kai aphes hêmin ta opheilêmata hêmôn,
> Hôs kai hêmeis aphêkamen tois opheiletais hêmôn;
> Kai mê eisenenkêis hêmas eis peirasmon,
> Alla hrusai hêmas apo tou ponêrou.
>
> Hoti sou estin hê basileia,
> Kai hê dynamis, kai hê doxa,
> Eis tous aiônas. Amên.

The assembly answers:

> Amen.

The Deacon presents the chalice and the bread to the Bishop. The Prelate puts on the Stole (when his Grace the Patriarch officiates, he is covered with the very august Pallium), raises the hands over those present and says:

> Eon Jesus prisquam pateretur mystice, accepit panem et vinum in stancias et venerabiles manus suas, et, elevatis oculis in coelum, fregit

(The Bishop breaks the bread)

> benedixit

(The Bishop makes the shape of the Tau over the bread and the chalice)

> et dedit discipulis uais, dicens:

(All prostrate themselves)

> Accipite et manducate et bibit omnes!

The Deacon carrying the plate and the Deaconess carrying the chalice precede his Eminence who advances towards the Perfect. The organ plays a slow religious march.

The Bishop, taking the bread, raises it above the assembly while saying:

> Touto estin to soma pneumatikon tou Christou.

Then he puts the bread back onto the plate, kneels and adores.
He rises, takes the chalice and raises it while saying:

> Calix meus inebrians quàm proeclaus est!
> Calicem Salutaris accipiam et nomen Domini invocabo.

He kneels and adores.
He rises and breaks a fragment of the spiritual body of Jesus and eats it.
He drinks from the cup of blood.
Pause. Organ plays.
He then advances towards each of the Perfect in turn and offers the bread and the cup to each.
Silence. Organ. Adoration.
Upon returning to the altar, the Bishop, extending his hands, proclaims:

> May the grace of the most holy Pleroma be with you always!

The remains of the consecrated host are burned in the chafing-dish, for the essence of the body of the Lord should not be profaned.

After this his Eminence gives the Gnostic benediction and retires between the two assistants who carry the candles.

Appendix VI
Cakes of Light

Ingredients:

1. Wine leavings, or if these are difficult to find, substitute two litres (half a gallon) of port wine
2. One & a half cups of whole-wheat flour
3. Honey (to taste)
4. One & a half tablespoons of olive oil
5. Abramelin oil (to taste - not much!)
6. Other ingredient (see AL III, 23 & 24)

Procedure:

Wine leavings are a by-product of the wine manufacturing process, and may be obtained from a vineyard if you have one locally. Otherwise, buy a good port wine and reduce it. Heat the wine at the lowest heat possible. Steam should be rising, but it should never boil. Let it simmer for approximately five hours. At the end you should have about a quarter of an inch (half a centimetre) of goo at the bottom of the pot.

Preheat the oven to a very high temperature.

In a mixing bowl add the flour, honey, wine leavings/goo, olive oil, and Abramelin oil. Knead until it becomes cookie dough - this takes a while. Add more flour if it's too sticky. You can get Abramelin oil from an occult supply shop - or ask your local O.T.O. body, frequently someone there will know how to make it or procure it.

Roll out the dough on to a floured surface. Flour the rolling pin and your hands too. When the dough has been flattened out, take a small ball of it and add in the Other Ingredient. Make the result into a small cake and bake in a very hot oven until it is black, or carcinate it with a bunsen burner (or any similar method for reducing it to ash).

Allow this cake to cool, then crumble a small amount of the resultant ash into the main dough. Do not add any of the raw Other Ingredient directly into the main dough, only use the burnt ash for this. Effectively you will be adding only a homeopathic, carcinated amount of the Other Ingredient to the final mix.

Reduce the oven temperature to 150°C (approximately 300°F, or Gas Mark 2).

Take the dough mixture and cut into cakes using a small circular cutter - a pill bottle top or lipstick top is ideal.

Place cakes on floured sheet and bake them in the oven for no more than five minutes. Usually 3-4 minutes is enough. The cakes won't look done when you take them out - just let them cool for a while and they'll be fine, hardening as they cool.

Bibliography

Apiryon, T, and Helena. *Mystery of Mystery: A Primer of Thelemic Ecclesiastical Gnosticism*. 2nd ed. Red Flame 2. Red Flame, 2001.

Baigent, Michael, and Richard Leigh. *The Temple and the Lodge*. Arcade Publishing, 1991.

Beta, Hymenaeus., ed. *The Equinox: Vol.III, No.10*. OTO / Thelema, 1990.

Blecourt, Willem de, Jean de La Fontaine, and Ronald Hutton. *Witchcraft and Magic in Europe, Volume 6 (History of Witchcraft and Magic in Europe)*. Athlone Press, 2001.

Budge, E. *The Gods of the Egyptians or Studies in Egyptian Mythology*. London: Methuen & Co., 1904.

"Catholic Encyclopedia: Gnosticism." http://www.newadvent.org/cathen/06592a.htm.

Churton, Tobias. *The Gnostics*. 2nd ed. Barnes & Noble Books, 1999.

Crowley, Aleister. *Commentaries on the Holy Books and Other Papers: The Equinox v.4, No.1*. Edited by Hymenaeus. Beta. Red Wheel/Weiser, 1996.

———. "Invocation of the Holy Spirit." *The Magical Link 5*, no. 3 (Fall 1991): 3.

———. *Little Essays Toward Truth*. London: Ordo Templi Orientis, 1938.

Crowley, Aleister, ed. *The Blue Equinox*. 1. Detroit MI: Universal Pub. Co., 1919.

Crowley, Alcister. *The Book of the Goetia of Solomon the King : translated into the English tongue by a dead hand and adorned with divers other matters germane delightful to the wise*. Translated by S. L. Mathers. Boleskine Foyers Inverness: Society for the Propagation of Religious Truth, 1904.

———. *The Book of the Law*. Centennial Ed. Red Wheel/Weiser, 2004.

———. *The Book of Thoth; A Short Essay on the Tarot of the Egyptians, being the Equinox, Volume III, No. V*. London: Ordo Templi Orientis, 1944.

———. "The Brazen Head." *The Magical Link 9*, no. 3 (Fall 1995): 4.

Crowley, Aleister, ed. *The Equinox*. 1-10. London, 1909.

Crowley, Aleister. *The Law Is for All: The Authorized Popular Commentary of Liber Al Vel Legis sub figura CCXX, the Book of the Law*. Edited by Louis Wilkinson. Thelema Media, 1996.

———. *Thelema: Holy Books Of Thelema*. Weiser, 1983.

———. *The Magical Diaries of Aleister Crowley*. Edited by Stephen Skinner. York Beach, Me.: S. Weiser, 1981.

———. "The Ritual of the Mark of the Beast (variant)." *The Magical Link 6*, no. 2 (Summer 1992): 3.

———. *The Spirit of Solitude: an autohagiography: subsequently re-Antichristened The Confessions of Aleister Crowley*. London: Mandrake Press, 1929.

———. *The Vision & The Voice - With Commentary and Other Papers: The Equinox v.4, No.2*. Edited by Hymenaeus. Beta. Red Wheel/ Weiser, 1999.

———. *The Works of Aleister Crowley*. Foyers: Society for the Propagation of Religious Truth, 1905.

Crowley, Aleister, Mary. Desti, and Leila. Waddell. *Magick : Liber ABA, Book Four, Parts I-IV*. Edited by Hymenaeus. Beta. York Beach, Me.: S. Weiser, 2004.

Dee, John, Meric Casaubon, and Edward Kelly. *A True & Faithful Relation of What Passed for Many Yeers between Dr. John Dee (a Mathematician of Great Fame in Q. Eliz. and King James their Reignes) and Some Spirits*. Edited by Stephen Skinner. London; New York: Askin Publishers; Samuel Weiser, Inc., 1974.

Deśapānde, Purushottama. *The Authentic Yoga : a fresh look at Patanjali's yoga sutras with a new translation, notes and comments.* London: Rider, 1978.

Disney, Walt. *Fantasia*, 1940. http://www.imdb.com/title/tt0032455/.

Durant, Will, and Ariel Durant. *The Story of Civilization.* New York: Simon and Schuster, 1935.

Euripides. *The Plays of Euripides, tr. into English prose from the text of Paley.* Translated by Edward P. Coleridge. London: G. Bell and sons, 1891.

Frazer, James George. *The Golden Bough: A Study in Magic and Religion.* London: St. Martin's, 1911.

Frédol, Bérenger, Étienne de Suisy, and Landolfo Brancacci. "The parchment of Chinon – the absolution of Pope Clement V of the leading members of the Templar order." Chinon. Diocese of Tours, August 17, 1308. http://asv.vatican.va/en/doc/1308.htm.

Fuller, J.F.C., and Aleister Crowley. *The Pathworkings of Aleister Crowley: The Treasure House of Images.* Edited by James Wasserman. New Falcon Publications,U.S., 1994.

Goodrick-Clarke, Clare, and Nicholas Goodrick-Clarke. *G.R.S. Mead and the Gnostic Quest: Western Esoteric Masters Series.* North Atlantic Books,U.S., 2005.

Goodwin, Charles Wycliffe. *Fragment of a Graeco-Egyptian work upon magic.* Cambridge: Cambridge Antiquarian Society, 1852.

Homer. *The Iliad of Homer and The Odyssey.* Chicago: Encyclopaedia Britannica, 1948.

Howe, Ellic. *Magicians of the Golden Dawn: A Documentary History of a Magical Order, 1887-1923.* Routledge & Kegan Paul Books, 1972.

Jaynes, Julian. *The Origin of Consciousness in the Breakdown of the Bicameral Mind.* Boston: Houghton Mifflin, 1976.

King, C.W. *Gnostics and their Remains Ancient and Mediaeval.*
    Kessinger Publishing, LLC, 1942.

Lachman, Gary. "Homunculi, Golems, and Artificial Life." *Quest Magazine*,
    February 2006. http://theosophical.org/publications/questmagazine/
    janfeb06/Lachman/index.php.

Mathers, S.L.MacGregor. *The Key of Solomon the King: Clavicula
    Salomonis.* New edition. Red Wheel/Weiser, 2000.

McIntosh, Christopher. *Eliphas Levi and the French Occult Revival.*
    Rider, 1972.

Mead, G. R. S. *The Mysteries of Mithra.* Theosophical Pub. Society, 1907.

Mead, G. R. S., and Albrecht Dieterich. *A Mithraic Ritual.*
    London; Benares: Theosophical Pub. Society, 1907.

Meyrink, Gustav. *Der Golem, ein Roman.* Berlin: Neufeld & Henius, 1915.

Morrison, Grant. *The Invisibles Vol. 1: Say You Want a Revolution.*
    New York: Vertigo, 1996.

Nabarz, Payam. The Mysteries of Mithras: *The Pagan Belief That Shaped the
    Christian World.* Inner Traditions Bear and Company, 2005.

Orpheus, Rodney. *Abrahadabra: Understanding Aleister Crowley's Thelemic
    Magick.* Red Wheel/Weiser, 2005.

Partner, Peter. *The Murdered Magicians: The Templars and their Myth.*
    Oxford; New York: Oxford University Press, 1982.

Patanjali. "The Yoga Sutras of Patanjali." Translated by BonGiovanni.
    http://www.sacred-texts.com/hin/yogasutr.htm.

Polyphilus, T. "Conditions for Eucharistic Magick."
    http://www.hermetic.com/dionysos/conditns.htm.

Regardie, Israel. *The Complete Golden Dawn System of Magic.*
    Phoenix, Ariz., U.S.A.: Falcon Press, 1984.

Sheldrake, Rupert. *A New Science of Life*. Icon Books Ltd, 2009.

Skinner, Stephen, and David Rankine, eds. *The Goetia of Dr Rudd: The Angels and Demons of Liber Malorum Spirituum Seu Goetia*. Golden Hoard Press, 2007.

Skinner, Stephen, and David Rankine, eds. *The Veritable Key of Solomon*. Llewellyn Publications,U.S., 2008.

Starr, Martin P. *The Unknown God: W. T. Smith and the Thelemites*. Teitan Press Inc.,U.S., 2003.

Tertullian. *The Chaplet, or De Corona*. Whitefish, Mont.: Kessinger, 2007.

Tyson, Donald. *The Power of the Word: The Secret Code of Creation*. Llewellyn Publications,U.S., 2004.

Ulansey, David. "Mithras and the Hypercosmic Sun." In *Studies in Mithraism*, 257-264. http://www.well.com/user/davidu/hypercosmic.html.

———. "Solving the Mithraic Mysteries." *Biblical Archaeology Review* 20, no. 5 (October 1994): 40-53.

———. "The Mithraic Mysteries." *Scientific American* 261, no. 6 (December 1989): 130-135.

———. *The Origins of the Mithraic Mysteries: Cosmology and Salvation in the Ancient World*. Oxford University Press, USA, 1991.

Various Authors. *Holy Bible*. Thomas Nelson, 1983.

White, Howard E. "A Rite of Isis." *The Magical Link* 6, no. 1 (Spring 1992): 2-4.

Willoughby, Harold Rideout. *Pagan Regeneration: A Study of Mystery Initiations in the Graeco-Roman World*. Chicago: University of Chicago Press, 1929.

To Our Readers

Weiser Books, an imprint of Red Wheel/Weiser, publishes books across the entire spectrum of occult, esoteric, speculative, and New Age subjects. Our mission is to publish quality books that will make a difference in people's lives without advocating any one particular path or field of study. We value the integrity, originality, and depth of knowledge of our authors.

Our readers are our most important resource, and we appreciate your input, suggestions, and ideas about what you would like to see published.

Visit our website at *www.redwheelweiser.com* to learn about our upcoming books and free downloads, and be sure to go to *www.redwheelweiser.com/ newsletter* to sign up for newsletters and exclusive offers.

You can also contact us at *info@rwwbooks.com* or at

Red Wheel/Weiser, LLC
65 Parker Street, Suite 7
Newburyport, MA 01950